SOWING BEAUTY

JAMES HITCHMOUGH

SOWING BEAUTY

Designing Flowering Meadows from Seed

Timber Press
Portland, Oregon

To my mother and father, who encouraged me
to be interested in these and all sorts of things

Published in 2017 by Timber Press, Inc.
The Haseltine Building
133 S.W. Second Avenue, Suite 450
Portland, Oregon 97204-3527
timberpress.com

Printed in China
Text and jacket design by Kristi Pfeffer

Library of Congress Cataloging-in-Publication Data

Names: Hitchmough, James, author.
Title: Sowing beauty: designing flowering meadows from seed / James
    Hitchmough.
Description: Portland, Oregon: Timber Press, 2017. | Includes
    bibliographical references and index.
Identifiers: LCCN 2016036943 | ISBN 9781604696325 (hardcover)
Subjects: LCSH: Meadow gardening. | Meadows.
Classification: LCC SB439 .H58 2017 | DDC 635.9/676—dc23 LC record
    available at https://lccn.loc.gov/2016036943

A catalogue record for this book is also available from the British Library.

CONTENTS

INTRODUCTION

This book is a little bit different from run of the mill gardening and planting design books. It's about utilizing an understanding of how naturally occurring plant communities function ecologically, and then transferring this understanding to help design, establish, and manage visually dramatic herbaceous vegetation in gardens, urban parks, and other urban greenspaces that is long persistent, given simple low-intensity maintenance. What's more, the book largely focuses on achieving this not through planting, but through sowing designed seed mixes. Planting is used as an embellishment but is not the main game.

As seen on this hillside in Diaobing Shan, Liaoning Province, north-eastern China, sometimes just being on a hill with poor soils and steep slopes allows species-rich vegetation to survive urban development.

The information in this book is derived from more than 30 years of university research mostly at the Department of Landscape Architecture, University of Sheffield. I describe how to produce meadows in ways that provide a substantial measure of control over the outcomes—not far, in fact, from the control you get with planting. Add on 20 years of applying these techniques to practice in a large number of prestigious projects, and you sort of have this book.

The vegetation discussed in this book is sometimes a facsimile of a naturally occurring plant community but generally not. More often it is an eclectic mixture of species drawn from parallel habitats around the world, resorted to create designed cultural plant communities that flower and look dramatic for much longer than most naturally occurring plant communities. This longer flowering season benefits native animals as well as people. The vegetation is, however, always naturalistic, in that it has the visual patterns and rhythms found in semi-natural vegetation. It is also party to the same ecological processes that are inherent in semi-natural vegetation, as these processes are blind to the species present and their origins.

On this hill, *Delphinium grandiflorum* and many other species survive. Elsewhere for tens if not hundreds of kilometres, these plants have been eliminated by intensive agriculture and urban development.

Prior to the development of highly intensive, fossil fuel–dependent industrial agriculture in the 20th century, flower-rich, meadow-like vegetation was much more abundant in human-settled landscapes. A visit to the low-intensity, more traditionally farmed meadow landscapes of the European Alps, or indeed almost any temperate mountain region, provides potent insight into what lowland areas once looked like and how such flowery vegetation was both aesthetically and economically important to agricultural societies. Remarkably accurate meadow depictions in medieval paintings and tapestries, such as "The Hunt of the Unicorn" (1495–1505), suggest that flower-rich meadows were highly valued for both their aesthetic and utilitarian qualities, such as the production of hay to keep livestock alive over winter.

The process of loss began in earnest in the 18th century with the use of clover to boost nitrogen in soils and the evolution of cultivation machinery that makes it much easier to plough up meadow vegetation. The invention of granular, manufactured fertilizers that make it cheap and easy to boost growth at the end of the 19th century and herbicides that allow the elimination of undesired plants in the 20th century are the final coup de grace. The subsequent elimination of flower-rich vegetation happened almost everywhere in the world, but to different degrees, depending on the affluence and ambition of the society in question. In many parts of Eastern Europe, for example, lowland flower-rich meadows are still common, as the traumatic political and economic events of the 20th century, two world wars, the remaking of nation states, and 50 years of communism froze agricultural development in time. Low-intensity traditional practices persisted long after they did in more affluent Western Europe, much to the benefit of meadows.

In the United States, one of the most extensive and in many ways most iconic of the world's flower-rich, meadow-like vegetation, the prairie, has been almost entirely

Květnice represents a half-way point between traditional cultivation and meadow. The meadow grasses around *Inula* species in Pruhonice Park, Prague, are carefully trimmed to manage competition and facilitate the satisfactory growth of the flowering plants.

eliminated and replaced by monoculture. The rapidity and thoroughness of this process and the immensity of the areas over which this transformation took place from the 19th century on are truly staggering. We know from contemporary accounts that even those who might later conspire to plough up prairie were astonished by its beauty and majesty. Patches survive across the American Midwest, often when some local visionary or romantic argued for keeping a piece of what the landscape had once been. The emerging commodity market economy in the west led to the destruction of the prairie. The Soviet Union did the same to its flower-rich steppes in the 20th century through collectivization. Two different economic agendas, but the same net result.

There is at least anecdotal evidence of the creation of meadow-like planting in gardens from the medieval period through a process known as enamelling. This involved closely planting small-flowering plants such as dianthus and primula hybrids in hand-clipped lawn grass to create a neat meadow-like flower border. This idea of herbaceous plants being deliberately planted in and emerging out of managed grass comes again to the fore as more ecological gardening in the 19th century, particularly in central Europe (Germany and what is now the Czech Republic), for example, where in the latter it is known as *květnice*.

In the English-speaking world, this approach was also championed by William Robinson and represented in his 1870 book *The Wild Garden*, although it seems likely that he borrowed these ideas from what he had seen during trips to continental Europe. The grass around groups of planted herbaceous plants is mown occasionally during the growing season to control grass vigour and to prevent it from outcompeting the planted species. This seems to work, but it produces a somewhat bizarre landscape appearance, quite different to what a semi-natural meadow looks like.

PLANT COMMUNITIES AS A DESIGN TOOL

A central idea in modern planting as a means of capturing the visual character of semi-natural meadows is the plant community. The idea of planting as a community of different species probably has its most distant origins in the ideas of 19th-century plant explorers and travellers such as Alexander von Humboldt. Their travels allowed these intrepid souls to recognize that different parts of the Earth support different assemblages of plant species, and that there is a predictability in how individual species group together to form repeating assemblages or communities. Within a geographic region, the same species is often found wherever certain environmental conditions occur. Areas with wet soils support a distinctive community of species that are different from the species found in communities in adjacent dry areas. The plants within these communities have been screened by natural selection to tolerate the specific environmental conditions and also one another. Species that cannot tolerate the other species or the conditions are eliminated from the community. Communities are the result of a very long road testing.

In the 20th century, this idea of coexistence leading to an intrinsic stability within plant communities became a very seductive one for designers of plantings. In conventional garden plantings, much of the work required to achieve long-term perpetuation of species involves targeted and intensive maintenance to manage competition between individual plant species and cultivars to prevent one from eliminating the other. If it were possible to design plantings that operated as semi-natural plant communities seem to, then much of the work involved in maintenance would disappear.

Conventional horticultural garden planting does not operate like semi-natural plant communities. This is because it uses species from all over the world (not fundamentally a major problem in itself), without much thought given to the habitats these plants evolved in. In the British tradition, these plants were often selected almost on flower colour alone. In nature the process known as natural selection sieves species from germination onwards, eliminating those individuals that are least suited or fit for the conditions in a given site. Over long periods of time, this creates populations of individuals of species whose tolerances are honed to that site. When seed is collected from these wild populations and grown on in gardens, the tolerances of these resulting plants strongly reflect those of the parents in the wild. These genetically based tolerances are hard wired in, and so seedlings of a species that need wet soil will continue to need wet soil in cultivation until some additional evolution or hybridization occurs to change this situation. If you completely disregard this and only chose plants, for example, on their flowering display, without thought about whether they share similar environmental or management requirements with their peers, such plantings will be inherently unstable from the outset. Stability of sorts can be achieved, but only by expending large amounts of labour in maintenance. So far so good, it seems, but unfortunately semi-natural communities are not really stable. Stability in nature is an illusion. Natural and semi-natural vegetation changes all of the time, but this is not evident unless you look very closely over a number of years, and most unscientific observers do not do this. What you do find, however, in semi-natural vegetation is that the rate and extent of change is less than in, say, a herbaceous border that you don't maintain for a year. Semi-stability is still a property worth aspiring to.

Interest in using naturally occurring plant communities as a model for design first becomes really evident early in the 20th century in the Netherlands and Germany. In the Netherlands, the invention of a type of designed urban nature park (*heem* parks, meaning habitat or home) was important in encouraging these ideas, as described by Gaston Bekkers in *Jac. P. Thijsse Park: Designed Dutch Landscape*. Initially, much of this type of planting was largely driven by the desire to create native or near-native plant communities in cities to provide opportunities for people to continue to experience the fast-disappearing attractive native vegetation of the region. There were similar developments in the United States (in part driven by northern European emigres, such as the landscape architect Jens Jensen), particularly associated with the midwestern prairie school. The plans that survive from this era do, however, suggest that this planting was an abstracted version of what actual prairie looks like. These design movements were inspired to a greater or lesser degree by people going and looking at semi-natural vegetation in the wild and then trying to represent the most attractive qualities of this through design and planting.

The large-scale examples of this process commenced in the 1930s in the state of Wisconsin with the restoration (the creation of facsimile vegetation) of native prairie on land that had been converted from prairie into crop or grazing land in the 19th century. This approach was and is mostly led by environmentalists, who are often more captivated by reinstating ecosystem processes than by the aesthetics of the resulting vegetation. It is sort of assumed, rather optimistically, that if you get the processes right the aesthetics will happen anyway. Although the restoration of prairie and meadow vegetation is clearly an important part of the naturalistic planting palette, it is not the main subject of this book.

THE ROLE OF THE NATIVE

In many western countries, restoration ecology using local native species to reinstate native plant communities is now a highly developed science and practice. The progress of this discipline is sometimes restricted by philosophical perspectives about nature and what is natural, plus a lack of political awareness about how people who are not restoration ecologists might see the world and, in particular, recreated native vegetation, especially in urban places. Some of the examples and case studies that this book provides are based on native species, but in the main I describe the work I do with species that are not native to the places I am working in.

This may seem to be a contradictory and odd idea to some, especially since I start this chapter with a lament about how the countryside was, until quite recently, a much more biologically diverse, flowery, native, and beautiful place than it now is. To me this is no contradiction at all. It seems almost a necessity to be able to simultaneously value native vegetation in places where it can and should exist and deliver the diverse range of benefits that it does, and to want to have vegetation in private gardens, parks, and other public spaces, while beautiful and pleasing to the ordinary urban citizen, that may be or is different from native plants in the countryside. This suggestion that it is entirely legitimate to have vegetation in cities that is not native to the region flies in the face of the sustainability perspectives that are particularly dominant in North America and that have been exported internationally.

The validity of the arguments as to why urban vegetation might differ from semi-natural vegetation of the region depends on the specific context of the site and culture, rather than universal truths. If you live in a geographically large country with a large native flora, such as the United States or China, then you might be able to get by working in urban places entirely within that flora, because there are so many species to choose from. In large countries, however, you may be using natives which are as geographically and ecologically distinct from the local environment that you are working in as species naturally occurring in an adjacent country and deemed to be exotics. An example of this might be Perth in Western Australia, where ecologically speaking some native plant species may have as much or more in common with South African species than they do with those in Sydney, 3000 km distant. Political and ecological concepts of natives and native-ness mean very different things. If the newly formed United States of America had not expanded across the Appalachians and acquired the Louisiana Purchase from France and California and Texas from Mexico, many species currently seen as natives would be aliens simply through political happenchance.

If you are designing a green roof in New York and you need species highly tolerant of summer drought (the local species are not this), is it more appropriate to use species from inland California or central Spain? If the species then subsequently escaped from the roof and naturalized would it be worse if they were Californian or Spanish? Just think about that and try to get beyond the idea that California is now part of the United States. The geographic origin of the escapee is less critical than the potentially adverse ecological impact. A highly aggressive Californian species would be worse than a not very aggressive Spanish one.

If you live in a small country such as the Netherlands or Britain, with a very small flora (about 1000 species), it is very difficult to meet your design needs solely from within this. One characteristic of the herbaceous flora of Western Europe is that there are very few species that flower in late summer and autumn. On the whole, semi-natural vegetation in these countries is visually rather dull at this time of year, yet in urban places people like to have flowers as late into autumn as possible. This situation is in stark contrast to, for example, eastern North America with many instances of *Aster*, *Rudbeckia*, *Solidago*, and the like.

I often use well-behaved asters and rudbeckias in my designed plant communities in Britain to benefit both people and British native invertebrates such as bees, butterflies, hoverflies, and other pollinators. These insects make no apparent distinction between these alien species and U.K. natives when both are flowering. Although these pollinators do make distinctions over which species they visit, it is largely not on the basis of whether they are native or non-native. Utilitarian properties such as the quality of the nectar (sugar type and concentration) and pollen type are what is important. A certain percentage of both natives and non-natives score highly and poorly on these characteristics.

Much of the large-scale interest in designing naturalistic community-based meadows and prairies has been to reinstate ecosystem processes, in part because some believe that only these can support native animals such as pollinating insects or seed-feeding birds. Because this habitat restoration approach to naturalistic vegetation has emphasized ecological function rather than how attractive a vegetation might be to ordinary people, it has led to the mindset that vegetation that is designed to be extremely flowery and attractive to people is by definition less valuable to wildlife. These widely held belief systems are largely false and are based on a misunderstanding of how ecosystems actually support animal populations.

One of the factors that creates this misunderstanding is the idea of the degree of naturalness in the vegetation, with vegetation that grows spontaneously being more natural and that designed by people being less natural. For most of the animal species that might live in or feed on plants in a meadow or prairie, the degree of naturalness is a completely meaningless concept. What these animals really need is access to food and shelter and a management regime which is compatible with their life cycle. These factors are not necessarily strongly related to naturalness. Ken Thompson's thoughtful and provocative book *No Nettles Required* is recommended reading for those who want to understand the scientific underpinning to these issues rather than simply cling to dogma.

Based on a number of large-scale ecological studies in Western Europe over the past 15 years, we now know much, much more about how plants support a diversity of invertebrates. In most cases, neither naturalness nor nativeness of the plants is very important. What is important for pollinating insects is the quality of the supply of pollen and nectar and duration of the supply (known as the supermarket effect: are you open 24/7 or do you close at 5?). For insects that are not pollinators the critical factor is the degree of spatial complexity of the vegetation, but again not necessarily naturalness or nativeness. In Western Europe, we now know that intensively managed vegetable allotments are better for native pollinator diversity and density than native wildflower meadows in a nature reserve. This may seem a staggering idea, but it is true because allotments are managed in a way that ensures greater continuity of supply for humans, as opposed to the rather short flowering season of the native meadow vegetation. Many books aimed at encouraging people to adopt a natives-only perspective in their gardens to save nature are political polemics masquerading as ecological truth.

The chief bête noire of the non-native is the potential to escape from beyond the site, although of course this is also a possibility with natives. Escapes involve a relatively small

A landscape in western Wales in which a handful of native species, bracken and some highly competitive grasses, competitively exclude many other species and restrict native biodiversity.

percentage of the total pool of non-native plant species, and an even smaller percentage of these has significant ecological impacts. While clearly the escape of exotic species is not something that anyone wants to encourage, these invasions are not, from a scientific perspective, always how they are represented in the media and popular culture. A recent study conducted in the United Kingdom by Chris Thomas and Georgina Palmer found that, at the national level, naturalized exotic plant species had no measurable negative impact on native plant biodiversity—and this is in a country with some of the most detailed data sets on what plants are where of anywhere in the world. At a local scale, of course, you will always see shocking invasions which are most probably eliminating native species, such as kudzu vine in the south-eastern United States. However, even here these plants stop and start, they do not invade everywhere. This is the point of Thomas and Palmer: it is a question of the scale.

Sometimes the picture is more complex than this. Many argue that one of the worst alien herbaceous weeds in the United States and Canada is purple loosestrife, *Lythrum salicaria*. However, if you review the evidence for the harm everyone feels they know it must surely do, the published scientific studies find little evidence of ecosystem harm. Areas that are heavily invaded generally have no lesser diversity of native species than those that are not invaded. This is because the competitive dominant role *Lythrum* plays is simply taken up by vigorous native species in the absence of the *Lythrum*, thus suppressing native diversity anyway. When abundant, large and leafy native plants cause harm to less vigorous native species. The most damaging plants to native plant biodiversity in Western Europe are the most common and aggressive natives, including bracken (*Pteridium aquilinum*) and grasses such as false oat grass (*Arrhenatherum elatius*). It's worth reading Ken Thompson's very revealing and at times amusing book *Where Do Camels Belong?* about these sorts of issues, as much a reflection on the foibles of our species as the risks from invasive species.

There is a whole industry in many countries in praise of the native, so it is difficult to challenge the mantra "native good, alien bad", but this is what the urban ecology scientific literature is increasingly doing. Once you move beyond romanticism and political native tags, ecologically speaking exotics and natives behave in pretty much the same sort of ways.

The good news is that, in general, the plants that you are most likely to want to use in making naturalistic vegetation in your garden and cities are typically relatively slowly growing, conservative species with low dominance potential, that is, they are highly unlikely to be invasive. Species that are the opposite of these characteristics quickly eliminate their neighbours and are pretty useless when you want to design complex long-flowering vegetation. I don't work with species with invasive characteristics.

For me the critical issues in making decisions on whether to use natives, exotics, or both in urban design projects is context and character. My main aim is to try to "get it right" (or at least as right as possible) in terms of how human beings other than myself might feel about what I make and, secondly, to make a positive contribution to providing resources to support biodiversity with as little collateral environmental damage as possible. In contrast to the traditional restoration ecology philosophy, I believe that in urban open spaces the key objective is to get it right for people first and then to shoe-horn in as many biodiversity benefits as possible. This is because, outside of your garden, if you don't get people who view or use the site on board, the political pressure for removal will often be too great for the sowing or planting to persist, and sooner or later it will be replaced by mown grass or similar. Everyone loses in this scenario.

Of course, this does not mean that I as designer completely hand over my decision-making to the public, but rather that I make my choices within an understanding of this background political and social-cultural context. So, for example, if I believe that the right thing to do is to use native species—perhaps to make connections with the native context outside the site boundary or to minimize the risk of escape of non-native species into a surrounding environment which is particularly sensitive in terms of possible diminution of character—I would create a gradient of nativeness in my design. This would work by having perhaps two or three native vegetation types.

In the cultural core of the site, the areas most used by people or perhaps the most developed or urban, I would design a native vegetation in which species were selected to be as floriferous, attractive, and long flowering as possible. I would probably leave out meadow grasses that visually dilute the flowering drama. This human-centred designed native plant community would then be surrounded by another in which flowering, while still important, would be counterbalanced more by a highly sustainable structure, perhaps using more grasses. This vegetation would have much more of the character of the semi-natural vegetation that was setting the overall context for the project. Depending on scale and perceived human needs, I might need to create two or three of these gradient plant communities to "get it right".

The same ideas can be used when not using natives or when using natives and exotics in the core cultural areas. Through a series of almost concentric rings of different designed communities, I gradually fade the exotics out and bleed more natives in, until by the time the site boundary is reached, there are no exotics present. This is a much more sensible, human-centred approach to take than dogmatic natives-only prescriptions allow.

Native plants and plant communities are very important in setting context. If you are in rural, semi-natural landscapes with few architectural cues evident as to where in the world you are, it is the plants and plant communities that tell you this, assuming you can read these cues. This is interesting, however, because anecdotal evidence suggests that many highly urbanized people who have grown up detached from the semi-natural world can no longer do this very well. Many landscape architects take as a given that because they can do this, so can everyone else, but this is not necessarily so. Even if this is so, I would still tend to want to respond to strongly native contexts by using at least some native material. But when one then transfers these ideas to urban landscapes, and in particular those populated by multi-ethnic communities, do these ideas continue to have any purchase?

My six-year stint working on the Queen Elizabeth Olympic Park in London gave me lots of time to observe and think about these sorts of issues in East London, an extraordinary cultural melting pot within probably the most global city on Earth. If you look at the character of the greenspace networks of parks in cities such as these, at either a large or small scale, how important is semi-natural native vegetation in terms of creating and informing a local sense of character and identity? What does this all mean to someone, for example, of Bangladeshi origin who lives in East London and rarely if ever ventures out to visit the countryside? We know from research that this and many other primarily urban-based ethnic groups are less well represented in visits to the countryside, and that notions of identity in these urban-based cultures are not strongly formed by romantic notions about the native landscapes. The tendency is to believe that these notions should be instilled through education, but this is surely just cultural hegemony that is out of kilter with the realities of migration and the future of the global city.

Native plants and native plant communities are very important in setting context and character, but this is not necessarily so in highly urban contexts. Perhaps what is more important in these contexts is simply to provide experiences that are meaningful to the multiplicity of local cultures at the point of experience or delivery.

ESTABLISHING PLANTING FROM SOWING SEED

Where this book differs, I think, from other books on designing naturalistic vegetation is that it shows how this can be achieved by sowing seeds of the desired species in combination with small amounts of planting or no planting at all. The advantages of doing this is to greatly reduce costs of plants and planting, allowing much larger areas of meadow to be created than would otherwise be possible. Sowing also allows much more complex planting to be created with many species per unit area that flower for longer and create extremely fine-grained change on almost a daily basis. At the scale of the garden, there is a nearly endless variation and change in such vegetation that creates an inherent fascination for human beings. It all seems magical: you start with almost nothing, and then gradually this vegetation (with your guiding hand and brain) just comes into being. Things just seem to happen spontaneously. Tom Stuart-Smith put it well, "It is an encounter with nature". Sown vegetation also brings improved ecological performance over planted, as the much higher density of plants make the vegetation much more resistant to weed invasion.

My own interest in meadow-like vegetation and how to design and construct it, be it in my garden or a public landscape, was prompted by the absence of this vegetation in my childhood. I grew up in the 1960s in a small mining community in north-eastern England in which, to my child's eyes, nearly all flowers seemed to have been wiped away by the apocalyptic industrialism of the previous 150 years. While at university, I was inspired by the research undertaken by Terry Wells on how to recreate native U.K. wildflower meadows.

When I moved to Melbourne, Australia, after completing my Ph.D., I was entranced by some of the roadside fragments of steppe-like native grasslands that once covered the volcanic plains to the west of Melbourne. I could see that these plant communities could form the basis of beautiful meadow-like vegetation for Australian gardens, parks, and road verges. Although there would be many situations in which a purely native version would be most appropriate, I was more interested in using the native species in my research as the basis for a hybrid vegetation that included compatible non-native species. This vegetation would flower for longer and be taller, more visually dramatic, and perhaps more usable in more intensely cultural environments while still providing a rich habitat for native animals. This set me on an early collision course with a more literal nativist agenda.

Unknown to me, cocooned in Australia, there were others who had had similar thoughts, while often arriving at these from different directions. When I returned to live in Britain in 1993, I soon became involved in a group organizing a series of conferences and field visits to designed landscapes across Europe know as "Perennial Perspectives". Much of the impetus behind pulling this together came from Brita Von Schoenaich, a German landscape architect working in London. Brita is a pretty indefatigable character who charmed and corralled a diverse array of Germans, Dutch, Swedes, Swiss, and Brits

Steppe-like grassland fragments still survive on some of the roadsides through the basalt plains west of Melbourne, Australia. The topsoil has been removed at this scrape site on the western highway, creating the low-productivity conditions in which these species prosper.

Knautia macedonica, *Salvia nemorosa*, and *Verbascum speciosum* thrive in this more Balkan-inspired steppe.

together to learn about the others' planting ideas. This group included current luminaries such as Piet Oudolf and Cassian Schmidt—indeed, most of the people who are now big names in the European planting scene. There were also a few Americans, including James Van Sweden, Wolfgang Oehme, and prairie man Neil Diboll.

In common with most British designers and ecologists interested in planting, I knew very little about the traditions of the fellow Europeans, written as they were in a language other than English. There was a long history of interest in ecologically based public landscapes (less so private gardens) in Germany. Such interest had been developed from the 1950s by Professor Richard Hansen of the University of Weihenstephan, Munich, and was known in Germany as the Hansen School. Sensational though a lot of the German planting was, at the time I think I was most inspired by the Dutch School.

In contrast to the Hansen School which was based on plantings organized around a more literal interpretation of world plant communities (see the splendid text by Hansen and Stahl, *Perennials and Their Garden Habitats*), the Dutch work and particularly that of Rob Leopold and Henk Gerritsen was much freer. Gerritsen had developed the Priona Gardens with his partner Anton Schlepers, creating communities by putting together plants from different parts of the world with a thoughtful artistic appreciation of habitats and compatibility but in ways that produced exciting, constantly changing visuals.

Onopordum emerging within plantings in the Priona Gardens, Schuinesloot, Netherlands. These gardens are inspired by nature, but designed and presented through a cultural lens.

Their book on their ideas *Playing with Nature: Nature as an Inspiration for Gardens* is still available and is much recommended.

Many of these people came from an arts, philosophy, or design background. I was just about the only ecological-horticultural researcher in the group. These experiences gave me the stimulus to think long and hard about how to try to integrate human aesthetic needs with ecological science, in essence the core of the research plan I have followed since the mid 1990s. My initial research, which commenced soon after my arrival in Britain in 1993, was to look at whether it was possible to create native wildflower meadows by sowing, into which other native and non-native species were added by planting. This was very much me following in the footsteps of William Robinson at Gravetye Manor just over a century later, albeit armed with a lot more understanding of ecological science. Much of this early research was on the effect competition has on which plants can establish, and if they cannot, why and can anything be done about this.

Christopher Lloyd's famous garden at Great Dixter on the Sussex-Kent border had a long history of trying to establish non-native plants in native meadow swards. I got to know Christopher Lloyd really well, as planting in meadows was one of his real passions, and I was a would-be devotee.

Initially the sowing idea was really just to fill in the space, but I increasingly became interested in sowing as the main method. This was all happening in the 1990s at a time in Britain of ever-declining budgets for urban greenspace management, with market forces ideologies very much in the ascendancy. One could see the effect of this all around: as vegetation that was too difficult to manage was simply edited out of parks, there was very little left to look at that was interesting and little seasonal change. In all but the most affluent local government areas, greenspace was all becoming mown grass and trees or monocultures of evergreen shrubs.

A sculpture floats within some wild parsnips.

This was happening not only because of cuts in budget but also because of a much more serious loss of ambition for public spaces. It was as if the largely horticulturally trained greenspace management industry was hunkering down in a bunker waiting for the budget cuts storm to pass, after which there would be a return to the halcyon horticultural days of the past. I saw no such halcyon days on the horizon. Even if they were, it was clear to me that there were new emerging agendas that would change the urban landscape scene probably forever. The first of these was the growing awareness that planting in cities had to be good for wildlife as well as people.

This awareness tends to arrive first in small countries where there are not great tracts of wildlands, so nature and people have to share. In British cities prior to the 21st century, the places where people lived were generally simply blanked out on Nature Conservation Strategy plans. The assumption was that where there are a lot of our species there could be few other species worth thinking about. It's true that many large animals find it difficult to live in dense cities, but if the food and habitat resources are present this is not a problem for many small animals, such as invertebrates, small mammals, reptiles, and amphibians, and many birds. There was a need to design vegetation that was of value to wildlife.

I wasn't the first person to have this realization; there were many others in mainstream urban and rural nature conservation who had had this idea. The problem with their version of this idea, however, was that it was often based on the premise that what this vegetation looked like did not really matter. People would learn to like it, to see the world as they saw it, to see their light. Education was all they needed. Unfortunately, all the available evidence suggested that this had not occurred since the emergence of the nature in cities movement in Britain in the 1970s and it probably would never happen.

In response to this, my colleague Professor Nigel Dunnett and I began to develop an alternative model. For ecologically valuable vegetation to become widely accepted in valued parts of cities, it had to look attractive (and that generally means flowers) for as long as possible. We put these ideas in a book called *The Dynamic Landscape: Design, Ecology and Management of Naturalistic Urban Planting*. Looking good does not make a plant look bad to the wildlife you want it to support. This view seems to be commonly held and is a perspective from the 19th century forged in observing the negative effects of industrialization and intensive farming on the land. We need to move on from this view and accept that we can do bad or good for nature; it is a choice for individuals and human societies. This is a simple but fairly radical thought, but one which in many urban areas is really important to adopt.

The reason for our view is that human beings see the world in cities and other urban places differently to how they see the same scene in rural landscapes. Because naturalistic vegetation, and in particular herbaceous vegetation, has no obvious structure (other than repeating patterns of individual species that may be too subtle to read), it is intrinsically seen as disordered, wild, and lying outside notions of appropriateness for cities. As a result, it is often very challenging for most people to value this sort of vegetation. The same vegetation in a rural landscape is generally seen as fine: it's just how rural areas are.

My research, although primarily concerned with how to design and manage naturalistic vegetation, has also looked at how human beings interpret and value the very same vegetation. What causes negative reactions or positive perspectives in urban situations other than context? Human responses are generally very complex, but there are patterns. It is perfectly possible for ordinary urban people to come to terms with the disorder of naturalistic herbaceous vegetation and even to love it. It is also important to recognize that people might love this vegetation at some times of the year but dislike it at others. Ambiguity is normal.

Some people might love meadows because they were exposed to wild vegetation as children or imagined they were and create a romanticized sense of connection between distant past and present. I have had conversations with elderly people, and in particular women (who tend to be more articulate about these things), in front of a sward of Russian meadow species in Sheffield, where they told me with complete confidence that they hadn't seen those species since they were children. Others are more deeply immersed in more nature-centric views of the world and this allows them to filter out the disorder and see the beauty either in the actuality of what is in front of them or the idea it represents: nature as paragon. Of course, it doesn't matter how or why you find something beautiful, only that you do is quite sufficient. It is not a competition about the nature of truth. There is often a gender aspect to these processes. Men seem, in general, to find the disordered appearance of urban nature more challenging than women do and are more likely to want to see more evidence of control, but the boundaries are pretty fluid, and all these responses can be changed by prior or future experiences.

For those people who are not able to perhaps value naturalistic vegetation, and this appears to be a large majority in most urban cultures, the most powerful inducement to do

Experiments in 1997 kicked off my research into sowing as a means of establishing perennial herbaceous vegetation. This North American prairie planting in Sheffield is in its second year of growth.

so is flower colour and drama. Plantings that are regarded by such people when green and flowerless as just weeds are often seen as rich, beautiful, and meaningful a month later when in flower. The transformation of attitude is truly extraordinary to witness. These transformations seem to stick in many people; the off winter season is subsequently accepted because of the glory of the spring and summer flowering. These experiences and understandings have shaped my work and that of my colleague Nigel Dunnett. Vegetation is typically most preferred by ordinary people when it is relatively short, say 750–900 mm tall or less, and flowers for a long period with dramatic episodes. As it happens, this pattern of flowering is also very good for native invertebrate pollinators: a win-win situation.

People trained or interested in design will of course read their own preferences into this type of vegetation. I personally like tall emergent species punching out of lower layers of vegetation, but my design colleagues and clients in China, for example, often see this, much to my frustration, as just too messy.

My experiments into creating vegetation types entirely from sowing commenced in 1997, with North American prairie vegetation. I was working closely with Marcus De La Fleur, a Sheffield master's student at the time, but one highly experienced with all things

INTRODUCTION

25

to do with plants. We tried to identify the key factors that would prevent these species from establishing successfully in Sheffield (as opposed to Chicago) and persisting in our experiments. There were already a lot of people in the United States working with these species as natives, such as Neil Diboll at Prairie Nursery, Wisconsin, so I was able to access seed and look at what they did. The critical initial task seemed to be suppressing weeds. As natives, prairie plants were sown into U.S. soil under the presumption that eventually they would come good. This doesn't always happen if the current site occupants are sufficiently aggressive, and in ecological processes prior site occupation is very difficult (often impossible) and slow to overcome. In the very cool summers of northern Britain, it seemed very unlikely that this could happen, so we had to find a way to stop weed seeds in the soil from spoiling things. In the urban contexts I wanted to use this summer- to autumn-flowering vegetation in, it simply wasn't politically tenable to wait 5 years for the desired species (even if they could) to begin to make their presence felt. It would be swept away as a messy failure long before this ever happened, and sowing would be consigned to the "it doesn't work" category and forgotten about.

We tested a 75-mm layer of sand as a sowing mulch in comparison with the inevitable car crash option of sowing straight into initially weed-free topsoil. It is possible to sow straight into soil. I did this once in our garden, but I almost died from exhaustion weeding it in the first year. The sand sowing mulch worked brilliantly and has been the mainstay of my practice ever since. We also tested different forms of simple management: cutting down in spring and removing, the same and burning, and the same and spraying a contact herbicide as a chemical equivalent to burning. Sand mulching and burning produced beautiful vegetation with few weeds. It could work.

After this I began to lay out a plan of what I was going to look at next in the research, so I compiled a list of the most extraordinary semi-natural herbaceous plants and communities in the world. On my must do (or at least must try) list were the *Primula*-dominated wet meadows of Yunnan and Sichuan in western China, dry steppe-like meadows from western North America and Eurasia, and the Drakensberg grasslands of high-altitude eastern South Africa. Most recently I have worked with my Ph.D. student Ye Hang on the niche steppe plant communities on the tops of mountains in western South Africa, a Mediterranean climate in which, because of winter cold, the vegetation behaves as if it were temperate. The model that allowed us to ultimately understand how to create a given vegetation type by sowing involved several steps.

Where it was possible to do so, I tried to identify good examples of the vegetation in question growing in the wild in its country of origin, which I then visited to gain a better understanding of the visual and ecological characteristics and potential. What were the outstanding aesthetic aspects? What were the aesthetic downsides? And likewise for the ecological characteristics? This allowed us to fast track our understanding of the range of vegetation types. In particular, we could produce a list of the species that we thought were the most important to work with to produce a functional but glamorous, long-flowering

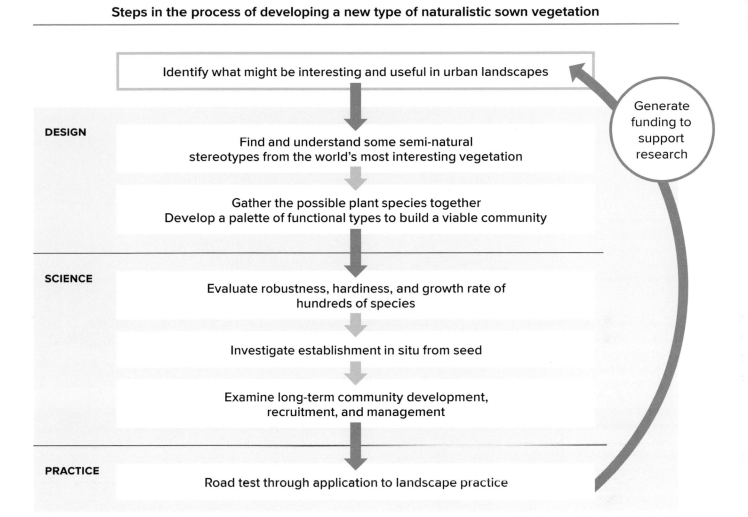

Steps in the process of developing a new type of naturalistic sown vegetation

Identify what might be interesting and useful in urban landscapes

Generate funding to support research

DESIGN

Find and understand some semi-natural stereotypes from the world's most interesting vegetation

Gather the possible plant species together
Develop a palette of functional types to build a viable community

SCIENCE

Evaluate robustness, hardiness, and growth rate of hundreds of species

Investigate establishment in situ from seed

Examine long-term community development, recruitment, and management

PRACTICE

Road test through application to landscape practice

vegetation. Following this, we then had to try and obtain seed of these key species. In some cases, it was possible to obtain species directly from the commercial seed industry; for example, Jelitto Perennial Seeds sells almost 4000 species. Where this was not possible, we had to try to obtain plants or seed of these species either from within the horticultural world, including botanic gardens, and from people growing those key species on a very small scale within the country of origin. Where a key species was not available from Jelitto or equivalents in other countries, this meant a long period of growing plants from seed and producing seed in sufficient quantity in Sheffield on research plots. We have used this latter process to the greatest degree in our work within the South African flora, and in some cases it has taken us more than 5 years of growing mother plants to have a sufficient volume of seed of species to use in experiments.

Small monocultural microcosms (300 × 300 mm) in Sheffield provide a basic understanding of what individual species (here South African Drakensberg species) do, including field emergence after sowing, seedling survival and robustness, growth rate, winter cold tolerance, years to flowering, and duration of flowering.

Much larger (2.4 × 2.4 m) microcosm experiments using sown communities of South African Drakensberg species were studied over a period of 5 years. Here the plants are shown at the end of the first year.

Once we had seed, we could then work on the germination and emergence characteristics of the species in Petri dish studies. We would then move to small scale, often 300 × 300 mm outdoor sowings into sowing mulches. These processes allowed us to become very familiar with the traits and behaviours of the species. Which ones were very slow to germinate and emerge, and which were quick? How fast did species grow relative to one another? How suited were they to the climate of Sheffield? These initial research investigations took between 2 and 5 years for each different community. We would then move on (generally as a Ph.D. study) and look at how the species which we had previously only grown in monoculture fared in much larger, but carefully controlled microcosm experiments, where they are mixed with other species. What plants do in monoculture is often very different to what they do in mixture. A plant which grows slowly in one climate is fine when it doesn't have to compete with an adjacent plant which is faster growing, but when you put them together, the previously slowly growing but satisfactory species is soon eliminated by the faster growing neighbour which intercepts most of the light. These microcosms experiments were generally kept, maintained, and monitored for at least 5 years, and when possible for longer.

These microcosm experiments give a very good indication of how the vegetation will develop and change, which species will become dominant, and which will fail and disappear. Very often these experiments are designed to incorporate different management techniques and to study the impact of these on both the community as a whole and the individual species.

After running microcosm experiments for 3 to 5 years, we would generally have enough understanding of that particular plant community to begin to road test it in the real landscape, applying the research-based understanding to practice. My first attempt to do this was in 1998–1999 at the newly created National Botanic Gardens of Wales, near Carmarthen, where I created a sown native wildflower meadow into which pot-grown herbaceous plants were planted. I also road tested a North American prairie community. Both of these schemes involved thousands of square metres and included stripping off the topsoil to reduce fertility and weed levels. It was all rather stressful, but it sort of worked, although perhaps not to the degree that I had hoped. As with all practice activities, however, it was a valuable learning experience as well as a terrifying exercise in self-doubt.

Since those early days, my practice has become more refined and the results more predictable. This book is an insight into how my thoughts, research, and practice over the past 30 years have fed off one another, and how you can use this understanding to design and implement your own meadows and similar naturalistic vegetation types in gardens and public landscapes.

ABOUT THIS BOOK

In the chapter "Looking to Nature for Inspiration and Design Wisdom", I describe what to consider when choosing plants for a particular cultivation location and how to use the appearance of plants as a guide to the conditions they require. Designing attractive vegetation involves working with the various layers of canopies that exist within plant communities. In addition, considering the ecological classifications of the members of a plant community (competitors, stress tolerators, and ruderals) is also important in my design practice. Finally, I describe important world plant communities that can be used as sources of inspiration for naturalistic perennial herbaceous planting, including summer-cut grassland and meadows, summer-uncut grasslands such as steppe and prairie, and woodland understorey and edge communities.

In "Designing Naturalistic Herbaceous Plant Communities", I discuss the importance of evaluating the planting site to inform your design decisions. This process involves considering both the macroclimatic factors, such as latitude, altitude, and continentality, and microclimatic factors, such as the degree of localized shade and moisture stress. Of course, a designer must also consider the key site user needs and preferences. When choosing plants for a particular herbaceous community, there are many species traits and characteristics to take into account: robustness and long-term persistence, potential naturalization and invasiveness, growth form and method of spread, growth rate, palatability to herbivores, drama and duration of the flowering season, plant structure in relation to attractiveness, and capacity to support native biodiversity. I discuss the use of spreadsheets to assist in making selection decisions based on all these traits. When formulating design objectives, you might include several communities within a single project and should consider the degree of structural and species diversity needed within a community, as well as the component species' attractiveness to people across the year and appropriateness in terms of local character and scale. Finally, I discuss design from the perspective of community spatial organization and how to use single-, two-, and three-layer communities effectively.

In the chapter "Seed Mix Design, Implementation, and Initial Establishment", I describe both the aesthetic and logistical aspects of designing seed mixes to fit the site conditions as well as the design aspirations. In addition to envisaging the appearance and performance of the community you wish to create, you must also consider the commercial availability and germinability of seed, the field emergence percentage of each component species, and seed dormancy constraints. Apportioning the total seedling target to individual species in the mix involves calculating the weight of seed of each species needed to achieve the target density. I describe how to perform these calculations and how to produce the seed mixes. Alternatively, of course, you could use one of the many seed mixes that are available commercially. Likewise, designing and implementing planting mixes is simpler than designing seed mixes because the plants already exist, and they simply need to be planted at the site and kept weed free. Sowing and planting a vegetation community involves site preparation, soil cultivation, and spreading sowing mulches. I describe the best times of the year to sow particular species, how to integrate planting and sowing at the same site, and the use of jute matting as a surface stabilizer. At the end of this chapter is a special section providing detailed emergence data to use in designing seed mixes. The data are the results of my research performed over many years in Sheffield, United Kingdom. The tables in this section list hundreds of species that showed particular percentages of emergence under the experimental conditions, ranging from those showing less than 10 per cent emergence to those showing more than 70 per cent.

In "Establishment and Management", I describe the key establishment activities in the first year, including applying irrigation to achieve target field emergence, applying nitrogen-only fertilizers to boost growth, minimizing slug damage to seedlings, and managing weeds and the sown species. Long-term management of naturalistic vegetation communities involves targeting weeds at the critical developmental stages to maximize long-term control. I also describe in detail the effect of community type on the subsequent management of forb-dominated, steppe-like, prairie-like, woodland understorey, and Mediterranean communities.

The final section of the book is a collection of case studies in which I describe eleven projects—ten in England and one in western China—that I have worked on over the past two decades. In these case studies I describe both what has and what has not worked in these sown communities or sown and planted hybrids. Each case study has tables that list all the species included in the project as well as notes on the sowing and planting densities.

The Resources section provides online sources of information on wild habitats and contact information for companies that sell Soil Saver jute matting, seed for individual species based on region and community type, and seed mixes.

LOOKING TO NATURE FOR INSPIRATION AND DESIGN WISDOM

If you want to create successful naturalistic herbaceous vegetation, it is really helpful to develop at least an appreciation of how this type of vegetation looks and works in nature. There are many reasons for looking to nature as a means of inspiring and refining design ideas, not least because semi-natural vegetation gives you a sense of what is possible and what can be sustained in the longer term and what cannot. The inconvenient truth is that it is not possible to wish away ecologically ill-informed plantings; sooner or later these just fail or require the expenditure of unsustainable amounts of time and effort in trying to prop up vegetation that is just not suited to where it has been used.

CHOOSING PLANTS TO BE FIT FOR A PARTICULAR CULTIVATION LOCATION

As a general principle, the closer the conditions under which you want to use a plant in a community are to those where a plant grows in its natural distribution, the better the "fit". By conditions I mean the entire range of what plants have to interact with, for example, the overall climate, local microclimatic deviations from this, soil types (really a surrogate for how much water and nutrients are available), the level of competition with other plants, and the herbivorous animals that might want to eat them.

Climate

Whatever the scale you are working at—whether a home garden or public park—the starting point in arriving at plants that can grow well in the area is to review the climate of the site in relation to where the plants come from in nature. To do this you need to find out where the species you are interested in are naturally distributed, through books and the internet. Comparisons are most difficult with species that have distributions over very large areas, because the climatic conditions in one part of the distribution will be very different to that in others. In addition, you will rarely know where in the distribution the seed that you eventually use originally came from. This sort of detective work is, however, the only sensible way to proceed, despite these ifs and buts.

Plants that are well fitted to the climate are likely to be the most robust as a rather crude generalization. The very best climate fit is likely to be found in local native species, which by definition have evolved in the region around the site. The key climatic factors to consider are how warm are the summers, how cold are the winters, when is the growing season, and what is the rainfall during the growing season. Finding information on these factors online is normally straight-forward.

Latitude, that is, distance from the equator or the poles, has a major effect on climatic parameters and particularly growing season and winter temperatures. Many places at the same latitude experience similar climatic conditions, for example, Oklahoma City, Oklahoma, United States, and Beijing, China, despite being thousands of kilometres apart geographically. Shanghai, China, and Athens, Georgia, United States, are another couplet. What this means is that species from China can theoretically be as well fitted to the climate of Oklahoma City as local native American species, and vice versa. The critical thing in making these comparisons is that you compare like with like. If you compare a city at the same latitude with another, but one is in the middle of a continent and the other on the edge of a landmass next to the sea, the oceanic effect will mean the climates are very different.

The other factor that corrupts simple latitudinal comparisons is altitude. Using the example of western China as a source of plant material for projects in Britain, although the British Isles lie between 50 and 55°N with the Sichuan Plateau far to the south between 30 and 35°N, because of its very high altitude the plateau climate is similar to that of Britain. A 1000-m increase in altitude is approximately equivalent to a 5° poleward shift

Altitude has a major impact on the nature of plant communities and the climatic tolerances of the component species. This alpine vegetation of Sichuan grows at 4000 m.

This evergreen broadleaf forest is 50 km distant at an altitude of 1000 m.

in latitude. Wild plants hone their biochemistry to align with local climatic conditions, so a population of a widespread species found at, say, 3000 m altitude will have evolved to grow well in the cool summers and low moisture stress conditions of that altitude. British gardens are full of plants from the mountains of Sichuan that are demonstrably well fitted. Indeed this flora is in fact better fitted to Britain than that of the low-altitude Chinese cities only 100 km from these mountains. Examples of this nature abound, and more information on this from a Western European perspective can be found in Jane Taylor's *Weather in the Garden*.

Such mismatches are often a major problem when trying to rely on only the native flora in large, low-altitude cities surrounded by high mountains. Many of the wild plant communities that have survived urbanization and agriculture are largely restricted to these mountains and potentially poorly fitted to the urban environment. Geographic proximity, when altitude changes are pronounced, is not a good measure of likely plant climatic fitness for your site.

As a result of these climatic phenomena and their effects on plant capacity to grow well on the site, you need not be restricted purely to the local plant communities. These ideas about fitness operate over a sliding scale: sometimes you need species that are extremely fit, perhaps where little care is possible, whereas in other cases plants that are much less climatically fit will be good enough because there will be enough maintenance available to make it all work. Plants that are extremely fit tend to have a greater capacity to naturalize beyond the planting site. The critical thing is to try not to mix species together in designed communities that have very different levels of fitness, because when you do this the least fitted species normally fail due to competition from the better fitted ones.

In my work in the cool oceanic climate of northern Britain, heat-demanding herbaceous plants like the North American *Ruellia humilis* just disappear when exposed to faster growing cool species. The same plant in southern China is relatively indestructible because the average midday temperature is over 25°C. Even in the United Kingdom this plant is almost satisfactory 200 km to the south of Sheffield's cool summers.

Soils and soil types

In addition to climatic match factors, being a geographically local native does not guarantee that the plant will work well on the particular site. This may sound counter-intuitive, but this is because plants have evolved to require, within the background climatic regime, relatively specific conditions in terms of soil wetness and dryness, soil fertility (productivity), and the intensity of invertebrate or vertebrate herbivores feeding upon them.

Plants growing in nature do not know about the complicated soil classifications devised by geologists and soil scientists. Instead, plants are found where they experience an appropriate level of soil moisture, soil oxygen, and soil nutrients to be able to grow robustly enough to compete with their neighbours. As a result they are often restricted to certain soil types, and the narrower the range of tolerance of these conditions the more restricted the distribution of a species. Common species tend to have broader

This shallow, highly unproductive limestone soil on a hillside in the Czech Republic allows a diversity of small plants to survive

soil tolerances than uncommon species. Soils that are very finely textured such as clays and finely decomposed organic soils typically hold a lot of water and very little oxygen, whereas those that are very coarsely grained (for example, those based on sand or gravels) contain little water but much oxygen.

In between these hypothetical soil extremes lie a huge diversity of soils that correspond to some sort of normal or average soil moisture and oxygen status. If the soils at the site are very dry, plants that naturally occur on wet soils will be of limited to no use, no matter how attractive they are. Throughout this book I will talk about soils and plants in terms of these simple but profoundly important gradients of soil moisture and oxygen.

Another aspect to consider is soil pH, a measure of how acidic or alkaline a soil is. Some plants are only associated with acidic soils and some only with alkaline soils. Relatively few herbaceous plants fall into the former category, as these conditions tend to be more the territory of acid-loving woody families, such as the Ericaceae (*Rhododendron*, *Erica*, *Calluna*, and *Vaccinium*). Quite a number of herbaceous plants are, however, associated with strongly alkaline soils, although they tend to grow perfectly well on many other soils providing they are not highly acidic. Very often these relationships are not what they might initially seem. For example, highly alkaline soils are very infertile, as high soil pH reduces the solubility of many key nutrients, including nitrogen, iron, and magnesium, in the soil water. This may be more important as to why a species grows at a site than the high pH itself. This idea of infertility or productivity is a very important one in understanding how both naturally occurring and designed plant communities work, but is rather confusing as it runs counter to many conventional ideas about gardening.

A core principle in conventional gardening is that by adding nutrients (primarily nitrogen, phosphorous, and potassium) you make plants grow faster and therefore

Where the soil gets deeper some 20 m further down the same hill, productivity goes up and these species lose out due to shading by taller and more productive grass species.

"better". More nutrients make leaves and plants larger and lusher. Plants are likely to have more stems and potentially more and larger flowers. These are all positive attributes for most people, and we know from psychological research that this is linked with our own evolution: places with lush vegetation speak to us of water and lots of things to eat. The capacity of a soil to allow plants to be leafy and vigorous is known in ecological jargon as productivity.

Soils that support only small amounts of aboveground leaves and stems, such as an acidic heathland or chalk grassland in Western Europe or a so-called goat prairie (which occurs on steep, dry slopes with thin soil) in the United States, are known as unproductive, whereas soils that contain lots of nutrients and water, such as an agricultural field or a garden, are known as productive. The acidic heathland on average typically supports about 300–400 g of dry biomass/m², whereas your garden will support about three to four times as much, because the soils are naturally more fertile and they have been fertilized by you and the previous householders, potentially for centuries.

In general, as productivity increases individual plants tend to become more attractive to people. The problem, however, when thinking about communities of plants as in a garden or meadow is as productivity increases, the species that produce the greatest amount of biomass most quickly begin to dominate, shading the smaller, slower growing species. After a couple of years these slower, smaller species are lost from the community, leading to ongoing decline of plant diversity in the planting. This loss is much reduced if the slower, smaller species are shade tolerant.

Because of this process, in the natural world the most diverse herbaceous plant communities—those with the greatest number of different species per square metre—are nearly always found on less productive soils. It's only possible in the longer term to have a lot of different species in each square metre where the growth of the fastest species is restricted by limited availability of nutrients and/or water. This is a fundamental rule in plant ecology that can only be breached when intensive inputs of maintenance are available. In a garden you stop one plant from eliminating a neighbour by either replanting it further away or clipping its shoots to reduce its shading of the other. This rule also explains why slowly growing or small local native species often don't persist well in gardens when mixed with other species, even within their native range. The more sun demanding a species is, the more likely that it will be eliminated by competition with taller, faster growing species.

In Western Europe, for example, many native wildflowers of dry, unproductive alkaline soils tend to persist poorly on moister more productive soils, not because these conditions are fundamentally hostile towards them, but because other species grow faster in response to these conditions and hence tend to shade out the species of unproductive habitats. In a garden context, this is essentially what is going on in a rockery or similar open planting of small slowly growing plants on productive soil. The rockery is constantly invaded by weeds, species of which can produce much more growth more quickly than the rockery plants. If you stop weeding, the rockery plants are eliminated within a year or so by the shade cast by the weeds. The more you fertilize the rockery, the more quickly you cause the extinction of the rockery plants if you don't weed.

The world's most unproductive soils are known as serpentines, in which the presence of high concentrations of naturally occurring heavy metals severely restricts growth rate or even the survival of intolerant species. These sites support very interesting communities of rare species, including some *Penstemon* species, because most of the common species of a region can't tolerate the toxic metal concentrations in the soil. The green roof on my potting shed supports (minus the heavy metals) structurally similar communities to those that occur on serpentines, through water and nutrient shortfalls.

Palatability to herbivores

The most problematic herbivores of herbaceous plants differ from country to country depending on the local climate and the effect this has had on evolutionary processes. In maritime climates with frequent rainfall, slugs and snails are normally the dominant herbivores, especially on herbaceous plants whose shoots have to push through the soil surface each spring, providing great dining opportunities for slugs. In more continental climates such as that of the American Midwest, slugs are a minor ecological factor and the invertebrate herbivores are mainly insects, such as grasshoppers. Insects tend to graze on a mass of leaves and their effect is spread across the community, whereas intense herbivory by slugs often results in the loss of the most palatable species either as seedlings or adult shoots pushing through the soil in spring. In heavily wooded landscapes in continental climates, deer tend to take over this role from the slugs, namely that of catastrophic repeated defoliation in spring.

USING THE APPEARANCE OF PLANTS AS A GUIDE TO THE CONDITIONS THEY REQUIRE

The structure or architecture of plants can tell you a lot about them and the environments they are designed to grow in, if you know what the cues are. Plants with small leaves are generally adapted to sunny, high-light environments where large leaves would overheat and are highly tolerant of soil moisture stress. Plants with large leaves are generally naturally associated with the other extreme, moist soil conditions and shade. If they are large and woolly, as in *Verbascum*, they are generally tolerant of drought.

These plant traits represent the ecological extremes. Most plants have intermediate sized leaves and are found in more mid-range conditions. Some low-growing plants, such as the temperate European *Primula veris*, have leaves that typically grow much larger as the growing season progresses and they are subjected to increasing amounts of shade from surrounding plants. This is a ploy to try to capture more light as shading increases.

Plants that have very low spreading foliage (for example, many *Thymus* species) or flat leaf rosettes (such as *Eryngium bourgatii*) are associated with low productivity soils and open sunny habitats. Unless species with these architectures are shade tolerant, as in the case of *Primula vulgaris* and to a lesser degree *Primula veris*, they would not be able to capture enough light to persist in competition with the taller plants favoured on productive soil. Plants with markedly hemispherical canopies are often associated with dry unproductive sites, which restrict the production of tall leafy stems, and the hemispherical leaf orientation allows the minimization of canopy surface area and hence water loss. Plants with taller leafy stems are normally associated with moister more productive soil, with the tallest leafiest stems of all associated with the giant plants (mega-forbs) of wetlands on highly fertile soils, such as *Eupatorium fistulosum*, *Filipendula* species, *Helianthus* species, *Leucanthemella serotina*, and *Rudbeckia laciniata*.

Most species clearly lie between these extremes, but architecture always reflects soil productivity conditions pertaining to a plant's natural distribution. Most plants with large rounded leaves are associated with the shaded moist edges of woodland or found in deep ravines or along drainage lines. This happens even in relatively dry climates; for example, the western North American drainage-line specialist *Darmera peltata* has large round leaves, but these are more thickened to cope with episodes of summer drought in a near-Mediterranean climate. In general, large leaves are uncommon in dry shade, with the conspicuous exception of some ferns, such as *Polystichum*.

CANOPY LAYERING WITHIN PLANT COMMUNITIES

Local site conditions such as soil moisture stress and soil productivity have a major effect on the overall appearance and character of different plant communities. In part, this is due to the individual architecture and growth patterns of the component plants. Equally important, however, is how these different architectures tend to be arranged into two or three layers of foliage, typically with a ground layer, middle layer, and tallest emergent

The hummock form and narrow hard leaves of the South African *Aptosimum spinescens* is common in extremely unproductive, dry, and sunny habitats.

A hummock form, but with larger leaves, is seen in drought-tolerant plants of dry but less extreme habitats such as this European sea holly, *Eryngium maritimum*.

At the other end of the spectrum *Aconitum lycoctonum*, with large soft leaves and tall leafy stems, is a plant of wet and shaded woodland edges.

The California native *Darmera peltata* has the large leaves of a wet species but is capable of coping with seasonal drought in stream beds.

Corydalis solida flowers in spring between the large emerging rosettes of *Veratrum* that will soon overtop it in mountain meadows of northern Italy.

layer. Not all of these layers may be evident at any given point of time. The evolution of these layers has often been driven by two key factors, the opportunities to gain advantage in utilizing light for photosynthesis and to compete with other plants in attracting insects to ensure flower pollination.

Many examples of semi-natural herbaceous vegetation show layering. The net effect is to increase the number of species that can coexist in the same area of ground by distributing species across two or more canopy layers. This form of spatial organization also has a major impact on appearance and plant use in designed landscapes, and it is discussed in greater depth from a design perspective in the next chapter.

The ground layer

Except on dry unproductive soils, which inhibit the development of tall overtopping canopy, the plants in the ground layer tend to be largely spring flowering and either highly shade tolerant or able to go dormant in summer as they become heavily shaded by taller species. Some species do both. Very often these species are either winter growing or start growing very early in the calendar year to utilize the light that is abundant before other species start growing. Examples of geophytic (bulbs, corms, and tubers) species include *Anemone nemorosa*, *Anemone blanda*, *Corydalis solida*, *Cyclamen coum*, *Cyclamen purpurascens*, and *Cyclamen hederifolium*. Herbaceous species that flower in spring and then

enter early dormancy include *Cardamine bulbifera*, *Cardamine enneaphyllos*, *Cardamine waldsteinii*, *Dicentra formosa*, *Dodecatheon meadia*, *Lathyrus vernus*, *Primula elatior*, *Primula sieboldii*, *Primula veris*, *Primula vulgaris*, and *Pulmonaria* species.

Species that don't go dormant but can survive in low light levels in summer, provided the amount of biomass of the taller canopy is not too dense, include *Ajuga reptans*, *Ajuga genevensis*, *Asarum europaeum*, *Geum* cultivars derived from *G. rivale* and *G. coccineum*, *Heuchera villosa*, *Impatiens omeiana*, *Lamium orvala*, *Melittis melissophyllum*, *Omphalodes cappadocica*, *Primula polyneura*, *Saxifraga* ×*urbium*, *Tellima grandiflora*, and *Tiarella wherryi*. The capacity of many of these species to survive in mixed plantings depends very heavily on how fertile the soil is and hence how much shade is likely to be cast by taller, emergent species.

The middle canopy layer

Plants in the middle layer usually commence flowering between late spring and summer. In communities which are very unproductive, this layer may represent the upper layer. In extremely productive systems this layer may be obscured by the upper emergent layer later in the season. Many of these species represent the average herbaceous plant: they often have some tolerance of shade but also grow well in sun. This is a large and diverse group of plants that are difficult to neatly categorize. Most flower between late spring

Heuchera villosa in May, when it is one of the taller components in this woodland edge planting at Queen Elizabeth Olympic Park in London.

The same scene in October, when *Heuchera villosa* has become a middle canopy species.

Asphodelus microcarpus and *Ferula communis* in central Sicily are striking emergents in April, but they enter dormancy in early summer and look pretty sad thereafter. They should be used with caution in designed plantIngs that need to look good in late summer and autumn.

and late summer, but a few, such as *Aster oblongifolius*, flower in autumn. Species that form a middle canopy layer and that flower in autumn are often associated with very dry, unproductive habitats, such as *A. oblongifolius*, or heavy shade, as in *Heuchera villosa*. In these situations these species may be the tallest in the community.

The upper emergent layer

Tall emergent layers are only possible when productivity in terms of soil nutrients and water are sufficient to allow the manufacture of tall flowering stems. To plants the payoff from investing so much of their growth in these tall structures is the opportunity to get noticed and attract pollinators who might otherwise visit other flowers. Many species with very tall flowering stems flower in summer or autumn, such as *Actaea* species, many *Aconitum*, *Eupatorium* species, *Filipendula* species, *Helianthus* species, *Inula* species, *Kniphofia multiflora*, *Kniphofia rooperi*, *Rudbeckia nitida*, *Silphium laciniatum*, *Silphium terebinthinaceum*, and *Vernonia* species. Most of these species are associated with damp sites on fertile soils with reliable summer rainfall. Some species with tall stems behave in a geophytic fashion and flower earlier in the year, say in late spring, and then enter summer dormancy after this. Many of these species come from climates that are too dry to support growth after early summer, including some *Delphinium*, such as the Rocky Mountain *D. glaucum* and the Californian *D. trolliifolium*. Mediterranean and central Asian *Ferula* and *Prangos* behave in this way, and on really dry sites the European *Laserpitium siler* does as well. The most extreme examples of species responding in this way are geophytes, such as some of the bigger *Allium* and *Eremurus*. In complete contrast, the June-flowering Spanish grass *Stipa gigantea* does not enter dormancy post flowering. Many of these species are very important visually to provide vertical design lines and create drama in plantings.

FORMS OF ECOLOGICAL CLASSIFICATION

Ecological classification helps us to understand individual species in greater detail. There are many ways to do this, ranging from observation based on what plants do through to far less obvious characteristics that would not be evident to the casual observer. The most obvious ecological classification of plants is how many years the plant continues to live after setting seed: annuals live for 1 year maximum and die after setting seed, biennials live for 2 years, monocarps typically live for 3–7 years, and perennials live for many years. Another familiar way to categorize is based on taxonomic lineage. For example, monocots include many geophytes and orchids, grasses, and graminoids (which are not members of the grass family, but share similar morphological characteristics). Then we have dicots, which comprise most of the trees and shrubs you know, plus all herbaceous plants that are not grasses, graminoids, or geophytes. These latter dicots are frequently referred to by ecologists as forbs. Clearly there are some crossovers between these classifications, for example, perennial forbs, biennial forbs, annual forbs, and similar for graminoids and so on.

Still fairly familiar are categorizations on the basis of how plant species make their living. We have nitrogen fixers that convert atmospheric nitrogen gas into nitrates via bacteria in their roots, parasites with no green leaves, hemi-parasites that are semi-parasitic and have green leaves, geophytes that seasonally die back to a subterranean storage organ below the surface of the ground, and C3 and C4 grasses that grow during cool or warm periods of the year, respectively. Much more obscure is Raunkaier's 1934 classification based on the positions of the resting buds during the season of dormancy. For herbaceous plants, the most important of these classes is hemicryptophyte, with the resting buds at the soil surface, and geophyte, with the resting buds below the surface. Again, there are a lot of crossovers between these classifications; for example, geophytes are associated with both taxonomic and bud position classifications. In essence, these classification terms are ways to try to create a language to describe or conceptualize ecological behaviour.

Aut-ecological frameworks

A key purpose of this chapter is to equip readers with a simple but effective ecological framework based on how species behave within semi-natural plant communities to help make better design decisions. This goal has been much advanced over the past 40 years by the introduction of aut-ecological ideas and frameworks. In many ways, these build on some of the more familiar classifications mentioned above. *Aut-ecology* literally means the ecology of the self, and it is really just about what a plant does, its strategies for getting by. An understanding of plants can be based on different ways of thinking and looking: an ecological perspective, a horticultural perspective, or a design perspective. In many cases, the most profound of these understandings is the ecological, whereas the most popular and widely understood is the horticultural.

If one looks in a textbook on plants of importance in cultivation, such as the *RHS Encyclopaedia of Perennials* by Graham Rice, a traditional horticultural perspective is revealed. Take the genus *Kniphofia*, for example. There is a lot of information on cultivars, but the cultivation information on these and the species that are covered is very generic. The take-home message is that *Kniphofia* all seem to require well-drained soil and sun and a site that is not too cold in winter. This is because horticultural understanding of plants is heavily skewed by the idea that one can amend the site to meet the preferences of a species or cultivar and use top-up maintenance to keep the plant growing well enough if it is still not sufficiently well suited.

If one takes an ecological perspective, which of course is mostly only really possible when the writer or observer is familiar with the plants in their wild habitats, a very different picture begins to emerge. The seventy-odd species of *Kniphofia*, in contrast to the impression given by Rice, are not very uniform, indeed they are extremely diverse visually and in ecological terms. Quite a few are wetland or drainage-line species, including *K. caulescens*, *K. linearifolia*, *K. multiflora*, and *K. uvaria* (in many populations). Other species are restricted to very dry sites, for example, *K. hirsuta* and *K. stricta*. Some species are colonial and form large monocultural clonal stands, including *K. caulescens* and *K. linearifolia*. Others are nearly always solitary, for example, *K. ritualis* and *K. triangularis*. This ecological perspective is much more revealing of what *Kniphofia* species really are and what they do and more importantly what they can tolerate, rather than what they might seem to prefer. The horticultural message is that *Kniphofia* need well-drained soil, so you will never see these plants used in sustainable drainage swales in wet places, yet some of these species have the genetic capacity to be used in this way.

This underplaying of the specific ecological characteristics of individual species is played out for nearly all genera you might choose at random. *Dracocephalum* is described as a genus for sunny locations, but *D. rupestre* is a relatively shade-tolerant species of moist shaded edges. In contrast, *D. peregrinum* is a species of highly xeric Mongolian and central Asian steppe; its small, heavily thickened leaves immediately give this away even if you didn't know where it came from.

These different ecological characteristics are often referred to by ecologists as characters or traits, and they represent adaptations, tolerances, and behaviours that have evolved in species over long periods of time in response to key environmental factors in the habitat. Traits include things that, once you get your head around these ideas, are

Kniphofia species often differ in ecological terms. ***Kniphofia stricta*** is a small solitary species of dry habitats. By contrast, ***Kniphofia caulescens*** (blue foliage, centre) is a colonial wet species, and ***Kniphofia northiae*** (edge of image) is a massive solitary wet species.

often evident in plants simply through looking or observing, such as growth rate and method of spread (for example, spreading rhizomes as opposed to a compact root system, mass regeneration from self-sown seed). Then there are traits that are really important but essentially invisible, such as how quickly plants close their leaf stomata to reduce the risk of desiccation in response to increasing soil dryness. Ecological traits are important when it comes to assembling plantings that are broadly compatible with one another.

Important ecological traits of herbaceous perennials that may be expressed across a gradient from low to high include:
- capacity to product seed
- ability of seed to germinate and establish seedlings
- palatability of seedlings and adults to herbivores
- capacity to form seed banks in the soil
- capacity to thrust shoots through leaf litter and overtopping plant canopies
- capacity to make vegetative spread via aboveground shoots
- capacity to make aboveground spread from shoots on the roots
- capacity to tolerate low light levels
- capacity to tolerate extreme moisture levels
- capacity for longevity

Another way of categorizing plants is through various functional type classifications. There is some overlap here with traits, as they have been developed by researchers looking at the same issues from differing perspectives. In *The Vegetation Ecology of Central Europe*, the German plant ecologist Heinz Ellenberg approached a functional type classification by developing indicator values that define the environmental conditions that circumscribe the distribution of the species of central Europe, and this has now been extended to other parts of Europe. For each species a value is set for important factors operating within the plant's natural habitat, such as the light regime, water regime, and nitrogen regime, on a predetermined scale. For example, a species requiring very wet soils might be scored as +2, a species from very dry soils as –2, and a species of average soils as 0.

Another aut-ecological approach to categorizing plants is how they will interact and compete with other plants and animals. This approach was developed by Professor Phil Grime at the University of Sheffield in the 1970s and described in his book *Plant Strategies, Vegetation Processes, and Ecosystem Properties*. It has proved to be really useful in planting design. It categorizes all plants as belonging to one of three primary strategies—competitors, stress tolerators, or ruderals—plus four secondary or intermediate strategies, such as stress-tolerant ruderals. This approach is particularly useful for designers because it is relatively easy to approximate species to one of the three primary strategies on the basis of informed guesses derived from looking at these plants and what they do.

Where soils are wet and fertile, the South African *Kniphofia linearifolia* competitively excludes other species via its voluminous biomass.

If you start thinking about the plants you design with in terms of the three primary strategies, it helps you get it right more often than getting it wrong. In particular, it begins to ring warning bells when you mix together, say, species with more competitive strategies with stress tolerators. In the longer term such mixtures are unstable, especially if the soil is productive.

Competitors

These are rapidly growing, highly competitive plants that produce a large standing biomass quickly. Competitors are perennial, are often very long lived, form large patches, and often spread by under- or aboveground stems or roots. They typically invest more energy in vegetative spread than in seed production. Many are weedy, and their strategy is to dominate by swamping other plants. They are, however, only really successful at doing this where soils are productive and there is plenty of light. Where the environment restricts their vigorous growth they are not nearly so competitive.

Some common weedy examples are nettles (*Urtica dioica*), rosebay willowherb (*Chamaenerion angustifolium*), creeping buttercup (*Ranunculus repens*), and Japanese knotweed (*Fallopia japonica*). *Anemone hupehensis*, *Kniphofia linearifolia*, *Macleaya cordata*, and *Monarda didyma* are examples of attractive cultivated species with this strategy, but many competitors produce too high a volume of foliage in relation to their flowers to be seen as hyper-attractive.

Stress tolerators

These plants are the direct opposite of competitors. Very few stress tolerators are weedy. Instead, stress tolerators grow slowly to very slowly, produce small amounts of biomass

Sonchus oleraceus and *Chenopodium album* are classic urban ruderal weeds, here producing a large messy biomass in the second year of a sown wildflower meadow in an urban park.

per unit time, and are generally restricted to unproductive environments, either in sun or shade. They generally do not have rapidly spreading rhizomes or stolons, and they tend to form tight clumps and stay put. Because of limitations of water and nutrients, stress tolerators generally have relatively small amounts of foliage relative to their flowers, so many of these are neat and tidy and typically highly attractive both to humans and invertebrate pollinators. When stress tolerators find themselves growing with competitors on productive soils, they are soon eliminated by competition for light unless they are also highly shade tolerant. Stress tolerators only have potential competitive advantage on unproductive to very unproductive soils or in the case of highly shade tolerant stress tolerators when light is very scarce. As a group, stress tolerators are in decline around the world due to the increase in soil productivity through intentional and unintentional human activity.

Many cultivated herbaceous plants that grow slowly and are small show aspects of stress tolerance, with many species drawn from these genera: *Eryngium*, *Euphorbia*, *Gentiana*, *Helleborus*, *Meconopsis*, *Origanum*, *Paeonia*, *Penstemon*, *Scabiosa*, and *Thymus*.

Ruderals

These plants share the rapid growth potential of competitors but with two important differences: they are short lived (generally annuals or biennials) and instead of investing in permanent rhizomes to colonize and hold territory, they invest in massive seed production and fast-growing seedlings that swamp the opposition. Ruderals differ considerably in their biomass production capacity, from huge in the case of weeds such as fat hen (*Chenopodium album*) and annual rye grass (*Lolium multiflorum*) through to relatively small biomass annuals that form dramatic sheets of spring colour in South Africa and

Dianthus grows with other stress tolerators on dry infertile soils in the Swiss Alps.

California. In temperate regions, most ruderals evolved to respond to the disturbance created by large herds of migrating herbivores. In Mediterranean climates (such as those in western South Africa and California), ruderals are mainly adapted to utilize resources during the autumn to spring period prior to a hot dry summer.

IMPORTANT WORLD PLANT COMMUNITIES AS SOURCES OF INSPIRATION FOR NATURALISTIC PERENNIAL HERBACEOUS PLANTING

One of the reasons why my academic research has made the successful transition from an idea to a reality in practice was the investment I made in travelling extensively to see and understand the world's most glamorous natural and semi-natural vegetation in the wild. This has been a powerful source of both visual inspiration and ecological understanding. The remainder of this chapter will provide a typology and overview of the types of semi-natural herbaceous vegetation that might be useful models for those wishing to design visually exciting herbaceous vegetation in gardens and urban greenspace.

Summer-cut grassland and meadows

The word *meadow* is so used and misused in everyday speech, as to render it almost meaningless. At its loosest it is often used to describe an uncut sward of grasses and flowers (flowering plants are *forbs* to ecologists), and at its more specific it is used, particularly in Europe, to describe a flowery, grass-based herbaceous vegetation that has been reordered by cutting in summer to produce hay to feed livestock during winter. Growth starts in spring, flowering typically peaks in June or July, and then it is cut in July and the cut material raked up. In agricultural situations, the regrowth is grazed in autumn and winter (snow cover permitting). In urban greenspace, remnant or designed meadows are sometimes mown once in late winter to tidy up in lieu of grazing.

It is the act of cutting and removing the cut material as hay that checks the invasion of weeds, including trees, and allows the meadow to perpetuate. These meadows are a hybrid natural-cultural vegetation and also occur in many parts of temperate Asia, especially at moderate to high altitudes. They were originally a key part of the traditional agricultural landscape from sea level to 1500–2500 m in Europe and the near east (for example, Turkey, Iran, and the Caucasian region), as the hay allowed farmers to keep at least some of their livestock alive over winter.

Above these altitudes, meadow confusion begins to set in. In many parts of the world from approximately 2000 m up to where permanent ice and snow is found, other meadow-like communities occur that are not cut, but rather grazed by various herbivores from deer and ibex through to marmots. These are often referred to as alpine and subalpine meadows, although subalpine meadows typically grade (especially in Europe) into the hay meadow regime.

Because of either being found at high latitude or high altitude, most of these meadows experience a cool, relatively short growing season. As a result, a common element

is that the grasses are all cool-season species (that is, C3, which grow from winter to summer) familiar as lawn grasses, such as *Agrostis*, *Festuca*, *Lolium*, and *Poa*. There are substantial differences in species composition as well as the height and luxuriance of the meadows, depending on aspect, rainfall, and soil productivity.

Low- to medium-altitude hay meadows

These meadows are particularly important in Europe from the British Isles eastwards to Turkey, with contemporary outliers in temperate eastern Asia. These came into being following forest clearance for agriculture, so in essence these are not a natural vegetation and depend on continual management (the hay cut) to persist. Despite this, in Europe hay meadows are often seen as a conservation and natural vegetation icon. These meadows have suffered very badly due to agricultural intensification since the beginning of the 20th century. In Britain less than 1 per cent of the original meadows of this type have survived.

Species composition in low- to medium-altitude hay meadows varies according to soil pH, soil moisture stress (affected by rainfall, evaporation, and aspect), soil fertility, altitude, and latitude. Species richness (that is, the typical number of species per square metre) tends to be greatest on relatively infertile limestone soils in those parts of Eurasia which have the most species in their flora. British meadows, for example, are not nearly as diverse—due to past glaciation and then sea level rise that prevented recolonization

Examples of forb and grass species found within the hay meadows of Eurasia

WIDESPREAD, MID RANGE, NEUTRAL GRASSLANDS	MOISTER SITES	MOISTER, MORE PRODUCTIVE	DRIER SITES, OFTEN ALKALINE
Forbs			
Achillea millefolium	Ajuga reptans	Campanula latifolia	Campanula glomerata
Centaurea nigra and C. jacea	Alchemilla species	Cirsium helenioides	Centaurea scabiosa
Knautia arvensis	Caltha palustris	Galium mollugo	Daucus carota
Leucanthemum vulgare	Cruciata laevipes	Geranium pratense	Filipendula vulgaris
Plantago vulgaris	Geranium sylvaticum	Geranium psilostemon	Galium verum
Primula veris	Geum rivale	Persicaria bistorta	Lilium bulbiferum
Prunella vulgaris and P. grandiflora	Ranunculus acris	Ranunculus repens	Linum viscosum
Rhinanthus minor and R. alolectorolophus	Silene flos-cuculi	Sanguisorba officinalis	Lotus corniculatus
Rumex acetosa	Succisa pratensis	Valeriana officinalis	Onobrychis viciifolia
Stachys officinalis	Trollius europaeus		Origanum vulgare
Taraxacum officinale			Ranunculus bulbosus
Trifolium pratense			Salvia pratensis
Trifolium repens			
Grasses			
Agrostis capillaris	Alopecurus pratensis	Dactylis glomerata	Arrhenatherum elatius
Festuca rubra	Anthoxanthum odoratum	Deschampsia cespitosa	Briza species
Lolium perenne	Festuca rubra	Holcus lanatus	Cynosurus cristatus
		Lolium perenne	Festuca ovina
			Koeleria macrantha

of many species—as other parts of Europe such as northern Italy or Germany which simply have much larger floras. Meadows in these latter regions are also often more diverse because of continentality. This often involves greater summer moisture stress and sometimes deep winter snow applying a brake to dominance of grasses, which in maritime regions often dominate at the expense of forbs.

Another factor that is important in determining what grows in meadows across Eurasia is the abundance of slugs. These herbivores tend to be most abundant in maritime climates (where rain events occur frequently) at relatively low altitudes. As altitude increases, slug abundance declines (as described by Brueldheide and Scheidel in the *Journal of Ecology*), and so species can grow that are eaten to extinction lower down the mountainside. Slugs are potent organisms.

These richer hay meadows in the foothills of the Carpathian Mountains, western Romania, are dominated by *Inula*, *Salvia*, and *Filipendula vulgaris*.

Phyteuma betonicifolium and *Cnidium silaifolium* dominate this meadow in Val di Cogne, northern Italy.

Lilium bulbiferum grows in a hay meadow near Arabba in the Dolomites of northern Italy.

What this means is that species that are found in meadows at higher altitudes in environments which support low slug densities have often evolved without investing in either toxic chemicals in their leaves or spiky hairs to dissuade slugs. Since most people who want to create meadows live at lower altitudes where slugs are generally more abundant, this is important as these species will quickly be eaten out. A classic example is the iconic orange lily (*Lilium bulbiferum*), which is particularly abundant in meadows in the Dolomites in northern Italy but quickly disappears if planted in designed meadows in northern Britain. Variations in this combination of environmental factors result in some species being found in one meadow but absent from others nearby. This also explains why some species work brilliantly in designed meadows in one location but fail completely in another meadow a short distance away.

Summer-uncut grasslands

There are many types of natural grasslands that are not cut in summer, in which grass varies from being dominant to barely present. Here they are arranged in approximate order of productivity from the least productive to the most.

High-altitude alpine meadows

Alpine meadows generally exist above the natural tree line. This occurs where the summers are too cool to permit trees to have sufficient photosynthesis to be able to make both wood and seeds, so production of the latter becomes very occasional. The altitude at which this threshold is reached depends on latitude and continentality. The tree line

Alpine meadow vegetation varies greatly, even within relatively small areas, according to soil productivity and aspect. A low turf-like community develops on unproductive soils, especially on south- or west-facing slopes. Here *Gentiana angustifolia*, *Viola*, and *Ranunculus kuepferi* grow in the Alpes-Maritimes, north of Nice.

on Mt. Elgon in Kenya on the equator is 3750 m above sea level, whereas in Scotland it is reached at approximately 500 m. Being above the tree line means that meadow-like vegetation can persist in the absence of human cutting, although many of these systems are grazed by domestic or wild ungulates to varying degrees.

Often these types of meadows grade into dwarf shrubs at their lowest altitudes. Many of the meadow species are adapted to relatively cool growing seasons and lower levels of moisture stress. Because the soils are unproductive, many of these species are classic stress tolerators and cannot compete with more vigorous species on fertile soils. Although both grasses and forbs are found in these meadows, forbs tend to make up a much larger percentage of the herbage than at low altitude and hence these meadows are often very flowery and visually dramatic.

EUROPE AND EURASIA

These meadows are often referred to as alpine grasslands and occur throughout the mountains of Europe and into western Asia where the rainfall is sufficiently abundant, as, for example, in north-western Turkey and throughout the Caucasian mountain chain. This can be a very beautiful vegetation type, but at the highest altitudes it is often so unproductive that the species tend to be rapidly displaced on productive soils at much lower altitudes. Some of the species from these meadows, such as St Bruno's lily, *Paradisea liliastrum*, are extremely palatable to slugs. Emergent large forbs such as *Gentiana lutea* are often conspicuous, as are hemi-parasites such as *Pedicularis*.

Tall meadows also occur where soils are productive and wet, as in the case of *Trollius europaeus* in the Dolomites of northern Italy.

On deeper, more productive soils taller species thrive, particularly on east- or north-facing slopes, as in the case of *Lilium martagon* on a mountain pass in the Italian Alps.

Examples of species with high design potential found within alpine meadows of Eurasia

UNPRODUCTIVE SOILS	PRODUCTIVE SOILS
Arnica montana	*Achnatherum calamagrostis*
Aster alpinus	*Aconitum napellus*
Campanula barbata	*Astrantia major*
Campanula glomerata	*Delphinium elatum*
Dianthus species	*Gentiana lutea*
Festuca amethystina	*Lilium martagon*
Gentiana acaulis	*Narcissus poeticus*
Gentiana verna	*Paeonia officinalis*
Geum montanum	*Persicaria bistorta*
Linum viscosum	*Phyteuma betonicifolium*
Paradisea liliastrum	*Ranunculus aconitifolius*
Potentilla aurea	*Rhaponticum scariosum* subsp. *rhaponticum*
Primula farinosa	*Senecio doronicum*
Pulsatilla alpina	*Thalictrum aquilegiifolium*
Pulsatilla halleri	*Trollius europaeus*
Trifolium alpinum	*Veratrum nigrum*

A more meadow-like community dominated by *Pulsatilla halleri* grows above Cret, Gran Paradiso National Park, northern Italy.

WESTERN NORTH AMERICA

Alpine meadows are found in both eastern and western North America, although generally the western meadows are the most interesting. They typically have a very high ratio of forbs to grasses and as a result are very spectacular. A particularly visually important group of plants in these are hemi-parasites from the genera *Castilleja*, *Orthocarpus*, and *Pedicularis*, with very colourful floral bracts. Relatively few of the species in these systems are entirely at home outside of this habitat, for reasons that are not particularly clear. It may just be that the populations that have been sampled are found in climatic conditions that are very disparate from those of the cultivation locations (mainly in the United Kingdom). This vegetation stretches, with changing species composition, from southern Canada to southern Colorado. Populations of species drawn from the more northern examples of these meadows are more likely to be successful in cool climates, such as that of maritime Western Europe. Some very attractive and relatively easy to grow plants from this community type are extremely palatable to slugs at lower altitudes, including *Helianthella quinquenervis* and *Helenium hoopesii*.

Examples of species with high design potential found within alpine meadows of western North America

UNPRODUCTIVE SOILS	PRODUCTIVE SOILS
Castilleja miniata	*Aconitum columbianum*
Castilleja rhexifolia	*Arnica latifolia*
Erythronium grandiflorum	*Arnica mollis*
Geum montanum	*Bistorta bistortoides*
Geum rossii	*Caltha leptosepala*
Hymenoxys grandiflora	*Delphinium glaucum*
Lupinus lepidus	*Dodecatheon jeffreyi*
Orthocarpus imbricatus	*Erigeron glacialis*
Penstemon procerus	*Geranium viscosissimum*
Persicaria vivipara	*Helenium hoopesii*
Polemonium viscosum	*Helianthella quinquenervis*
Pulsatilla occidentalis	*Mimulus lewisii*
Ranunculus adoneus	*Pedicularis groenlandica*

Castilleja species (here *C. miniata*) are key in many western North American alpine meadows.

Castilleja miniata also grows in high-altitude, much moister meadows that typically have very low grass content.

ASIA

As in other mountain ranges around the world, alpine meadows in Asia vary hugely in composition and form depending on soil productivity, rainfall, and aspect. For example, on the Balang Shan in Sichuan, China, above 4000 m the vegetation is essentially turf-like (grazed by yaks) but flower-studded meadow. The predominant height of the flowers is 100–300 mm on sunny slopes, due to the thin layer of soil. The general appearance is very similar to the meadows found in the European Alps, although species composition is completely different. On the Balang Shan, these meadows are dominated by *Codonopsis*, *Corydalis*, *Delphinium*, *Geranium*, *Meconopsis*, *Pedicularis*, and *Primula*. Along drainage lines and other areas of impeded drainage, taller candelabra and sikkimensis primulas can dominate. On slopes that are north- or east-facing, but still on thin soils, taller vegetation up to 600–800 mm is found, with many *Anaphalis*, *Aster*, *Ligularia*, *Pedicularis*, *Trollius*, and *Veratrum*. Finally, the gully or very wet soil vegetation is dominated by very tall, large-leaved forbs. Hemi-parasites in the guise of *Pedicularis* are very important elements in all of these meadows. Generally speaking, many Asian alpine meadow species seem to be less palatable to slugs in Western Europe than, for example, are many of their western North American equivalents.

Examples of species with high design potential found within alpine meadows of Asia (western China to the Tien Shan of central Asia)

UNPRODUCTIVE SOILS	PRODUCTIVE SOILS
Anemone narcissiflora	*Codonopsis clematidea*
Aster souliei	*Delphinium grandiflorum*
Caltha scaposa	*Erigeron aurantiacus*
Corydalis pseudobarbisepala	*Erigeron multiradiatus*
Gentiana sino-ornata	*Euphorbia jolkinii*
Geranium farreri	*Geranium pratense*
Incarvillea mairei	*Ligularia macrophylla*
Ligularia pleurocaulis	*Meconopsis integrifolia*
Pedicularis variegata	*Morina longifolia*
Potentilla cuneata	*Persicaria macrophylla*
Primula nutans	*Primula sikkimensis*
Silene davidii	*Salvia wardii*
Stellera chamaejasme	*Trollius altaicus*

At around 4000 m on the Balang Shan in western China, the same gradients of meadow height and plant size occur as in Europe. Here *Aster*, *Corydalis*, *Primula*, and *Pedicularis* (purple red) form a flower-rich turf on unproductive wet shale soils.

Corydalis pseudobarbisepala, with its gentian blue flowers, is an extraordinary species.

On more productive soils 1 km distant, rosette-forming *Ligularia pleurocaulis*, *Geranium*, and *Anaphalis* produce a taller meadow.

The shifting patterns between steppe and woodland in central Sicily are mediated by goat grazing and wood cutting. *Euphorbia rigida* is dominant because it is the least palatable species to goats.

Steppe

Among meadows, prairie, and steppe, the last is the driest of the major world grassland types. Indeed, some steppe is so dry that the cover of grasses is almost nonexistent. Rainfall patterns vary considerably, from year round to winter rainfall only, spring rainfall only, and summer rainfall. The critical point is that moisture stress is often very high at various times of the year, due to hot summers, so plants have to be sufficiently drought tolerant to survive this. Moisture stress can be because of low rainfall, soils that store little water, or a combination of both. Steppe is also generally associated with continental climates, with very cold winters, although steppe also overlaps with montane Mediterranean plant communities that experience far less cold winters.

The stereotypic, central Asian image of steppe consists of tussock-forming grasses (often dominated by *Stipa*) with a high diversity of forbs, sub-shrubs, and sometimes geophytes (for example, *Tulipa* and *Eremurus*). The plant community is often quite open, with bare soil visible due to the shortage of water, but on highly fertile clay-based soils steppe can support quite a luxuriant biomass. Steppe vegetation is normally grazed by agricultural and wild ungulates. As with prairies, steppe on more productive soils has often been converted to agricultural production, as has occurred in Romania and Ukraine, and is lost. The typical flowering peak is spring to mid summer but this is strongly correlated with rainfall patterns.

Many steppe species consist of small stress tolerators, with flowers that are often large in relation to the plant, and highly attractive to people. Steppe is, however, often difficult to use as a design model for vegetation types in moist-summer climates on productive

soils, as its open structure potentially makes it highly invasible by weed species. But it is often ideally suited to dry situations such as green roofs.

The origin of steppe outside of the central Asian region is something of a conundrum. In older ecology texts, steppe is often explained as occurring in situations where summer drought is too severe to support trees. This is, however, patently nonsense, as a walk through steppe areas in south-eastern Europe reveals that this often contains trees such as *Quercus pubescens* that are far more drought tolerant than the majority of the forbs and grasses. It seems much more credible that much steppe in Europe and Eurasia is the product of tree clearance in the distant past followed by long periods of regular extensive burning. The initial clearance probably involved felling by axe, followed by burning to kill the seedlings. Grazing by livestock was then used to eventually eliminate trees over large areas, making recolonization even after the cessation of grazing extremely slow.

CONTINENTAL EUROPE

The European steppes have been a powerful inspiration for planting design in Germany since the early 20th century. The most western extension of authentic steppe in Europe is found on the island of Gotland in Sweden, although there are near-steppe communities on sandy soils in Norfolk, U.K. Chalk grassland is a relatively common vegetation type in southern England, found on highly infertile free-draining soils, that has many steppe characteristics, is grazed by animals, and is highly species rich, but in most ecological texts is not considered as steppe. The boundaries between what is steppe and what is dry meadow are not very clear in practice.

Examples of species with high design potential found within European steppe

UNPRODUCTIVE SOILS	PRODUCTIVE SOILS
Adonis vernalis	*Clematis integrifolia*
Ajuga genevensis	*Clematis recta*
Aster linosyris	*Dictamnus albus*
Convolvulus cantabrica	*Echinops ritro*
Dianthus carthusianorum	*Euphorbia illirica*
Euphorbia seguieriana	*Inula ensifolia*
Iris pumila	*Inula helenium*
Melica ciliata	*Phlomoides tuberosa*
Polygala major	*Salvia nemorosa*
Pulsatilla halleri subsp. *slavica*	*Salvia ringens*
Pulsatilla vulgaris	*Stachys recta*
Sedum album	*Stipa gigantea*
Teucrium chamaedrys	*Stipa pulcherrima*

Romanian steppe with more productive soil is much more luxuriant, here dominated by *Euphorbia illirica*, *Salvia nemorosa*, and *Stachys recta*. In the background, the steppe has been converted to crops.

Steppe becomes more extensive as one moves south and east in Europe, into Spain and Eastern Europe, for example. The composition of steppe depends very heavily on the productivity of the soils in question. The surviving steppe in Europe tends to be most commonly associated with very infertile soils that are not suitable for agriculture, such as karst limestone in Croatia, the Czech Republic, and Puglia, Italy. In Austria, a train ride due east from Vienna reveals limestone rail embankments dominated by steppe, whereas out of the railway cutting, the flat landscape is now entirely dominated by productive agriculture. A limestone hill coming out of these agricultural fields (the Hunzheimer Berg) is still covered in rather short steppe.

In Romania, because of the lower intensity traditional agriculture, it is still possible to find steppe on productive soils. This vegetation is much taller and more closed than the very sparse open vegetation found on karst limestone. Where grazing pressure is especially intense, European steppe—particularly in southern Europe—tends to be composed of the most unpalatable and xeric species, giving a rather misleading image of what the more natural community might actually be.

European steppe typically has its peak flowering period from spring to mid summer, although there are species that flower in late summer or even autumn, such as *Aster oleifolius*, *Aster sedifolius*, and *Sedum telephium*.

EURASIA

Steppe is an extensive vegetation throughout Turkey, perhaps most famously on the central Anatolian Plateau, where it supports a very large number of highly xeric species (*Salvia* species in particular are very numerous). This vegetation continues through into the mountains of Iran and into the Caucasus and southern Russia. Precipitation in these regions is largely restricted to the winter months, and in the higher altitude regions falls mainly as snow. The soils are either wet in winter or rewet in spring following snowmelt. The moisture stress in these areas in summer is of a similar order of magnitude as that of the Mediterranean garigue-steppes associated with the Greek Peloponnese, although the steppes become less dry with altitude, as the likelihood of summer thunderstorms increases. Goat and sheep grazing is often intense in these regions, and this tends to restrict species to the least palatable. Some of the species of these landscapes are highly sensitive in cultivation to excess moisture during the growing season. Many of the Turkish *Salvia*, for example, are prone to fungal root-stem rots in wet summers in climates such as the United Kingdom, unless grown in free-draining soils, such as crushed brick on green roofs. Other species from these steppes are very easy to grow even in wet-summer climates, for example, *Papaver bracteatum* and *Papaver orientale*. Access to many of these species is limited and largely restricted historically to small-scale Czech seed collectors, who were most interested in alpine plants, but also made access available to a range of herbaceous *Phlomis* species, for example.

Examples of species with high design potential found within Eurasian steppe

UNPRODUCTIVE SOILS	PRODUCTIVE SOILS
Acantholimon species	*Achillea filipendulina*
Arnebia pulchra	*Alcea rugosa*
Convolvulus compactus	*Astragalus alopecurus*
Dianthus webbianus	*Echium russicum*
Dracocephalum multicaule	*Eremurus* species
Globularia trichosantha	*Ferula orientalis*
Hedysarum species	*Papaver bracteatum*
Onobrychis cornuta	*Phlomis armeniaca*
Onosma species	*Prangos ferulacea*
Pelargonium endlicherianum	*Salvia absconditiflora*
Salvia canescens	*Salvia hydrangea*
Scutellaria orientalis	*Stipa pulcherrima*
Stachys lavandulifolia	*Verbascum* species (many)

Papaver bracteatum grows in montane steppe in northern Iran.

Tall luxuriant steppe grows at Chong Kemin Tal, Kyrgyzstan, following the cessation of agriculture. The *Salvia* species is *S. deserta*.

CENTRAL ASIA TO CHINA

Many of these steppes occur in rain-shadow areas in an otherwise largely summer-rainfall climatic belt, albeit with often heavy winter snow. This is true of the central Asian republics of Kyrgyzstan, Tajikistan, and Kazakhstan south to Afghanistan through to Tibet and into the Chinese provinces of Xinjiang, Qinghai, Gansu, Inner Mongolia, and Mongolia. At the lowest altitudes, steppe in these countries grades into desert and at higher altitudes into subalpine woodland and alpine grassland.

From an English-speaking perspective, these steppe zones are not particularly well known because most of the ecological literature is written in Russian or Chinese. In recent years ease of access to some of these countries has improved, and the plant communities of this region are potentially very attractive.

Examples of species with high design potential found within steppe of central Asia to northern China

UNPRODUCTIVE SOILS	PRODUCTIVE SOILS
Arnebia fimbriata	*Caryopteris mongholica*
Aster alpinus	*Ceratostigma willmottianum*
Convolvulus tragacanthoides	*Clematis hexapetala*
Dracocephalum grandiflorum	*Clematis tangutica*
Dracocephalum peregrinum	*Delphinium semibarbatum*
Goniolimon speciosum	*Echinops latifolius*
Hedysarum species	*Eremurus* species
Heteropappus altaicus	*Ligularia macrophylla*
Incarvillea potaninii	*Paeonia anomala*
Iris lactea	*Perovskia abrotanoides*
Lagochilus species	*Rhaponticum uniflorum*
Limonium aureum	*Salvia scabrida*
Scutellaria rehderiana	*Stipa pulcherrima*

This sparse, open, and grazed steppe on Big Sheep Mountain in Mongolia is dominated by *Dracocephalum peregrinum*.

Penstemon species—in this case *P. barbatus*, *P. cobaea* (a more eastern species), and *P. strictus*—are particularly charismatic in the western steppe regions.

ROCKY MOUNTAINS

Steppe occurs at lower altitudes in the Rocky Mountains of North America, below the alpine meadows, and often consists of a mixture of forbs, sub-shrubs, and shrubs. In these habitats, cacti such as *Echinocereus coccineus* are often very numerous. Rainfall events tend to be widely spaced and erratic, with reliable moisture associated with spring snowmelt. Many of the plants in these systems are at least somewhat fire tolerant, and fire tends to be a regenerating agent in these plant communities. As in Asia, at the lower altitudes these communities grade into desert and at higher altitudes into pine woodland and meadows. Very few of these species are well known or widely used in Europe and eastern North America, in part because of poor adaptation to year-round rainfall, although this is not true of all species. Reliability in cultivation is increased by using free-draining soils, such

Charismatic plants in the western steppe regions of North America include *Castilleja integra*.

Artemisia tridentata is a characteristic species in this steppe.

as sands or the coarse granular mineral composts used on green roofs. These species do, however, have much potential for use in drier parts of Europe that typically experience cold to very cold but relatively dry winters, including East Germany, the Czech Republic, and central Spain.

In the past 20 years this flora has become increasingly explored and utilized in dry designed landscapes in the western United States, through collectors of seed in the wild such as Ron Rathko (now retired) and currently Alan Bradshaw of Alplains.

Examples of species with high design potential found within the Rocky Mountain steppe

UNPRODUCTIVE SOILS	PRODUCTIVE SOILS
Berlandiera lyrata	*Agastache rupestris*
Calylophus species	*Amsonia jonesii*
Castilleja integra	*Argemone hispida*
Echinocereus triglochidiatus	*Clematis hirsutissima*
Eriogonum species (many)	*Iliamna rivularis*
Lomatium grayi	*Lomatium columbianum*
Melampodium leucanthum	*Penstemon palmeri*
Oenothera macrocarpa subsp. *incana*	*Penstemon venustus*
Oxytropis lambertii	*Salvia pachyphylla*
Penstemon linarioides subsp. *coloradoensis*	*Sphaeralcea parvifolia*
Penstemon pinifolius	*Stanleya pinnata*
Tetraneuris scaposa	*Tradescantia occidentalis*
Zinnia grandiflora	*Wyethia amplexicaulis*

The cushion form common in plants of xeric central Asian steppe are replicated in Patagonian steppe. The scarlet gorse, *Anarthrophyllum desideratum*, is one of the most dramatic species.

SOUTH AMERICA

If one extends down the Americas to the Andes of South America, there are extensive areas of steppe-like vegetation, particularly in the Argentinian rain-shadow regions on the eastern side of the Andes. Virtually none of the species are commercially available as either seed or plants except in very small quantities. This flora is very cold tolerant but appears to generally be sensitive to soil wetness in year-round rainfall climates. An excellent account of the flora can be found in *Flowers of the Patagonian Mountains* by Martin Sheader.

Many species of *Junellia* (here *J. toninii*) form ancient cushions.

Slightly more familiar are *Tropaeolum* species, such as the sprawling *T. incisum*.

Rennosterveld can produce extraordinary flowering experiences. *Bulbinella latifolia* subsp. *doleritica* grows near Nieuwoudtville on the Roggerveld Plateau at approximately 850 m.

SOUTH AFRICAN WINTER-RAINFALL REGION

Although I have included this essentially Mediterranean vegetation under the heading of steppe for organizational convenience, in South Africa the highly diverse vegetation of this region is known as either Fynbos or Rennosterveld. At altitudes above 1500 m, however, the Mediterranean description is rather inappropriate as it is often too cold for most species to grow in the winter. Instead, growth is pushed more into the spring or even the early summer, a process facilitated by the much cooler temperatures and extension of spring rainfall at such altitudes.

Fynbos is essentially dominated by shrubby species. Although it also contains a large number of forbs, geophytes, and graminoids, relatively few of these are actually grasses. The herbaceous element is at its most dominant in the first 2 years after a fire, and then

This high-altitude shale Rennosterveld in deep gullies on the Matroosberg at almost 2000 m is home to *Gladiolus cardinalis* and *Bulbinella nutans* subsp. *turfosicola*, in autumn post flowering.

declines as the taller shrubby species reassert their dominance. In the first year after fire, the herbaceous element can be extraordinary. Key genera are mainly geophytes, including *Aristea*, *Dilatris*, *Gladiolus*, *Lanaria*, and *Watsonia*. There are, however, also long-lived forbs, such as the bizarre daisies within *Corymbium*. Fynbos is a highly nutrient deficient community. The soils are essentially pure sand, and growth of the species is only rapid post fire when nutrients previously locked up in the biomass are released from ash.

Fynbos-like vegetation is found at up to 2300 m on western Cape mountains, although at these altitudes the species present are often highly specialized and unlikely to be particularly useful for planting designers unless dealing with green roofs.

Rennosterveld is found on clay- and silt-based soils that hold more nutrients and water. As a result this vegetation has been almost completely converted to agriculture at

After fire, mountain Fynbos is often dominated in the first year by geophytes, such as this woolly white *Lanaria lanata* near Kleimond, western Cape, at 850 m.

Gladiolus cardinalis is almost hardy in Britain, even when seed was originally collected from populations at lower altitude.

Examples of species with high design potential found within the western South African steppe (Fynbos and Rennosterveld)

UNPRODUCTIVE SOILS	PRODUCTIVE SOILS
Anemone tenuifolia	*Aristea capitata*
Aristea spiralis	*Aristea inaequalis*
Bulbinella cauda-felis	*Brunsvigia josephiniae*
Corymbium species	*Bulbinella elata*
Dilatris ixioides	*Bulbinella latifolia*
Dimorphotheca nudicaulis	*Gladiolus buckerveldii*
Gazania krebsiana	*Gladiolus cardinalis*
Gladiolus splendens	*Kniphofia sarmentosa*
Heterolepis aliena	*Kniphofia uvaria* western Cape forms
Romulea komsbergensis	*Lanaria lanata*
Wachendorfia paniculata	*Wachendorfia thyrsiflora*
Watsonia schlechteri	*Watsonia borbonica*
Watsonia spectabilis	*Watsonia marlothii*

lower altitudes. At higher altitudes, however, what remains of this vegetation is relatively intact, although substantially modified and suppressed by sheep grazing. This is the case on the Roggerveld Plateau, where it is dominated by shrubby succulents such as *Ruschia*. At lower altitudes, Rennosterveld is dominated by shrubs such as the daisy bush *Elytropappus*, plus many other species. This vegetation is extremely rich in geophyte species, but also forbs and succulents. Prior to intensive sheep grazing, grasses were historically much more dominant in Rennosterveld. This vegetation is also highly dependent on fire, although dramatic flowering displays also occur in the absence of fire, often due to the more productive soils. A range of other niche vegetation can also be lumped in with Rennosterveld, including high-altitude (up to 2000 m) mountain gully vegetation on organic debris of *Gladiolus cardinalis* and *Bulbinella nutans* subsp. *turfosicola*, and high-altitude seasonal wetlands (known as Fluctas) dominated by *Kniphofia uvaria* and other species.

The main issue with these species in Europe and North America is cold tolerance. Most South African literature is written from a low-altitude Cape Town perspective and suggests that these species are likely to be intolerant of frost. This is true of low-altitude populations but not for those above 1400 m, where severe winter frosts as low as –15°C occur on the Roggerveld Plateau. My research with Helen Cummins on this provided some useful data on the actual cold tolerance of these species.

AUSTRALIAN GRASSLANDS

The grasslands that occur on the basalt-derived clay soils that historically ran from the west of Melbourne to the South Australian border are very reminiscent of steppe, although not described as such in Australia. As with elsewhere, many of these communities have been converted to agriculture and lost, but relatively extensive remnants remain mostly on roadsides. Rainfall is potentially year round, but summer precipitation is often sporadic and air temperatures high. The grass that dominates these communities is the same as that which dominates eastern and to some degree western South Africa, *Themeda triandra* (known as kangaroo grass in Australia). Many other species are present, with *Austrostipa* species particularly conspicuous in flower. The grassland is most open where rainfall is lowest, and the gaps between the tussocks support many small but highly attractive forbs, such as blue pincushion, *Brunonia australis*, yellow *Chrysocephalum apiculatum*, and purplish pink *Pelargonium rodneyanum*, plus a number of geophytes such as chocolate lily, *Arthropodium strictum*, and milkmaids, *Burchardia umbellata*. Horticultural ecology research at University of Melbourne over the past 20 years has led to a substantive understanding as to how to create these grasslands in designed landscapes, as described by Nicholas Williams and colleagues in *Land of Sweeping Plains: Managing and Restoring the Native Grasslands of South-eastern Australia*.

Examples of species with high design potential found within southern Australian steppe grassland

UNPRODUCTIVE SOILS	PRODUCTIVE SOILS
Arthropodium strictum	Bulbine bulbosa
Brachyscome basaltica	Chrysocephalum semipapposum
Brunonia australis	Craspedia paludicola
Burchardia umbellata	Dianella longifolia
Calocephalus citreus	Dichelachne crinita
Chrysocephalum apiculatum	Eryngium ovinum
Convolvulus angustissimus	Pelargonium rodneyanum
Craspedia variabilis	Poa labillardierei
Leucochrysum albicans	Podolepis jaceoides
Microseris lanceolata	Ptilotus exaltatus
Rutidosis leptorhynchoides	Teucrium racemosum
Stackhousia subterranea	Themeda triandra
Thysanotus tuberosus	Wahlenbergia stricta

At the town common at Woorndoo, Victoria, grasses are dominated by *Themeda*, *Austrostipa*, and the yellow daisy *Chrysocephalum apiculatum* in early December.

Exquisite sky blue *Brunonia australis* is a part of this community.

Several geophytes are also present, including purple-flowered chocolate lily, *Arthropodium strictum*.

Warm-season prairie grasses are the dominant plants in naturally occurring prairies. *Sporobolus heterolepis* is a slowly growing species of dry to wet unproductive soils.

Medium to tall forb- and geophyte-rich grassland

As compared to steppe, this type of grassland is generally found on more productive soils in regions with higher rainfall. As a result, the constituent plants are typically individually larger and in many cases better fitted to the more productive soils of urban landscapes. Being larger sometimes means they are more robust and potentially dramatic in flower, and hence these communities can be important as design models.

NORTH AMERICAN PRAIRIE

Prairie derives from the French word for grassland and in practice is applied to a relatively diverse range of grasslands found in North America. There are two classic types: tall-grass prairie, found on more productive soils with an upper height of between 1 and 2 m, and short-grass prairie, found on much less productive soils. This lack of productivity may be due to either very shallow soils (known as goat prairies) or because of low rainfall, as occurs in the western Midwest in the rain shadows created by the distant Rocky Mountains. These latter very dry prairies are probably best considered as steppe. The term *prairie* is also applied to quite distinctive grasslands in Oregon, which would probably be better described as steppe or meadow, that are composed of western species rather than those of the midwestern prairies proper. These moisture gradients give rise to further subdivision of prairie into wet, mesic, and xeric, with xeric describing the goat and western rain-shadow prairies.

Where prairie borders onto woodland or around clumps of trees, it begins to intergrade with more shade-tolerant species. Most true prairie plants are generally relatively intolerant of shade. Prairie in some form or another originally stretched from Saskatchewan in Canada south to Texas, east to the eastern forests, and west to the Rockies. Because

By contrast, *Sorghastrum nutans* is a large, potentially competitive dominant of more productive soils.

much prairie grew on moderately to highly productive soils (tall-grass prairie), it has largely been replaced by maize fields. Only relatively small remnants survive in more or less original form.

Prairie is important as a model for designed naturalistic vegetation in that it provides many attractive species from a huge diversity of different climate and soil types and does not need cutting in summer. Some genera (particularly *Aster* and *Solidago*) flower very late in the year, and this is a hugely valuable property in urban designed landscapes. Nearly all of the species are commercially available as seed or plants. With the exception of the higher latitude Canadian prairies, a consistent characteristic of prairie is the dominance of warm-season (C4 in ecological terms) grasses, including *Andropogon gerardii*, *Panicum virgatum*, and *Sorghastrum nutans* on productive soils and *Schizachyrium scoparium*, *Bouteloua curtipendula*, and *Sporobolus heterolepis* more typical on less productive soils. These C4 grasses start growing late in spring, as they require heat to grow vigorously, and hence the asteraceous forbs that dominate the prairie escape competition from these in spring. Where the dominance of these grasses is reduced, the forbs in prairies are a very dramatic sight. Given that prairie is associated with cold continental winters, almost all prairie species are winter deciduous, although some species retain dwarf leaves over winter in milder climates (for example, *Geum triflorum* and *Rudbeckia fulgida*).

Slugs were originally largely absent from prairie ecosystems and hence many prairie species are extremely palatable to these herbivores. Thus, in slug-rich environments prairie species may be eaten out. This is especially true where plantings invade with cool-season grasses, which compete with the prairie forbs in spring and also provide ideal cover for slugs, increasing their local abundance. This leads to the extinction of the most palatable species, such as *Arnoglossum atriplicifolium*, *Asclepias tuberosa*, *Echinacea*

**Examples of species with high design potential found within
North American prairie communities**

UNPRODUCTIVE, DRY SOILS	INTERMEDIATE SOILS	PRODUCTIVE, MOIST TO WET SOILS
Aster sericeus	Amorpha canescens	Andropogon gerardii
Coreopsis palmata	Asclepias tuberosa	Asclepias incarnata
Dalea purpurea	Aster oblongifolius	Aster laevis
Echinacea tennesseensis	Baptisia australis	Aster novae-angliae
Euphorbia corollata	Echinacea pallida	Coreopsis tripteris
Geum triflorum	Echinacea purpurea	Eupatorium maculatum
Helianthus occidentalis	Eryngium yuccifolium	Liatris pycnostachya
Liatris aspera	Monarda fistulosa	Ratibida pinnata
Liatris scariosa	Parthenium integrifolium	Rudbeckia subtomentosa
Pulsatilla patens	Phlox glaberrima	Silphium integrifolium
Ruellia humilis	Silene regia	Silphium terebinthinaceum
Schizachyrium scoparium	Solidago speciosa	Vernonia fasciculata
Sporobolus heterolepis	Sorghastrum nutans	Veronicastrum virginicum

purpurea, *Liatris aspera*, *Monarda fistulosa*, and *Ratibida pinnata*. Unpalatable plants include many *Aster* species, *Geum triflorum*, *Rudbeckia subtomentosa*, *Solidago rigida*, *Veronicastrum virginicum*, and most grasses.

In the wild habitat, prairie species typically commence flowering in late spring to early summer, with *Phlox pilosa* and *Echinacea pallida*. There is also a spring-flowering element, although this is mostly associated with highly unproductive sites (either dry infertile or wet infertile), which restricts the upper canopy layer from casting too much shade later in the growing season. Spring-flowering species are always small and low growing and include *Dodecatheon meadia* (wet and dry), *Lithospermum incisum* (dry), *Pulsatilla patens* (dry), and *Viola pedata* (dry). These latter three species are generally difficult in cultivation other than on green roofs and similar dry unproductive habitats. *Dodecatheon* is able to grow in a wide range of sites in designed plantings because it behaves like a geophyte, going dormant after flowering, and hence is not restricted by dense over-canopy.

Prairie is a fire-adapted vegetation and was historically burnt in spring by native North Americans to make it easier to travel through and to attract game that fed on the new post-fire shoots. As a nature conservation vegetation or restored public park element, prairie is typically managed by burning in spring (normally late March) in the United States to prevent colonization by trees and shrubs and to defoliate invading spring-growing, cool-season European grasses.

Species composition fluctuates according to soil moisture. *Liatris pycnostachya* and *Eryngium yuccifolium* are indicative of moist to wet conditions.

The grass *Sporobolus heterolepis* is abundant in this prairie, but the site is not too productive and hence good densities of the relatively low *Dalea purpurea* are supported.

Prairie is typically at its most flowery when the density of grasses is relatively low, as in this woodland edge dominated by *Echinacea purpurea*.

Themeda triandra is the dominant grass throughout eastern South Africa and is an extremely attractive plant in cultivation.

SUMMER-RAINFALL SOUTH AFRICAN GRASSLANDS

These grasslands are found from relatively low altitudes close to the sea in the eastern Cape and Kwa-Zulu Natal up to the top of the Drakensberg Plateau at over 3000 m. Although composed of completely different plant species with no evolutionary relationships with prairie species, these grasslands share some basic characteristics with prairie. They are dominated by C4, warm-season grasses and at low to medium altitudes are burnt in spring by indigenous people to provide fresh spring growth for livestock. This burning is often on a biennial or even annual basis. At high altitude these grasslands are burnt occasionally either through human accident or intention or are ignited by winter lighting strikes. Winter rainfall is almost absent, and the grasses become tinder dry. Originally these grasslands would have supported large populations of antelope, zebra, and wildebeest, but these species are now absent except in national parks and game reserves where they have been reintroduced.

The dominant grass throughout the altitudinal range of these grasslands is red grass (*Themeda triandra*), intermixed with *Cymbopogon* and *Heteropogon*. Above 2700 m, cool-season (C3) grasses such as *Merxmuellera* and *Deschampsia* become more dominant

Almost nonflowering clones of *Themeda triandra* were used at the Queen Elizabeth Olympic Park in London.

under wetter cooler conditions, in a vegetation known as Afro-alpine. In contrast to prairie, many of the flowering plants are monocots rather than dicots, geophytes such as *Crocosmia masoniorum* and *Crocosmia pearsei* (both with very restricted distributions), *Dierama*, *Eucomis*, *Galtonia*, *Gladiolus*, *Tritonia*, and *Watsonia* and many intermediates between geophytes and herbaceous plants such as *Agapanthus*, *Kniphofia*, and *Moraea* species. *Agapanthus* species are ultimately large and very long lived, but all grow very slowly. There is also a forb component. For example, many *Helichrysum* and *Diascia* species are often associated with the first few years after a fire, temporarily disappearing as the dominance of the grasses is reasserted. There are, however, also long-term forbs, such as *Barleria monticola*, *Berkheya*, and *Geranium*, many of which are sub-shrubby (such as the lavender blue *Geranium brycei* and pale pink *Geranium pulchrum*). The latest flowering species in these communities are generally *Gladiolus oppositiflorus* and *Nerine bowdenii*.

Winter cold tolerance of these species varies considerably depending on the altitude a population of a species was originally collected from. The highest altitudes generally experience temperatures below −12°C, with parts of the eastern Cape as cold as −18°C. Cold tolerance is generally less than this in designed plantings in regions with wet winters.

The distribution of geophytes and forbs in summer-rainfall South African grasslands is much affected by altitude. Here *Kniphofia angustifolia* grows on a roadside at 1400 m near Nottingham Road, Kwa-Zulu Natal.

Dierama dracomontanum grows below Sani Pass, Kwa Zulu Natal, at 1700 m.

Anemone fanninii, with its 300-mm-wide leaves, thrives in drainage lines at 1700 m.

Vast sheets of *Kniphofia caulescens* grow at 2300 m, below Ben Macdui, eastern Cape.

The 100-mm-wide flowers of *Anemone fanninii* are spectacular in early summer.

Examples of species with high design potential found within montane eastern South African grassland communities

UNPRODUCTIVE SOILS	INTERMEDIATE SOILS	PRODUCTIVE SOILS
Agapanthus species	*Anemone fanninii*	*Berkheya macrocephala*
Cyrtanthus epiphyticus	*Crinum bulbispermum*	*Berkheya purpurea*
Diascia integerrima	*Dierama pulcherrimum*	*Cymbopogon caesius*
Dierama mossii	*Eucomis comosa*	*Eragrostis curvula*
Geum capense	*Gladiolus oppositiflorus*	*Eucomis pallidiflora*
Gladiolus saundersii	*Kniphofia caulescens*	*Galtonia candicans*
Helichrysum aureum	*Kniphofia northiae*	*Geranium brycei*
Kniphofia hirsuta	*Merxmuellera drakensbergensis*	*Geranium pulchrum*
Kniphofia triangularis	*Moraea alticola*	*Hesperantha coccinea*
Nerine bowdenii	*Moraea spathulata*	*Kniphofia linearifolia*
Tritonia drakensbergensis	*Themeda triandra*	*Kniphofia multiflora*
Watsonia strubeniae	*Watsonia latifolia*	*Kniphofia uvaria* eastern Cape forms
Xerophyta viscosa	*Watsonia pillansii*	*Senecio macrospermus*

Nerine bowdenii as it comes into flower on the shaded, wet slopes of the Sentinel (3000 m) among *Merxmuellera* grassland, northern Kwa Zulu Natal.

On wet drainage gullies on the
Balang Shan in western Sichuan,
the vegetation is dominated by tall
mega-forbs such as *Ligularia* and
Angelica species.

Summer-uncut, tall forb communities

These forb communities are found in many parts of the world, normally on highly productive, summer moist to wet soils. In parts of the world where either less fertile soils are the norm or where summer rainfall is less reliable, they are often restricted to drainage lines or even to very small areas enriched by the deposition of grazing animal manures. The forbs are often very tall, potentially with large leaves. As a result they tend to shade out invading grasses, which are often almost absent, especially at altitude, where deep and persistent snowfall further inhibits grass growth in winter and spring.

Many of these forb species have a competitor strategy. In addition to their height and physical size, they use laterally spreading canopies, stolons, or laterally spreading subterranean shoots to form patches and swamp their neighbours.

In Britain and Western Europe, classic examples are rosebay willow herb (*Chamaenerion angustifolium*) on urban brownfield sites (the same species is also found across the northern hemisphere, in North America and northern Asia in pristine natural environments) and nettles on former allotment or garden sites. In less human influenced environments, such as subalpine woodland in the Rocky Mountains, tall herb communities often include *Delphinium* species, particularly *D. glaucum*, and *Helianthella quinquenervis* along drainage lines. In the Caucasus, the equivalent vegetation is dominated by 2-m-tall *Campanula lactiflora* and *Telekia speciosa*.

Patrinia scabiosifolia, *Aster tataricus*, and gigantic forms of *Campanula glomerata* grow in developing *Miscanthus* grasslands at 800 m following woodland edge coppicing in Liaoning Province, north-eastern China.

Asian summer-rainfall forb communities

In summer monsoonal rainfall climates in China, Korea, and Japan, these forbs often grow at relatively low altitudes within what is naturally a forest ecosystem as a temporary vegetation following coppicing of native woodlands or on abandoned agricultural land. They also contain large C4 grasses such as *Miscanthus*, *Saccharum*, and *Spodiopogon* species and can initially support a diversity of forbs prior to the woodland canopy reasserting itself.

In the mountains of western China with very wet conditions in summer, species of *Angelica*, *Ligularia*, *Phlomis*, and tall *Corydalis* are found at gullies up to 4500 m. In the mountains of Japan, communities of very tall leafy forbs such as *Aconitum* and *Filipendula* are particularly striking and occur over very large areas. Outside of areas with very high rainfall, many of these tall leafy meadow species are likely to struggle to grow well.

Woodland understorey and edge communities

Nearly all the communities discussed in this chapter thus far are mainly composed of plants that, to varying degrees, are intolerant of shade. Trees and shrubs create a gradient of shade at ground level from intense directly beneath canopies to almost full sun at the margins on their southern side (in the northern hemisphere) or northern side (in the southern hemisphere). The presence of a green under-canopy of herbaceous plants in summer largely depends on the amount of rainfall received during this time. In temperate to Mediterranean climates with dry summers, most shade-tolerant species—be they forbs or geophytes—grow during the winter and enter dormancy during summer. Woodland

A halo of *Paeonia lactiflora* and *Dictamnus albus* grows around the edges of the canopies of *Ulmus pumila* groves in steppe landscape in Inner Mongolia.

understories that maintain their leaves and structure during the summer are normally associated with deciduous woodlands in climates with high rainfall during this time.

The leafless period in deciduous woodlands allows light penetration in winter and spring, and this permits a wider range of species to persist. The winter-growing species in these deciduous woodlands are generally geophytes, and spring to summer-growing species are forbs and graminoids. A number of species that have high shade tolerance are also able to grow in full sun, such as *Aruncus dioicus*, whereas others are more restricted to shade. Some species are therefore more commonly found as under-canopy species, whereas others are also found on the edges. Most of the plants of very heavily shaded sites are slowly growing, evergreen stress tolerators, such as *Asarum* species. Some species generally thought of as woodland species, such as *Corydalis solida*, are also found in full sun in meadows, where they form an understorey beneath later emerging forbs such as *Veratrum nigrum* and *Gentiana lutea*. These species can be used in designed landscapes in exactly the same way.

Species that grow very slowly but are very long lived are often associated with the edge of woodland, as the shade and root competition of the trees disadvantages grasses and other species that are most competitive in full sun. Species with these ecological characteristics occur in communities from southern Europe right through to north-eastern China, as in the case of *Paeonia lactiflora* and other members of the genus. Where soils are productive, slowly growing species in genera such as *Dictamnus*, *Delphinium*, and *Paeonia*, and other genera often cannot compete with neighbouring plants in full sun.

EURASIA

The richness of woodland edge and understorey communities tends to increase in Europe as one travels eastwards and southwards. Many species are found across these large distances, but particularly diverse understories are found in the mountains of the Caucasus. Most species flower between spring and early summer.

Examples of species with high design potential found within Eurasian woodland communities

UNDERSTOREY SPECIES	EDGE SPECIES
Adenostyles alliariae	Ajuga reptans
Anemone nemorosa	Aquilegia species
Aruncus dioicus	Dictamnus albus
Asarum europaeum	Digitalis grandiflora
Brunnera macrophylla	Geranium sanguineum
Cardamine pentaphyllos	Geranium sylvaticum
Convallaria majalis	Helleborus species (most)
Epimedium perralderianum	Omphalodes cappadocica
Lathyrus vernus	Paeonia species
Melittis melissophyllum	Primula veris
Omphalodes verna	Pulmonaria species
Primula elatior	Silene dioica
Primula vulgaris	Succisa pratensis

The central European species *Cardamine pentaphyllos* grows in spring and later goes dormant.

Cardamine pentaphyllos is a very handsome, clump-forming species that flowers in late spring.

In contrast, the highly shade-tolerant *Aruncus dioicus* maintains its leaves throughout the summer.

Melittis melissophyllum, here growing in grassy woods in the Czech Republic, is a very attractive species.

TEMPERATE ASIA

Much of temperate Asia has its rainfall peak between May and August, and hence the growth and flowering period of many species is in summer. This is also the case with some geophytes of heavily shaded woodland understories, such as *Arisaema*. Evergreen genera highly tolerant of both moisture and shade stress, such as *Epimedium* and *Ophiopogon*, are important components, as are largely winter-deciduous genera such *Begonia*, *Corydalis*, *Impatiens*, and *Primula*. There are also, particularly on edges, a diversity of summer- and autumn-flowering geophytes from genera such as *Lilium* and *Lycoris*. Ferns are extremely diverse in many of these habitats.

At high altitudes as the tree canopy begins to open up, these vernal species are followed by a sheet of summer-flowering *Ligularia jamesii*, *Aster ageratoides*, and the orange *Lychnis cognata*, here enjoyed by our weary guide.

In north-eastern China, the climate is cold temperate, and species are largely winter deciduous, as in the case of *Astilboides tabularis* growing on wet rock faces under trees in Jilin Province, north-eastern China.

Asian woodland understorey vegetation varies considerably depending on the degree of winter cold. At 800 m in the largely evergreen broadleaf forests of western China, winter minima are rarely below −5°C, and both winter-deciduous and semi-evergreen species such as *Begonia* and *Boehmeria* abound.

Exotic looking evergreen *Hedychium* species are also common in these woodlands.

Examples of species with high design potential found within Asian temperate to warm temperate woodland communities

UNDERSTOREY SPECIES	EDGE SPECIES
Adonis amurensis	*Anemone tomentosa*
Arisaema species	*Astilbe chinensis*
Aruncus dioicus	*Astilboides tabularis*
Begonia species	*Clematis heracleifolia*
Boehmeria species	*Hedychium* species
Epimedium species	*Hosta* species
Hylomecon japonicum	*Iris tectorum*
Impatiens species	*Ligularia* species
Liriope species	*Lilium* species
Ophiopogon species	*Lychnis cognata*
Paris species	*Lycoris* species
Podophyllum delavayi	*Rodgersia* species
Primula polyneura	*Roscoea* species

In Liaoning Province, as in much of eastern Asia, *Hylomecon japonicum* is a common spring-flowering species.

EASTERN NORTH AMERICA

This region parallels temperate Asia in that it has, particularly at altitude, high summer rainfall. These conditions permit a rich woodland herbaceous layer that potentially flowers over a long time period, as seen in the Appalachian Mountains. Some of the early-spring species include *Polemonium reptans* and *Senecio aureus*. The understorey is often florally spectacular, with *Phlox divaricata*, *Phlox stolonifera*, and *Tiarella cordifolia* usually flowering in unison. These communities also include quite a number of autumn-flowering species, such as *Aster divaricatus* and the evergreen *Heuchera villosa*, something of an oddity in temperate woodlands. There is also a rich, tall herb woodland edge flora, including *Aster cordifolius*, *Monarda didyma*, and *Helianthus divaricatus*.

Galax urceolata is a highly shade tolerant evergreen species associated with strongly acidic soils.

Dicentra cucullaria is a vernal forb that goes dormant in early summer.

Examples of species with high design potential found within eastern North American woodlands

UNDERSTOREY SPECIES	EDGE SPECIES
Actaea racemosa	Aster cordifolius
Actaea rubra	Chasmanthium latifolium
Aster macrophyllus	Coreopsis major
Caulophyllum thalictroides	Dicentra eximia
Chrysogonum virginianum	Geranium maculatum
Galax urceolata	Gillenia trifoliata
Heuchera villosa	Helianthus divaricatus
Hexastylis shuttleworthii	Monarda didyma
Phlox stolonifera	Phlox divaricata
Polemonium reptans	Phlox paniculata
Tiarella cordifolia	Rudbeckia fulgida
Trillium grandiflorum	Solidago sphacelata

Trilliums such as *Trillium grandiflorum* are the classic spring flowers of the woods of eastern North America.

Where summer rainfall is high,
Rudbeckia laciniata and *Monarda
didyma* grow on woodland edges
and underneath the canopy.

My colleague Nigel Dunnett is up to his neck in this tall forb vegetation.

WESTERN NORTH AMERICA

Rainfall patterns vary considerably across western North America, from a near Mediterranean climate in the south with precipitation falling mainly as snow at altitude to year-round rainfall in south-western Canada. In the more southerly regions, understorey growth is normally limited to winter and spring, in conjunction with the rains. Some of the understorey and edge species in this region deal with summer drought by going dormant in early summer, as seen in *Dodecatheon hendersonii* and *Delphinium trolliifolium*, a behaviour similar to many of the geophytes present in these communities, for example, *Erythronium* species. Species tend to be more evergreen further north where summers are cooler and wet.

Examples of species with high design potential found within western North American woodlands

UNDERSTOREY SPECIES	EDGE SPECIES
Actaea rubra	*Aquilegia formosa*
Anemone oregana	*Balsamorhiza sagittata*
Arnica cordifolia	*Boykinia major*
Aruncus dioicus	*Darmera peltata*
Asarum species	*Delphinium glaucum*
Cornus canadensis	*Delphinium trolliifolium*
Dicentra formosa	*Dodecatheon hendersonii*
Erythronium species	*Geranium richardsonii*
Geum macrophyllum	*Geranium viscosissimum*
Maianthemum canadense	*Heracleum lanatum*
Maianthemum racemosum	*Heuchera cylindrica*
Tellima grandiflora	*Mertensia paniculata*
Tiarella species	*Penstemon serrulatus*
Trillium chloropetalum	*Veratrum californicum*

Many different semi-natural herbaceous communities exist in different parts of the world, but they share broadly similar environmental and management regimes. If we look at steppe-like vegetation, for example, species from Chinese steppe communities are likely to work pretty well with the species present in European steppe communities. They evolved to deal with broadly similar habitats and are often adapted to similar management pressures. Conversely, American prairie plants that have not evolved to tolerate being cut for hay in July are unlikely to be successful mixed together with European meadow species that have. Even more telling, native species that naturally occur in short, light-demanding native meadow communities (regardless of where you live) will not be compatible with species drawn from tall forb communities just by virtue of being native. The former will quickly be shaded and eliminated by the latter when mixed together. Evolution for specific habitat conditions is more important in a designed plant community than politically constructed notions of nativism.

EVALUATING THE PLANTING SITE TO INFORM YOUR DESIGN DECISIONS

As a precursor to developing an ecologically informed planting concept and selecting plant species and communities to realize this, it is important to undertake a thorough site analysis which culminates in a series of site characteristics overlays of the site plan. These overlays will be shown as a series of zones, based on key environmental parameters, such as moderately cool and moist; wet, shady, and productive; or dry, sunny, and highly unproductive.

A simple matrix to clarify thinking about how soil moisture and shade come together to shape the likely conditions experienced by plantings on a site

SOIL MOISTURE	LIGHT		
	Full sun	Semi-shade	Dense shade
Dry			
Intermediate			
Wet			

These compilation zones are valuable, as they highlight the conditions plants needs to be able to tolerate at various points on the ground. They also inadvertently create an ecologically informed ground pattern, which can then be used to define where the plant communities designed to handle these conditions are distributed in space—in essence, where one plant community stops and another begins. In conventional, non-ecologically informed design practice, ground patterns for planting are inspired by factors other than these ecological zones and usually ignore the invisible (to the unthinking designer) ecological conditions intrinsic to the site. Where this mismatch occurs it is common for areas of the planting to fail in the longer term, as plants find themselves placed in locations to meet the needs of the designed ground pattern which cannot meet their ecological needs in terms of soil moisture or shade and sun. Both macro- and microclimatic factors should be considered during the site evaluation process.

Macroclimatic factors: latitude, altitude, and continentality

The location of the site on the surface of the Earth is a really profound site evaluation consideration, as this influences all aspects of climate, including background solar radiation levels, growing-season and winter air and soil temperatures, precipitation, and evaporation characteristics. Plants that come from similar latitudes can sometimes be very well fitted to sites that are extremely distant from one another, for example, Kansas City and Beijing. Where altitude and continentality of two sites at similar latitude differ greatly, this leads to large differences in the climatic conditions experienced even when the sites are at similar latitudes. Glasgow, Scotland, for example, is at a similar latitude to Moscow, but because of its maritime location on the edge of the Atlantic, Glasgow has very mild winters (−5°C the normal minimum) and mild, moist summers (July mean temperature 14.0°C, April–September rainfall 400 mm). In contrast, Moscow has very cold winters (−25 to −30°C are normal minima) and warm summers (July mean temperature 18.5°C, April–September rainfall 370 mm). Although total summer rainfall is similar, in Moscow summer rainfall often involves widely spaced heavy downpours as opposed to light and very regular rain in Glasgow. When these conditions are combined with the warmer summers in Moscow, very few plants would be equally well fitted to these two places.

Altitudinal differences often allow many plants to be used in designed plant communities that come from far south (or in the southern hemisphere far north) of the proposed planting site. Western China, at 3000–5000 m, experiences a similar climate to the British Isles some 15–17° of latitude to the north. A 1000-m increase in altitude is approximately equivalent to 5° of latitude. Hence, plants from the Drakensberg Mountains in South Africa at 28°S (the equivalent latitude in the northern hemisphere is North Africa) and 2000–3000 m altitude are actually quite well fitted to the climate of maritime Western Europe. These climatic rules of thumb allow you to undertake an initial scoping evaluation of what plants might or might not be suitable for use on any given site.

Microclimatic factors operating at the site level

Within the overall climate of the site generated by latitude and altitude, there are often wide variations driven by local or microclimatic factors. These are really important in practice and ultimately determine what can grow well in a particular place.

Degree of shade

Shade is most obviously generated at the site level by buildings and trees, but also at a much more localized level within the community by the plants you are designing with. These shading zones are not eternally fixed as they are on the day you carry out the site analysis. On most sites, shade at the ground level only ever increases beyond what an initial site analysis records, as shrubs and trees expand in size. Sites are nearly always at their sunniest at the implementation of a design project. For a planting that is currently in sun, but likely to be increasingly shaded in the future, to be resilient, species must be used at the outset that can also tolerate shade in the future. These changes occur at all scales, large and small. As small shrubs and clumps of evergreen monocots like *Libertia* develop, they create highly localized shaded and drier conditions on their northern side (in the northern hemisphere) that will lead to the decline of moisture-demanding and shade-intolerant species. Individually these shaded zones may seem trivial, but together they drive significant undesirable change across the planting as a whole.

Aspect

Aspect refers to the direction (north, south, east, or west) a sloping site faces. It affects plant growth by influencing how much solar radiation is incident on plants and the soil, leading to changes in air and soil temperatures as well as light. In temperate regions, maximum solar radiation absorption occurs on south- and west-facing slopes approximating to 45°. Where slugs are common, aspect also affects the intensity of their grazing, a really important factor for the persistence and regeneration of many herbaceous plants. Plant communities from more continental, warm- to hot-summer climates perform much more reliably on south-facing slopes, whereas species from cool montane climates perform best on north-facing slopes. The experiences of highly skilled growers of alpine plants, such as Peter Korn, show that plants that thrive on a south-facing slope may fail on a north-facing slope only 1 m or so distant precisely for these reasons.

Likely soil moisture stress

Soil moisture stress is the situation that arises when there is insufficient water available to plant roots. It is related to all of the above locational and climatic factors, plus highly localized factors such as soil type and proximity to the root plates of trees and large shrubs. The largest localized reductions in the availability of water in soils are driven by root uptake and subsequent evaporation through the leaves by trees and shrubs. Moisture loss through evaporation from the soil itself under trees is negligible compared to loss

Growth of plants placed directly into a 200-mm-deep mulch of crushed limestone (8- to 12-mm diameter) overlying productive soil as a means of reducing weed invasion and maintaining tight attractive canopies. The adjacent plot contains the same species in similar-sized pea gravel. (Michael Livingstone's Ph.D. research, Department of Landscape, University of Sheffield)

to evaporation through tree canopies. As a result of these phenomena, moisture stress is always least when a project is first planted and becomes greater and more extensive year by year as tree roots ramify through the soil. If designed plant communities are to be resilient and long persistent, this needs to be taken into account at the plant selection stage.

Soil productivity

A key factor in designing naturalistic planting, soil productivity can be thought of as the capacity of soil to produce plant biomass, in terms of grams of dried plant per square metre of soil surface. Soil productivity is typically high to very high in gardens (800–1500 g/m²), the legacy of intentional and unintentional soil improvement practices. Highly productive soils limit some of the effects that can be created using naturalistic designed plant communities and tend to lead to very floppy soft vegetation with weak design lines. On sites which have been stripped of soil as part of a past or current development process, requiring new substrate materials to be brought in, there is the opportunity to drastically reduce productivity by importing much less productive materials, such as sand in lieu of topsoil.

The use of sand-only beds has become increasingly popular particularly as a means of cultivating alpine plants of dry habitats. Sand and similar materials (including crushed building rubble on public and commercial sites) can be used to create a mosaic of different productivity levels that will in turn create highly contrasting plant communities. This might include maintaining high soil productivity under trees, where soil moisture stress from the trees will in itself reduce productivity irrespective of intrinsic soil productivity, while using deep sand to create low-productivity areas in full sun to facilitate the creation of hard, sharp looking herbaceous plant communities as a contrast. These may seem to be radical contrasts to traditional horticultural practice, but are quite sensible, particularly when dealing with construction sites, be they domestic or commercial, and where earth-moving equipment is available on site. At a small garden-like scale, these approaches can be undertaken with a wheel barrow. Peter Korn's garden in Sweden is probably the most interesting example of application of these ideas to an entire garden landscape.

Soil pH

Species that naturally grow on soils derived from limestone often perform better in high-pH soils in designed landscape. In some cases, however, equally important for these species are good drainage and low levels of productivity. Relatively few herbaceous plants appear to have an obligate need for acidic soils, and those that do are mainly woodland or alpine species.

KEY SITE USER NEEDS AND PREFERENCES

By the end of the site analysis process, you will have developed a plan of ecological zones making up the site, based on combinations of factors such as moisture stress, shade, and soil conditions, which can then be used as a template to overlay cultural and other design needs.

If you are designing plant communities for your own garden, then you don't need to read any further, as you will either know or come to know what is important or acceptable to you and what is not. Where you are designing for a household or small group of people whom you can sit down with and have a discussion, it is relatively easy to work out what their aesthetic preferences and thresholds of acceptability are. You show them images of planting styles, and a style that seems appropriate is negotiated. The main difficulty in this process is that most of the pictures that garden photographers and designers take are when the vegetation is at its most attractive.

Clients who do not have much first-hand experience of seasonal change in designed planting tend to assume that peak appearance goes on for much longer than it actually does, so the challenge is to find out how long must really attractive flowering last for, and at what time of year is it most preferred.

When you design in public sites, where it is often difficult to meaningfully consult with the breadth of site users, it is generally wise to design in order to maintain flowering seasons for as long as possible. Research indicates that drama and duration of drama are two of the key factors driving attractiveness of vegetation in these situations. Some research studies have suggested that plant diversity is the key factor, but much of this work confuses diversity with drama and flowering duration. Designed meadows with more species tend to flower for longer, although not always as dramatically as those with few species.

Probably the main user issue in naturalistic herbaceous vegetation is winter effect. If left to stand all winter, vegetation that grows in summer and is dormant in winter, such as North American prairie vegetation, is very brown and challenging for many people. This is especially so in wet-winter climates such as north-western Europe. If it has a lot of grasses in it, like little bluestem (*Schizachyrium scoparium*), which is intolerant of shading so difficult to retain except on drier, unproductive sites, then the persistent, orange-red dead foliage can make for quite an attractive winter presence. Meadow-like plant communities typically contain more plants with evergreen or near evergreen winter foliage and can be mown off in autumn—becoming a sort of textured lawn over winter—and this may be more palatable to some people.

Winter effect is much more important in mild-winter climates, where people are out and about much more in winter than in the more frigid zones, where there will often be persistent snow cover. In milder climates using more species from Mediterranean or near Mediterranean climates which grow in winter or are at least wintergreen is one strategy, although some of these go into summer dormancy, so the point of unattractiveness may just shift to another time. People often latch onto winter effect as a sort of "ah-ha, caught you out" moment. This seems odd to me, as in Western Europe, for example, standard horticulturally based plantings of winter dormant herbaceous plants are in almost everyone's private garden and no one blinks an eye about this. Most of these perceived problems can be satisfactorily addressed in many landscapes by integrating herbaceous plantings with trees and shrubs, which have good winter presence.

CHOOSING PLANTS TO FIT BOTH SITE AND HUMAN PREFERENCES

The choice of plants is the central challenge in all planting design, but it is particularly important in naturalistic planting design. This is especially so when creating naturalistic communities in situations where the capacity to intensively manage the vegetation is relatively limited.

Plant communities as the initial design reference point

Whether you are going to design biogeographically or not, communities provide a reference frame at which to undertake a first assessment of the likely suitability of constituent species for the site and their compatibility with other species chosen. The table indicates the typical range of climatic, soil, and management conditions that are tolerated or required by the different species that make up the naturally occurring vegetation communities.

Environmental and management limitations for naturally occurring meadow-like plant communities and species to work successfully as designed vegetation

PLANT COMMUNITY	KEY CLIMATIC LIMITS	KEY SOIL LIMITS	KEY MANAGEMENT LIMITS	ADDITIONAL COMMENTS
Summer-cut, low- to medium-altitude hay meadows				
Maritime	Reliable summer rainfall, cool summers, cold tolerant to −30°C; most species shade intolerant	Various, many subcommunities from dry to wet, mostly neutral to alkaline, moderately productive	Must be cut during growing season for persistence as a community	Most species relatively unpalatable to slugs as adults
Continental	Reliable summer rainfall, warmer summers, cold tolerant to −30°C; most species shade intolerant	Various, many subcommunities from dry to wet, mostly neutral to alkaline, moderately productive	Must be cut during growing season for persistence as a community	More species are palatable to slugs as adults in maritime climates, for example, *Salvia pratensis*, *Lilium bulbiferum*; lengthy winter snow cover suppresses grasses in their habitat
Summer-uncut, high-altitude meadows				
Europe and Eurasia	Reliable summer rainfall, relatively cool summers, relatively dry in winter due to snow cover; most species shade intolerant	Various, many subcommunities from dry to wet, mostly neutral to alkaline, low to very low productivity	Species probably more intolerant of grass competition than lower altitude meadows; intolerant of hay cutting	More species are palatable to slugs as adults
Western North America	Reliable to little summer rainfall, relatively cool summers, relatively dry in winter due to snow cover; most species shade intolerant	Various, many subcommunities from dry to wet, mostly neutral to alkaline, low to very low productivity	Species probably more intolerant of grass competition than lower altitude meadows; intolerant of hay cutting	Many species sensitive to winter wet soils and to slug grazing
Asia	Very wet in summer, warm to cool, relatively dry in winter due to snow cover; some shade tolerance	Various, many subcommunities from moist to wet, mostly neutral to alkaline, low to very low productivity	Species probably more intolerant of grass competition than lower altitude meadows; intolerant of hay cutting	Many species relatively intolerant of summer dryness; many species appear relatively unpalatable to slugs
Summer-uncut, medium to tall forb				
North American prairie	Warm to hot summers, reliable summer rainfall; tolerate cold and wet winters, some shade tolerance	Various, distinctive wet to dry subcommunities, moderate to very high productivity	Burnt in spring in habitat, otherwise sensitive to colonizing winter- and spring-growing grasses	Many species highly palatable to slugs in cultivation, damage increases with winter weed density; most species completely winter deciduous, invade quickly in maritime mild winter climates

PLANT COMMUNITY	KEY CLIMATIC LIMITS	KEY SOIL LIMITS	KEY MANAGEMENT LIMITS	ADDITIONAL COMMENTS
Summer-uncut, medium to tall forb				
Summer-rainfall, South African grasslands	Warm to hot summers, reliable summer rainfall, dry winters; tolerance of winter minima below −10°C reduced in wet winters, most species shade intolerant	Various, distinctive wet to dry subcommunities, moderate to high productivity; most species more reliable in wet-winter climates on well-drained soil	Burnt in spring in habitat, but annual burning disadvantages some species	Many species relatively unpalatable to slugs; some species winter evergreen or semi-evergreen, reduces winter weed invasion
Tall forb communities	Cool to warm summers, wet to deep snow winters; tolerate −20°C, many species have some shade tolerance	Mostly wet soils in summer, soils productive to highly productive	Cut down in spring in cultivation, rapid biomass production restricts weed invasion	Most species are not very palatable to slugs and have rapid shoot thrust to escape the slug feeding zone
Asian summer-rainfall grasslands	Warm to hot summers, reliable summer rainfall; tolerate cold and wet winters	Various, distinctive wet to dry subcommunities, productivity high to very high	Cut down in spring in cultivation, rapid biomass production restricts weed invasion	Most species are not very palatable to slugs
Summer-uncut steppe				
Continental central Europe	Warm to hot summers, rainfall low or unreliable, winter snow cover common; tolerate low to very low winter temperatures, most species shade intolerant	Productivity varies from very low to moderate, soils mostly alkaline	More productive types burnt in spring in central Europe; grass cover typically sparse in habitat	Largely winter dormant, low-productivity types have very open structure prone to weed colonization on productive soils in mild winter climates
Southern Europe and Eurasia	Hot to very hot summers, rainfall low to very low, winter snow cover limited to high altitude, such as Anatolian steppe; most species shade intolerant	Productivity varies from very low to moderate, soils mostly alkaline	Mainly grazed by goats and sheep, potentially very open structure	Many species evergreen to semi-evergreen; most species unpalatable to slugs; very open structure, prone to weed colonization on productive soils in mild winter climates
Central Asia to Mongolia and northern China	Warm to hot summers, summer rainfall various low to moderate, prolonged winter snow cover common; tolerate low to very low winter temperatures, most species shade intolerant	Productivity varies from very low to low	Mainly grazed by goats and sheep, potentially very open structure	Some species highly palatable to slugs; very open structure prone to weed colonization on productive soils in mild winter climates

PLANT COMMUNITY	KEY CLIMATIC LIMITS	KEY SOIL LIMITS	KEY MANAGEMENT LIMITS	ADDITIONAL COMMENTS
Summer-uncut steppe				
Rocky Mountains	Warm to hot summers, summer rainfall low, irregular, to moderate, prolonged winter snow cover common; tolerate low to very low winter temperatures, most species shade intolerant	Productivity varies from very low to low	Mainly grazed	Species vary from palatable to unpalatable to slugs; very open structure prone to weed colonization on productive soils in mild winter climates
North American dry prairie	Warm to hot summers, summer rainfall low to moderate, prolonged winter snow cover common; tolerate low to very low winter temperatures, most species shade intolerant	Productivity low, soils often alkaline or neutral	Burnt in spring	Most species not very palatable to slugs; very open structure prone to weed colonization on productive soils in mild winter climates
South African winter-rainfall region	Warm to hot summers, summer rainfall low to absent; winter cold tolerance varies from −1°C (low altitude) to −10°C highest altitudes, most species shade intolerant	Productivity varies from very low to low, soils mostly acid to neutral	Some species sensitive to summer wetness, especially on slowly draining soils	Most species not very palatable to slugs; most species winter evergreen or grow between autumn and spring, which reduces weed invasion in winter
Australian grasslands	Warm to hot summers, summer rainfall low to absent; winter cold tolerance to −4°C, most species shade intolerant	Productivity varies from low to moderate, soils mostly acid to neutral	More productive types burnt in spring	Some forb and geophyte species highly palatable to slugs
Woodland and scrub edge and understorey				
Eurasia, temperate	Cool to hot summers, rainfall either year round or summer; high to moderate shade tolerance	Soils normally have high organic matter content, plants intolerant of compaction; soil moisture varies from wet to dry, depending on location; productivity normally moderate	Some species disappear in summer as they enter dormancy; problematic	Species tend to be stress-tolerant, slowly growing evergreens or summer dormant; edge species are more diverse
Eurasia, Mediterranean and dry continental	Warm to hot summers, moisture either from rainfall in autumn to spring or spring from snowmelt; high to moderate shade tolerance	Much lower organic matter levels; tolerate very high levels of moisture stress in summer	Under Mediterranean tree canopy often evergreen, understorey tolerates moderately low light levels in winter	Species that are not seasonally dormant are highly tolerant of moisture stress (such as *Iris unguicularis*); some species may show some intolerance of soils moist year round

PLANT COMMUNITY	KEY CLIMATIC LIMITS	KEY SOIL LIMITS	KEY MANAGEMENT LIMITS	ADDITIONAL COMMENTS
Woodland and scrub edge and understorey				
Asia	Warm to hot summers, rainfall year round but with distinct wet summer peak; high to moderate shade tolerance	Soils high in organic matter and typically very moist during the growing season; productivity moderate	Species are often highly shade tolerant but require moist soils in summer	*Begonia* and *Impatiens* are classic genera from this habitat
Eastern North America	Warm to hot summers, rainfall year round but with distinct wet summer peak; high to moderate shade tolerance	Soils high in organic matter and typically very moist during the growing season; productivity moderate	Species are often highly shade tolerant but require moist soils in summer	Some species are palatable to slugs, such as some forms of *Phlox stolonifera*
Western North America	Warm to hot summers, moisture either from rainfall in autumn to spring or in spring from snowmelt; substantial summer rainfall at altitude, especially in the north; high to moderate shade tolerance	Much lower organic matter levels; generally high levels of moisture stress in summer; productivity generally low to moderate	Some of these species are highly palatable to slugs in maritime climates	Most of these communities are summer dry, but at altitude there are also very wet communities, dominated by tall forbs such as *Delphinium glaucum*

This table can be used as a guide to help identify semi-natural communities that are going to be most appropriate to draw from to match the environment of the site. The community approach also gives you the capacity to get a sense of what the overall characteristics of a community are (is it tall and dense or short and open?) and how this relates to management and maintenance capacity. The information in the table also helps you to get a sense of which communities share common environmental and management characteristics that might allow constituent species to be mixed with species from other communities. Adopting a community approach is, however, only part of the picture because even communities that appear poorly fitted to a given site sometimes contain species that work much better than might be expected from the wild habitat. Conversely, even when you work with a local native plant community, it is normal for some species to prove to be poorly fitted in practice to the specific site, in either the long or short term. Ecological fitness is very much a fine-grained, capricious lottery.

In addition to developing communities to deal with ecological conditions, on many sites there will be a desire to develop a range of communities to create additional patterning and contrasting seasons of display. At the University of Oxford Botanic Garden (see case study), we used three plant communities to create contrasting experiences and flowed these into a ground pattern composed of wedge-like alternating shapes to give the informal, chaotic vegetation a sense of structure and modernity.

Selecting species

Sometimes you may wish to bypass the community approach and jump straight to selecting a palette at the species level. Even when you use wild plant communities as a range-finding frame, you still have to review and make decisions on the actual species you intend to use. The first step in doing this is to try to characterize the conditions likely to be prevailing on the proposed planting site. This is most easily done when the site is in its near finished form, and it is most difficult when dealing with construction sites where there may only be a large hole or a flat base that has to be built up. In commercial design projects, it is nearly always necessary to design the planting before the final site conditions are really known, throwing a substantial degree of chance into the process. Designing in your garden is a much more informed process. Although selecting plant species to develop a planting palette is often portrayed as a relatively linear, flow-chart-like process, in reality it is multi-directional and highly iterative.

Sometimes it starts with a very rational survey, analysis, and design process: look at the site, understand it, and respond to it, including selecting the plants. In many cases, however, looking at some of the plants you think might be appropriate, before you do all of the surveying and analysis, may be helpful. If you do this, it is essential that you reject species to which you have an emotional attachment but which are clearly inappropriate for other reasons.

If you are not very knowledgeable about plants and you want to maximize the chances of success, you need to engage in as much research as is possible. In this book, there are many examples given of plants for particular ecological or aesthetic roles. Much of the horticultural literature about which plants tolerate what conditions—or more precisely, the breadth of conditions they will tolerate—is rather limited. The most notable exception to this is some of the alpine gardening literature, which seeks to use understanding of the wild habitat to inform cultivation of the plants. This work is sometimes excessively literal, but a welcome contrast to the vagueness of the rest of the literature.

This unsatisfactory situation within the horticultural literature prevails for a number of reasons. The most compelling is that most authors have insufficient understanding of the wild habitats of plants to be confident about thinking beyond generic horticultural recipes. This is compounded by proffering advice on cultivation in the context of the optimal conditions for those plants, rather than what will they tolerate before they cease to work well enough to do what is expected of them. If we take, for example, a common plant like *Aruncus dioicus*, it is mainly described as for full sun to light shade in well-drained soil. This species is circumpolar, so you will find it in Europe, Asia, and North America, often as an understorey plant in densely shaded woodlands, where it continues to flower, but it flowers best in full sun. It will also tolerate very wet soils through to quite dry soils, but the latter only when heavily shaded. So I guess this means that *A. dioicus* prefers moist soils in sun to semi-shade but will tolerate very dry soils in dense shade and very wet soils, too.

There is very little philosophical or scientific discussion of these issues within horticulture, such as how tolerances of plants differ from needs or requirements, and this is reflected in the literature. This situation leads to a horticultural literature in which only plants at the very extremes of the soil moisture–shade–productivity continuum are identified as thus. Most plants are just described as needing sun to semi-shade in well-drained soils. Although this may sometimes be reasonable advice, it is clearly a cop out.

Horticulture and gardening books generally arrange plants from A to Z by botanical name. Some of the books written by authors with a much more profound understanding of cultivated plants and how they respond to designed environments, such as Hansen and Stahl's landmark *Perennials and Their Garden Habitats*, organize plants in terms of the environmental conditions they need to be successful. This text is based on a lifetime of critical observation of practice. Such treatments are rare, however, so many readers will need to visit the websites of native seed companies (such as Emorsgate Seeds and Rieger-Hofmann in Europe and Prairie Moon Nursery in the United States). Other good sources on habitats are iSpot, an international website to which people upload images of plants (whose identification is then discussed) with quite a few details of habitats they grow in. The U.S. Department of Agriculture maintains the excellent USDA Plants website on the habitats for North American species. Likewise, the Eflora of China gives some clues for most species. In addition to these, increasing numbers of countries now have field identification guides for their floras, which normally give details of the wild habitat.

Among mainstream horticultural books, the series of photo-based texts on various plant groups by Phillips and Rix, including *Early Perennials* and *Late Perennials*, often refer to the habitat and are most useful. Most of the rest do not. The Royal Horticultural Society's series of encyclopaedias are particularly disappointing from the perspective of making connections with plant habitats.

Google Images is a hugely useful tool when selecting plants for use in designed plantings. Given a list of possible species, at a stroke you can view dozens or sometimes hundreds of images of a certain plant. You will quickly notice that some of the images are clearly wrongly identified, but this aside there is much information to glean, although this does require you to bring a critical mind to the process. Google Images is particularly good for assessing morphology, as you potentially see a plant from all angles and seasons. For example, is it mound like? Or does it have basal leaves in a rosette with naked flowering stems or tall leafy stems?

It is really useful to put the emerging palette of names into a spreadsheet, to which you can then add extra columns for information such as drought and shade tolerance, leaf height, and flowering time. You can then easily sort the spreadsheet based on these column headings as you evaluate and refine your selection and design process. Having the planting palette as a spreadsheet also allows you to enter values into a column as to how many plants of that species you might want per square metre and gets you to interrogate yourself as to why this many or this few.

Moisture and shade tolerance

A plant's tolerances of moisture and shade conditions interact strongly, limiting what can be grown under different combinations of these factors. Examples of species' tolerance of these combinations are shown in the accompanying three tables, providing reference points against which to compare other cultivated species. Species with a wide range of moisture tolerance will generally be satisfactory in at least the adjacent moisture category. In the medium category, this means sites which are potentially both wetter and drier. Plants listed in more than one table are examples of species that can tolerate a wider range of shade levels. Species listed under semi-shade and shade will generally grow satisfactorily in sites with more light where there is a commensurate increase in soil moisture. Conversely, many species requiring wetter soils in full sun will tolerate somewhat drier soils in shade, such as *Primula bulleyana*, as this reduces leaf transpiration and subsequent leaf overheating caused by moisture stress.

The climatic regime in which you make these judgements strongly colours the outcome. The tables provided here are from a Western European perspective. Some of the species in dry soils would move to medium soils if the site were located in Colorado, for example.

Soil moisture tolerance levels of species that tolerate full sun

Species with a wide range of moisture tolerance are marked by an asterisk.

SOIL MOISTURE LEVEL	FOLIAGE HEIGHT		
	Low (50–200 mm)	Medium (300–600 mm)	Tall (900–1500+ mm)
Dry	Delosperma basuticum Dianthus carthusianorum* Diascia integerrima Dracocephalum peregrinum Festuca punctoria Oenothera macrocarpa* Penstemon barbatus* Pulsatilla species* Sedum species Thymus species* Zinnia grandiflora	Asclepias tuberosa Aster sedifolius* Echinacea pallida* Eryngium bourgatii* Festuca mairei* Hyssopus officinalis subsp. aristatus* Inula ensifolia* Muhlenbergia capillaris Salvia nemorosa* Stipa gigantea*	Echinops ritro* Cephalaria dipsacoides* Perovskia atriplicifolia*
Medium	Geranium wallichianum	Echinacea purpurea Geranium sylvaticum* Molinia caerulea* Oenothera tetragona* Stachys officinalis	Helianthus 'Lemon Queen'* Miscanthus sinensis*
Wet	Dodecatheon jeffreyi Gentiana triflora Primula bulleyana Primula pulverulenta Succisa pratensis*	Caltha palustris Deschampsia cespitosa* Hesperantha coccinea* Iris laevigata Sanguisorba officinalis* Trollius europaeus	Aster novae-angliae* Aster umbellatus* Eupatorium maculatum* Euphorbia palustris* Veronicastrum virginicum*

Soil moisture tolerance levels of species that tolerate semi-shade

Species with a wide range of moisture tolerance are marked by an asterisk.

SOIL MOISTURE LEVEL	FOLIAGE HEIGHT		
	Low (50–200 mm)	Medium (300–600 mm)	Tall (900–1500+ mm)
Dry	Geranium macrorrhizum*	Euphorbia epithymoides*	Aruncus dioicus*
	Heuchera sanguinea*	Geranium ×oxonianum*	
	Lathyrus vernus*		
Medium	Polygonum affine	Geranium sylvaticum*	Anemone hupehensis*
		Hakonechloa macra	Meconopsis grandis
		Stachys officinalis*	
Wet	Dodecatheon jeffreyi	Caltha palustris	Aconitum carmichaelii*
	Geum coccineum*	Gentiana asclepiadea	Actaea racemosa*
	Geum rivale*	Ligularia dentata	Astilbe chinensis var. taquetii
	Polemonium reptans*	Rudbeckia fulgida*	Ligularia przewalskii
	Succisa pratensis*	Trollius europaeus	Persicaria amplexicaulis*
	Saxifraga fortunei*		Rodgersia aesculifolia var. henrici

Soil moisture tolerances of species that tolerate dense shade

Species with a wide range of moisture tolerance are marked by an asterisk.

SOIL MOISTURE LEVEL	FOLIAGE HEIGHT		
	Low (50–200 mm)	Medium (300–600 mm)	Tall (900–1500+ mm)
Dry	Epimedium ×rubrum*	Epimedium perralderianum*	Carex pendula*
	Geranium macrorrhizum*	Euphorbia amygdaloides subsp. robbiae*	Polystichum aculeatum*
	Helleborus orientalis*		(in general, very few species)
	Tellima grandiflora*		
Medium	Asarum europaeum*	Aster divaricatus	Aster cordifolius
	Primula vulgaris*	Heuchera villosa*	Helianthus divaricatus*
	Tiarella cordifolia		
	Tiarella wherryi		
Wet	Primula polyneura	Hosta species	Aconitum carmichaelii*
	Primula sieboldii		Aruncus dioicus*
	Saxifraga fortunei*		Astilboides tabularis*
			Ligularia sibirica

Robustness and long-term persistence

A designed community's robustness and long-term persistence is often strongly influenced by the overall suitability of the community types and the fitness of the species found within these for the proposed sowing and planting site and the likely management regime. Species that are well adapted or ecologically fitted to a site tend to be more robust and persistent. Robustness is, however, a relative concept. For example, it would be absurd to try to rank all of the world's temperate herbaceous plants from most to least robust, as the position of any species would change in the ranking depending on the conditions under which it was planted. Thus, one might argue that all plants are potentially robust under the appropriate planting conditions.

There are problems in this argument, however, in that there are other factors that affect robustness. The first of these is what is known as ecological amplitude, the breadth or specificity of environmental conditions under which a species grows well. Very common, widespread species are thus because they often have evolved wide ranges of tolerance of light level, growing-season temperature, soil moisture content, nutrient levels, and degree of competition with other plants and animals. That is, they have wide ecological amplitude. Then there are plants which have much narrower tolerance ranges, occurring in nature only where specific combinations of their environmental needs come together. As a result, these species are not common and often have relatively predictable and specific habitats. On our hypothetical robustness ranking scale, while these plants might be as robust in their chosen habitat as the more widespread species, they are statistically less likely to be so on any given design site.

The other important factor that affects these notions of robustness is the plants' ecological strategy. All plants have been shaped by evolution to adopt one of three primary ecological strategies, by which they make their way in the world. It's useful to draw analogies between ecological strategy and how human beings develop their cultural strategies to get what they want in the world. Some people adopt an aggressive confrontational approach, by which they hope to bully or scare people into submission, others a consensual approach to appeal to the better judgement of others, and so on.

The competitor strategy requires plants to be long lived and quickly produce large amounts of biomass, which they then use as a weapon to shade and eliminate competing neighbours and, in doing so, to form large colonies. Nettles (*Urtica dioica*) and many tussock-like grasses, such as Yorkshire fog (*Holcus lanatus*) or in climates with hot summers Johnsons grass (*Sorghum halepense*), are classic examples of competitors. Then there are short-lived plants which have evolved a similar high biomass strategy, but because of strongly fluctuating environmental conditions, they put much of their energy into producing very large amounts of seed which will ensure their long-term reoccurrence when conditions permit. This is the ruderal strategy, and plants with this inevitably show poor vegetative persistence. Finally, there is the stress tolerator strategy, in which plants grow slowly but tend to be long lived.

Because horticulture has historically judged robustness by growth rate, we are most likely to see competitors and ruderals as most robust. This is only likely to be so in the short term, however, in highly productive environments where there are lots of nutrients, light, and water to fuel growth.

Robustness can also be driven by morphological characteristics. Species with either evergreen or persistent dead winter foliage are often robust in practice (all other things being equal) because this inhibits competition during the winter months with adjacent planted species or would-be invading species. *Iris sibirica* and *Geranium ×magnificum* are two examples of species that use their dead but persistent winter foliage in this way.

One of the key principles in designing for long-term persistence in naturalistic plant communities is not mixing together species with strongly different ecological strategies, where it is not possible to use maintenance to control the excessive growth of ruderals and competitors.

Looking out for signs of potential naturalization and invasiveness

Whenever you use a plant outside its native distribution, there is a risk that in a new habitat it will be either more or less aggressive. The latter is much more common than the former. In Britain, among the cultivated flora of more than 70,000 species and cultivars only around five to ten species have shown significant aggressive behaviour over the past 100 years. Most naturalization events with herbaceous plants are transient. There are thousands of species that do this in Western Europe, but nearly all eventually decline or disappear following competition from native species. As a general principle of my work, I am extremely cautious about using species that show signs of aggressive behaviour. Scientific attempts to screen exotic floras for likely capacity to show invasive behaviour when grown in another country have not been very successful, because this has been done, for efficiency, mainly based on the analysis of traits, such as seed weight and relative growth rate.

When you actually grow species, you get a much better idea of the risks, that is, which species have massive seed production and high germination within and outside the immediate planting and sowing site, high seedling survival to reproductive maturity, or rapidly spreading roots and/or stolons. The species that are most likely to do these things are those with ruderal or competitor strategies. Anyone who has ever grown *Lythrum salicaria* on a wet site will after a year have noticed how the spaces are filled by literally thousands of seedlings, and it is no surprise that this species became a major wetland weed in North America. But, in my experience, this does not happen on drier sites.

As a group, the greatest potential for invasive behaviour is generally found in grasses and, as a rather broad generalization, in daisies (Asteraceae), a classic weedy family. Grasses often have high seed production and very high seedling establishment, and the seedlings are unpalatable to seedling herbivores such as slugs that eliminate many dicotyledonous seedlings. Although many daisies have massive seed production and very effective wind dispersal, many are not the least bit invasive, such as *Rudbeckia fulgida* in north-western Europe. The risk generally depends on the combination of species and the environmental conditions of the site, rather than just the species itself. As with other warm-season grasses, the very widely cultivated *Panicum virgatum* and its cultivars goes from being a mass seeder to producing no seedlings at all when it is grown in cooler climates. Seed production more or less ceases when the mean July temperature is less than 17°C, the temperature, for example, of northern England. In southern England *P. virgatum* seeds a little, whereas in central Germany it seeds a lot. 'Shenandoah' seems to be the least self-seeding *Panicum* cultivar, even in hot summer climates. *Miscanthus* species and cultivars typically show very similar patterns. The genus has naturalized in the south-eastern United States, but it is largely incapable of doing this effectively in Britain.

Nearly all of the species mentioned in this book are stress tolerators that do not have rapidly spreading roots and can only seed aggressively under low productivity conditions in very open communities. Under more productive conditions they typically cannot do this outside the site due to more closed native vegetation: they have nowhere to go. Be vigilant. If a species shows signs of these undesirable behaviours, stop using it and warn others of your experiences.

Growth form and method of spread

As a general principle, the most useful plant growth form to be used in naturalistic sowings is the tight clump, that is, plants that hold a space occupied by their foliage but do not constantly expand into the territory occupied by adjacent species. Plants whose basal foliage occupies a space little bigger than a dinner plate are ideal. This gives greater predictability to how species will behave, and it allows you to pack a lot of different plants in to create very diverse, long-flowering vegetation.

Plants that spread endlessly via aboveground stolons or self-rooting shoots or belowground by rhizomes to form monospecific patches are extremely undesirable plants for seeding. *Geranium* species and cultivars that spread enormously laterally each year from a central growth point are equally annoying and undesirable. They shade out their smaller neighbours and then retreat.

Growth rate

Rapid growth is a double-edged sword. The desire to fill in space and make plantings look full and mature as quickly as possible is very important to most people. However, plantings that grow slowly and are less full, at least initially, are more likely to maintain a diversity of species for longer. Mixing species together with very different growth rates is a source of potential disaster. The most stable designed plant communities will be composed of species with broadly similar growth rates.

In some commercial meadow mixes, short-lived rapidly growing ruderal species are included with perennials to provide more initial impact, but when you look at this in scientific experiments, it is normal for these species to eliminate many of the slower species in the first or second growing season. As a result, the intended longer-term vision is never actually realized. If you must use rapidly growing species in designed communities dominated by slowly growing species, they need to be present at low densities and preferably upright and slender. Fast-growing species with dense basal foliage—even when highly attractive, as in the case of *Coreopsis lanceolata* cultivars—essentially behave as weeds.

Palatability to herbivores

The most troublesome herbivores of herbaceous plants vary between different parts of the world. The most problematic species are those that feed selectively on the emerging shoots in spring; in well-wooded continental climates this is often deer, and in maritime climates this is often molluscs. Because of the potentially repetitive nature of the defoliation, highly palatable species have very low persistence in environments subject to these herbivory pressures. Deer are very difficult to deal with, and just avoiding the most palatable species is the best strategy. With molluscs you have a few more herbivore management options, for example, sand mulching is very helpful in reducing their impact. When sand is dry, slugs are disinclined to slither over this surface, hence the number of days of grazing per unit time is reduced. The comparative palatability to slugs of a wide range of species is given in the eight tables at the end of the next chapter.

Drama and duration of the flowering season

Species vary hugely in terms of the drama of their flowering display and how long this display is typically present. Although attractiveness of one species over another is at least in part in the eye of the beholder, a good way to think about this when designing plant communities for public sites is to consider what impact the flowers would have on a visiting Martian, who was initially free of any human, culturally constructed aesthetic positions. Flower impact and drama are often driven by the percentage of the plant surface that is not green at peak flowering, combined with much more nuanced factors such as the shape of the flowers and how they are presented in space. As a result of their intrinsic psychological preferences and cultural upbringing, people prefer certain flower colours over others.

White appears to be generally regarded as a noncolour; in many Asian cultures it symbolizes death, for Westerners purity. Yellow appears to be a negative for many people, whereas blue seems to be almost universally liked. Reds and oranges are strongly noticed by the human optical system, but some people have learnt to believe that such colours are crude or lacking refinement and are somehow less good. Red is, however, seen as lucky and much preferred by Chinese people and so it goes on. The writings of Gertrude Jekyll and others have unintentionally reinforced the rather preposterous idea that such vivid bright colours are problematic, because they offend good taste, whatever that might be.

It's perhaps useful to think of plants in flower as potentially belonging to three categories, dramatic, intermediate, and low key, based on the percentage of the plant in which the green foliage is obscured at peak flowering, the size of individual flowers, and finally how impactful the flower colours are. Species in the dramatic category might include

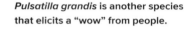

The flowers of *Gladiolus cardinalis* are dramatic.

Pulsatilla grandis is another species that elicits a "wow" from people.

Asclepias tuberosa, Aster sedifolius, Diascia integerrima, Kniphofia uvaria, Paeonia lactiflora cultivars, *Papaver orientale, Pulsatilla slavica,* and *Rudbeckia fulgida* var. *sullivantii* 'Goldsturm'. These are the sort of species that are likely to elicit a "wow" reaction in people who have very little inherent interest in plants.

At the other extreme, low-key species might include *Eucomis bicolor, Fragaria vesca, Geum rivale, Geum triflorum, Heuchera americana, Sanguisorba* species, *Tellima grandiflora,* and *Veronicastrum virginicum.* The flowers are typically small, not very brightly coloured, or sparse in relation to the vegetative mass of the plant. If you see "less as more" you may disagree with this assessment, but you will be in a substantial minority in relation to the public at large. Try designing a public scheme based largely on these types of species

At peak flowering, *Diascia integerrima* forms a pink, seemingly leafless dome.

and watch their response. Low-key species are often valuable in naturalistic plantings, however, because of the merits of their foliage or architectural lines. They are potentially very pleasing or charming to the initiated, but not necessarily to Joe Public hankering for a more visceral experience.

Species intermediate between over- and under-whelming might include those that are attractive in flower as detail but not dramatic, including *Aster divaricatus*, *Dianthus carthusianorum*, *Dierama* species, *Gillenia trifoliata*, *Silene regia*, *Silphium terebinthinaceum*, and *Thalictrum* species. In these species, while the flowers might be beautiful in themselves they are normally less densely borne or individually small, so the overall drama of each plant is reduced. People who are both passionate and knowledgeable about plants may see these as in the first category, but this requires the observer to share their constructed aesthetic values, rather than just looking at the plant dispassionately in terms of what it actually is.

Some species that are very dramatic at peak flowering, including many *Paeonia* species, flower for very short periods. With *Paeonia daurica* subsp. *mlokosewitschii*, for example, you probably only get 5 days. *Iris* species, as a crude generalization, also flower for a short period, typically 7–12 days. *Jeffersonia* and some *Penstemon* are also relatively brief moments in time. When you are selecting species for naturalistic plantings, it is important not to use too many short-flowering species, otherwise the planting will struggle to generate high levels of drama. In contrast, many species flower continuously for very long periods, some for up to 8 weeks or more. Examples of these include *Echinacea purpurea*, *Knautia macedonica*, *Leucanthemum ×superbum*, and *Rudbeckia fulgida* var. *sullivantii* 'Goldsturm'. *Heuchera villosa* flowers for a long time, but in an on-and-off fashion. On average, most species flower for about 2–3 weeks. Unless you have convincing information to the contrary, this is a reasonable assumption.

You can quantify decisions regarding plant selection based on flowering impact by giving a ranking to flowering duration (1 for short, 3 for long) and ditto to flowering impact (1 for low, 3 for high) in an Excel spreadsheet table. These values can then be multiplied together to help you identify real workhorses as opposed to prima-donna species. For example, *Rudbeckia fulgida* var. *sullivantii* 'Goldsturm' with 3 for impact and 3 for duration would have an overall score of 9, whereas *Paeonia lactiflora* would get 3 for impact but only 1 for duration for an overall score of 3. *Dierama pulcherrimum* would get a 2 for impact and a 2 for duration for an overall score of 4. These scoring systems are only a guide. Attractive vegetation requires including species that are long-flowering workhorses, but also seasonally extraordinary talking-point species such as *Dierama*. Some of these extraordinary moments will come through combining different species: in autumn, for example, creamy white *Actaea* intermingled with purple-blue *Aconitum*.

Plant structure in relation to attractiveness

The capacity to perceive plants with attractive structure or architecture depends to a substantial degree on sowing or planting density. The closer the plants are packed together, the harder it is to do this. Sowing at really high density (with sowing targets greater than 200 plants/m²) tends to result in almost flat-topped vegetation. At much lower densities (say, less than 50 seedlings/m²), the surface topography of the community and the component species is much more evident. Scoring approaches can also be applied to divide up plants on this basis. Species with interesting and attractive architecture and leaves such as *Rudbeckia maxima* would get 3, amorphous blobs such as *Helianthus* 'Lemon Queen' 1, and species with interesting lines such as *Kniphofia uvaria* 2.

There is also the issue of whether flowering structures post flowering are ugly, essentially invisible (as in *Dierama*), or somewhere in between. I really like the flowers of *Stipa gigantea*, but I don't much like the persistent chaffy seed heads. Ditto with what become very brown floral bracts in some *Eryngium*. This is important because in designed naturalistic plantings physical access for cutting off spent flower bits is generally very limited, even if you have the maintenance capacity to do this.

Capacity to support native biodiversity

While the media and popular culture bombards us with the belief that native animal biodiversity can only be supported by native plants, the scientific literature is increasingly suggesting that this is far from true. Native animal biodiversity is most effectively conserved by large volumes of vegetation composed of many plant species arranged in spatially complex arrangements. The latter means multiple layers of foliage overlying each area of the ground, which is discussed from a design perspective later in this chapter. Bird and mammal species are highly adaptive and adapt readily to both native and non-native species. Although reviled in the popular press, *Eucalyptus* trees are now extremely important habitat for Californian native birds. The main issues lies with invertebrates, whose capacity for the adaptive behaviour shown in birds and mammals has generally been regarded as much reduced. Native species are highly valuable in this role of supporting invertebrates, but scientific studies are now showing so are non-natives. Value can only really be assessed at the level of individual species: some native plant species are highly attractive to invertebrates, whereas other native plants are not. The same is true of non-native species. Many invertebrates are detritivores (feeding on dead plant tissues), parasitoids of other insects, or predators and clearly have no preference for the plants that provide the surfaces or substrates on which they undertake these activities.

Herbivorous insects are either generalists, which feed on a wide variety of plants, or specialists, which have specific preferences for food plants. Classic examples of the latter include the caterpillar larvae of many butterflies and some leaf-mining insects. Many pollinator invertebrates are generalists, and indeed generalism is very common. It is a smart evolutionary strategy, particularly within common species. The caterpillars of moths, in contrast to their more specialized butterfly cousins, feed on a very wide range of plants. A. M. Shapiro reported that many butterflies in the western United States have moved from their original native larval food plants to feed upon non-native species, as the former have become increasingly rare in urban places.

If you want to support the life cycle of a specialist insect with a limited range of larval food plants, then you may need to use a specific native plant. To support populations of the marsh fritillary butterfly, for example, you need *Succisa pratensis*. To support generalist pollinators, you need plants from anywhere that produce nectar with a high sugar concentration and pollen over as long a season as possible. To identify these species, just look at plants in nature or a garden in summer and watch the pollinator traffic.

Using matrices to assist selection decisions

When choosing the plant palette for the site, a matrix can be developed using a spreadsheet such as Excel, as previously suggested to help review and manipulate information on plants to assist selection decisions. The first column contains the names of the plants and subsequent columns information on the plants, such as height, typical spread, robustness, growth habitat, foliage and stem attractiveness, flowering impact, flowering duration, and so on. The process of doing this is straight-forward, but the difficulty lies in sourcing accurate information on issues that cannot just be inferred from observation.

Example of a plant selection matrix for a mixed steppe and prairie community, with canopy height the primary sorting factor

Species with a flowering impact score in excess of 5 are shown in bold.

SPECIES	CANOPY HEIGHT	FOLIAGE POSITION	FLOWER DRAMA	FLOWER DURATION	OVERALL FLOWER IMPACT (DRAMA × DURATION)
Dodecatheon meadia 'Goliath'	low	rosette	2	1	2
Dracocephalum rupestre	low	mound	2	2	4
Geum triflorum	low	mound	1	2	2
Oenothera missouriensis	low	prostrate	2	3	6
Phlox pilosa	low	semi-erect	3	2	6
Asclepias tuberosa	medium	semi-erect	3	2	6
Aster oblongifolius	medium	semi-erect	3	3	9
Baptisia bracteata	medium	mound	2	2	4
Baptisia australis var. *minor*	medium	mound	2	2	4
Castilleja coccinea	medium	mound to semi-erect	2	2	4
Euphorbia corollata	medium	semi-erect	1	2	2
Liatris aspera	medium	erect	3	2	6
Oenothera tetragona	medium	mound	2	2	4
Penstemon cobaea	medium	rosette	3	2	6
Penstemon cyananthus	medium	rosette	2	2	4
Penstemon strictus	medium	rosette	2	2	4
Schizachyrium scoparium	medium	semi-erect	1	1	1
Scutellaria baicalensis	medium	mound	2	2	4
Sporobolus heterolepis	medium	mound	1	2	2
Amsonia hubrichtii	tall	semi-erect	1	2	2
Echinacea pallida	tall	basal to semi-erect	3	3	9
Echinacea paradoxa	tall	basal to semi-erect	3	3	9
Eryngium yuccifolium	tall	erect rosette	2	2	4
Penstemon barbatus 'Coccineus'	tall	rosette	2	3	6
Silphium laciniatum	tall	semi-erect	2	2	4
Silphium terebinthinaceum	tall	semi-erect	1	2	2
Solidago speciosa	tall	semi-erect	3	2	6

FORMULATING YOUR DESIGN OBJECTIVES

Once you have developed an outline plant palette for each of the distinctive plant habitat types identified by your site analysis, it is possible to begin to design plant communities for each of these habitats.

How many communities do you need?

On sites that are topographically complex and/or have marked gradients of soil types or degrees of shade and sun, you could end up with a large number of main and secondary communities. Given that you are generally making lots of assumptions in a site analysis rather than carrying out an exacting study of actual soil moisture and shade conditions, a balance needs to be struck between excessive numbers of communities, which make the seed mixing and sowing process overly complex, and insufficient numbers to achieve a good fit with the site conditions. No matter how many communities you design, it is inevitable that some species will prove to be poorly fitted in the medium to long term.

One of the ways to address this conundrum is to share some species between each community. In a drainage swale, for example, there are three distinctive sets of conditions: the wet base of the swale, the dry shoulder of the swale, and the wet-to-dry slopes in between. You know that in relative terms all of these conditions must exist, but the difficulty is identifying where a damp site becomes wet or dry. Even with experience this involves informed guesswork. If, however, you include some species more tolerant of damper soils in the dry shoulder community, some drier and wet species in the slope community, and finally some damp species in the wet base community, this will provide the capacity for the species to fit themselves to where the anticipated moisture gradients actually prove to be.

The same approach can be used with a woodland edge, but the situation is more complex because as well as soil moisture there is also a gradient of shade. Another approach that can further assist with this is to include species that are mobile, such as through surface-rooting stems (like *Ajuga reptans*, *Fragaria vesca*, or *Tiarella cordifolia*) and can actually reposition themselves where conditions best suit. Very few species that have these surface-rooting stems can reliably and economically be established by sowing, so this is an example of when planting might be integrated with sowing to improve long-term persistence. An alternative strategy is to include species which reliably reproduce from self-sown seed, for example, in Western Europe *Primula elatior*, *Primula vulgaris*, *Succisa pratensis*, and *Aquilegia* species, to allow plants to readily reposition themselves as conditions change.

Designing communities gets most complicated when it is necessary for the edge of a community to cross over an ecologically meaningful boundary. Imagine, for example, that you wanted to use a Mondrian-inspired rectilinear ground pattern which you create by pouring a series of different communities into the rectangles. This might work fine on a site with no appreciable ecological gradients of light or soil moisture. But how do you do this where this is not the case? The answer is probably that starting with a culturally as

Gradients in drainage swales are most critical with planting rather than sowing, due to the far smaller number of plants and species per unit area. Here in Burgess Park in London, I designed the planting palette for a shallow series of swales only to discover post planting that the swales were deep with very dry sides and a permanently wet base. Fortunately, the plant species and cultivars used have sufficient tolerance of both wet and dry to work adequately in most years.

In Burgess Park in London, 2 m in from the path (left) there is a drainage swale with a sown wet mix. The slope beyond this is sown with a dry slope mix. After 4 years there is no apparent boundary between the two, as the species were able to re-sort themselves to form a seamless transition between two very different soil moisture regimes.

opposed to ecologically responsive ground pattern on sites with marked ecological gradients probably just isn't a sensible way to work. In my project at the University of Oxford Botanic Garden (see case study), the site was adjacent to a river, almost flat, and all of it was in full sun. The soil seemed to be a relatively homogenous alluvial loam. Three plant communities were used in alternating wedge ground patterns to provide three repeats of each community. In the winter of the first year the site flooded, and again in the second year. Flooding had previously been rare, so we did not take it into account as a major factor. It had no obvious effect on the Eurasian plant community, but in the South African and dryland U.S. communities, an extra week of being under the water nearest the river completely eliminated some species, significantly changing the planting.

Degree of structural-spatial complexity and plant diversity within a community

It is possible to design naturalistic plantings as one-, two-, or three-layer communities. The advantage of more layers is that this creates the canopy space to pack in more species per square metre than is possible in a single layer. More layers provide the potential for a longer season of flowering and greater spatial complexity, which is likely to help the vegetation provide more habitat opportunities for invertebrates and wildlife in general. On the negative side, the more species you have per square metre, the fewer plants that will be in flower on a given day, so the impact of flowering may be less but continue for longer. It's also more challenging to design, because many more variables need to be handled. A balance needs to be struck.

Disorder versus order

As spatial complexity increases—in this case, that deriving from layers—so does the potential for the planting to look disordered. A plant community designed with many species and three layers, with very tall emergents in the tallest layer, will be perceived as the most disordered. A single-layer short community with low species diversity will be perceived as the least disordered. In conventional horticultural planting, diversity is reduced down to one species per block or group, giving the least possible disorder. These factors are important to human perception, as for many people disorder in planting is very challenging in urban contexts, even when the same people find it acceptable in rural contexts.

By its very random nature, naturalistic planting tends to have relatively few cues that the vegetation is designed, meant to be, and cared for. There is strong evidence from psychological research that people's tolerance of spatial disorder in planting is increased when that vegetation has a dramatic flowering season. If you are designing planting for your own garden, you will know the level of disorder that is acceptable to you. If you are designing for others in public spaces, you need to try to decide how much disorder might be acceptable to the average user of the space. Even with thoughtfulness, clearly it is impossible to please everyone in this regard.

Attractiveness to people across the year

An ideal naturalistic plant community would flower for as long as possible (in temperate regions from spring to late autumn), with key peaks of high visual drama. This is facilitated by selecting species that flower for long periods of time and that are as dramatic as possible. The more planting spaces given to these types of species, the more this will be so. The thresholds of attractiveness of naturalistic vegetation do, however, depend heavily on location and context. Vegetation that is judged to be unattractive in one context may be seen to be acceptable or even attractive in another context. People who are familiar with naturalistic vegetation tend to become more accepting of the off season, as they become aware of the cycles of high and low impact across the year and appreciate that what may be unexciting now may be spectacular in a few months' time.

A relationship exists between how many species are used and the drama of flowering. Generally speaking, selecting triplets of species to flower together in spring, late spring, early summer, summer, late summer, and autumn is a good design strategy, leading to a minimum of about fifteen different species per community. There is lots of opportunity to build in really exciting colour and form contrasts within these. In largely winter dormant communities such as prairie, grasses such as *Schizachyrium scoparium* and

Pairs or triplets of species that flower at the same time can be used to extend the flowering display of a planting mix, as illustrated in this sown and planted scheme which I created at the University of Oxford Botanic Garden. The images are all of the same area of Eurasian steppe-like planting. In April and May, *Euphorbia epithymoides* catches the end of the purple bells of *Pulsatilla vulgaris* (the fluffy seed heads).

In mid June, acid yellow *Galium verum*, purple *Salvia nemorosa*, and bronze *Stipa gigantea* come into bloom.

In July and August, the flowers of blue *Eryngium planum*, pink *Malva alcea*, and violet *Limonium platyphyllum* dominate the community.

Pennisetum alopecuroides, with beautifully coloured persistent dead winter foliage, can play an important role in dormant-season attractiveness.

Evergreen species are sometimes problematic in terms of management when mixed with winter-dormant species, as they may compromise cutting down in spring as a tidy-up measure. Grasses such as *Themeda triandra* are passably wintergreen and yet do not absolutely require this old foliage to be cut away in spring to look attractive as growth recommences, and so these can be used with truly year-round evergreen genera such as *Beschorneria*, *Dietes*, and *Yucca*. Grasses with these characteristics, however, are rather uncommon. Creating communities in which these compatibilities are fully worked out and matched up is a critical aspect of designing novel naturalistic plant communities not based on a wild occurring stereotype. Mediterranean plant communities dominated by wintergreen species are likely to be most attractive in winter, but they still need their summer-dormant messy foliage removed by cutting or burning in late summer. Many of these species are, however, much less winter cold tolerant.

The dead leaf tissue of Mediterranean (winter-growing but not yet re-emerged) *Watsonia borbonica* mars the appearance of the September-emerging shoots of the winter-growing *Kniphofia sarmentosa* (blue-grey leaves). In this combination, there is a need to cut the vegetation to the ground to remove *Watsonia* in early September before the *Kniphofia* growth is too advanced. (Ye Hang's Ph.D. research, Department of Landscape, University of Sheffield)

Appropriateness in terms of local character

The design of nature-like vegetation may need to respond to local character, whether derived from natural or cultural cues. In the case of natural cues, this is most likely to be when the sowing or planting is close to the urban edge or next to a natural feature such as a river or woodland. In these situations, the most appropriate strategy may be to use local native species to tie in visually with the existing vegetation and to reduce both actual risk and perception of species from the planting potentially invading the surrounding habitat. As one moves away from these natural character cues along a character gradient, it may be reasonable to use plants that are not local natives but which share common morphological features with them. These species might be near natives or from very distant parts of the world, but which share the desired appearance. In locations that are distinctly cultural, there is much greater opportunities to adopt a more relaxed approach to character notions.

Appropriateness in terms of scale

Many of the sown communities described in this book cover relatively large to very large areas. I don't normally get asked to design sown vegetation for gardens unless those gardens are really large, that is, not really like gardens. This should not put you off if your garden is small. Because naturalistic sown vegetation has a repeating pattern, it tends to look good at a variety of scales. I have sown an entire home garden that is not very large—that of my partner and me—and it was very successful. These design approaches are relevant to all sized spaces.

The smaller the space, the more you reduce the height of the layers. You might have, for example, a base layer of up to 300 mm and then some emergent coming out of that to 750 mm. What you are making becomes akin to what you might do on a green roof on a shed using alpine plant species. With very small areas, you can really play with it to produce a finely grained, diverse vegetation that is endlessly changing. Almost every day something else will pop up and flower. It is hugely engaging.

DESIGNING WITHIN COMMUNITY SPATIAL ORGANIZATION

This is where at last we begin to deal with making the decisions that are typically seen as planting design: how many of this species in relation to that species and so on. It's about creating a design vision of what is to come forth, in terms of height, texture, surface topography, and character. Drawing cross sections through the vegetation is a great way to test and refine your ideas.

Single-layer communities

The single layer is the building block for all other types of communities. The inherent characteristic of single-layer sowing or planting is that plants are used that essentially maintain their foliage in the same layer of space. These layers can range from perhaps 50 mm deep on a green roof through to 2 m on very moist fertile soil. Designing with species with approximately equivalent foliage heights reduces the capacity of species to eliminate one another rapidly through competition for light. It also limits some of the visual effects that can be achieved.

Single-layer planting can be used in full sun, on the edges of trees or buildings that result in intermittent shade, and finally in the more permanent shade under trees. There are three key design decisions in a single-layer community: the target number of plants (irrespective of species choice) per square metre, the planting palette (that is, which species are to be used), and how many of the target number of plants per square metre are to be occupied by which species. The first and last of these decisions have a big effect on how far apart different species are from one another. This affects the grain of the inherent repeating pattern when plants flower, which becomes visually evident as individuals emerge from the anonymity of their neighbours.

The target number of plants per square metre largely depends on whether the community is to be created by sowing or planting. Sowing allows very high densities of seedlings at low cost. Typically the target range is from 50 to 300 seedlings/m². As density increases, the capacity of the community to resist weed invasion and compete with invading weed seedlings increases. High densities are particularly attractive on sites where levels of maintenance are likely to be lower. High target densities also build in resilience to failure. If you have a target seedling density of 200 seedlings/m², even if 75 per cent of seedlings fail to establish you will still have enough plants to produce an effective plant

The low, 600-mm single-layer structure that the mix in the table on pages 148–149 would create.

community. These desirable qualities of high seedling density have to be offset against the negatives of higher cost for seed and increased competition between the sown seedlings.

Competition leads to a situation known as self-thinning, in which the first to germinate or fastest growing seedlings typically outcompete the smaller, later emerging or growing species, leading to their elimination from the community. This seriously disadvantages slowly growing or late-germinating species from the outset, hence limiting the capacity to establish these in a community. Using North American prairie vegetation as an example, 200 seedlings/m² thins down to a more or less stable density of about 50–100 seedlings/m² in about 2 years, with most of the thinning (that is, death) involving the slower, potentially most desirable species. The smaller the individual species making up the sowing palette, the higher the sustainable density, and vice versa. Sustainable plant density is also affected by soil productivity, with less productive soil having a higher sustainable density because the plants are individually smaller.

Density also affects the appearance of the vegetation above and beyond the absence of some species due to self-thinning. It is common for vegetation sown at high densities to look rather flat topped with much reduced variation in surface topography. In essence the vegetation looks a bit like a table top, a distinctively different appearance than that of much planted vegetation.

In planted vegetation, it is rarely possible for economic reasons to plant at densities greater than 16 plants/m² where plugs and 9-cm-diameter pots are involved and 9 or 10 plants/m² when 9-cm square pots are involved. A density of 9 or 10 plants/m² results in a physical space for each plant of between 250- and 330-mm diameter (a large dinner plate). This much lower density compared to sowing means that the capacity of the planted material to compete with weed seedlings is much reduced both initially and in the long term, leading to reduced community resistance to weed invasion. Other than the fact that density of plants is obviously always going to be lower in planted schemes, all of the design principles mentioned in this chapter are equally applicable to planting.

Making decisions on the relative abundance of each species present in a planting palette is a highly iterative process. Assuming that in a single-layer community you are trying to work with plants with similar heights and growth potential (very different heights and growth patterns are discussed later for two- and three-layer communities), then one way would be to evenly split the target number of seedlings or plants per square metre among the species in the palette. To do this, however, it will be vital for you to have

The same structure shown in reality using the example of U.K. native sown meadow. Relative flatness and low surface textural variation result from similarity of plant size, plus intense competition. This is further exacerbated in this meadow by the summer cutting process which causes disproportionate stress to the larger species, further encouraging flattening.

thoroughly researched the growth and other characteristics of the species. This would involve drawing sketches of the growth form of the species relative to one another both in plan and in section.

Hence if you have a target of 100 seedlings/m² for a sown plant community and twenty species in your palette, five of these seedlings would be allocated to each species. If you have already selected those twenty species to have four species flowering in spring, four in late spring, four in summer, four in late summer, and four in autumn this might work out fine. Even if you have done this, then you will need to enter the species into a spreadsheet to nuance the design process and ultimately to calculate how much seed to include of each species or to calculate how many plants need to be purchased.

In many cases, you probably won't want to have this even distribution of species in the planting or sowing mix. You might, for example, want to reduce the number of places allocated to spring-flowering species and transfer the spare spaces to the autumn-flowering species. The reason for doing this in temperate climates is that it is politically useful in public spaces to have a good, highly floral autumn, something that many people find cheering in the approach to winter. If there are too many spaces given to spring- or summer-flowering species, there will not be enough left for the autumn species.
Alternatively there might be specific colour effects that you want to achieve by apportioning more spaces to given species or to species that flower for a very long time (the workhorses), while reducing other species which are fun but are more moments in time. Or you might just want to give more spaces to species that you really like.

A chart aiding decision-making on plant selection and sowing and planting density in the creation of a hypothetical single-layer plant community for well-drained moist to dryish soils established either by sowing or by planting at 12 plants/m^2

The orange areas show when the species flower, and the grey areas represent species whose main contribution is attractive foliage or form.

FLOWERING SEASON

SPECIES	FLOWER COLOUR	JAN	FEB	MAR	APR	MAY	JUN	JUL	AUG	SEP	OCT	NOV	DEC
Euphorbia epithymoides	acid yellow				■	■							
Primula veris	yellow				■	■							
Pulsatilla vulgaris	violet or red			■	■								
Buphthalmum salicifolium 'Alpengold'	yellow						■	■					
Dianthus carthusianorum	cerise pink						■	■					
Dracocephalum peregrinum	violet							■	■				
Galium verum	acid yellow						■	■					
Oenothera tetragona	yellow						■	■					
Salvia ×sylvestris 'Blaukönigin'	violet						■						
Anaphalis triplinervis	white								■	■			
Aster amellus	mauve-violet									■	■		
Hyssopus officinalis subsp. *aristatus*	dark blue								■	■			
Inula ensifolia	yellow							■	■				
Limonium platyphyllum	mauve							■					
Origanum vulgare	pink-purple							■	■				
Teucrium chamaedrys	pink							■	■				
Aster spectabilis	violet									■	■		
Sedum telephium 'Emperor's Waves'	purple red										■	■	
Sesleria autumnalis	pale green							■	■	■	■	■	■
Zauschneria cana	orange-red									■	■		

IF SEEDED: 100 SEEDLINGS/M²	IF PLANTED: 12 PLANTS/M²	IF PLANTED: 120 PLANTS/10 M²	RATIONALE FOR NUMBERS, ESPECIALLY WHEN LARGE OR SMALL	SPECIES
2	0.2	2	plants large	*Euphorbia epithymoides*
14	1.7	17	plants small	*Primula veris*
6	0.7	7	very attractive	*Pulsatilla vulgaris*
3	0.4	4		*Buphthalmum salicifolium* 'Alpengold'
10	1.2	12	plants small, long flowered	*Dianthus carthusianorum*
3	0.4	4		*Dracocephalum peregrinum*
5	0.6	6	visually exciting with salvia	*Galium verum*
3	0.4	4	evergreen basal leaves	*Oenothera tetragona*
3	0.4	4	relatively large, not too many	*Salvia* ×*sylvestris* 'Blaukönigin'
7	0.8	8	long flowering, silver leaf contrast	*Anaphalis triplinervis*
3	0.4	4		*Aster amellus*
3	0.4	4		*Hyssopus officinalis* subsp. *aristatus*
5	0.6	6	good structural hummock	*Inula ensifolia*
3	0.4	4	good evergreen leaves	*Limonium platyphyllum*
5	0.6	6	long flowering, very attractive to bees	*Origanum vulgare*
7	0.8	8	relative small, evergreen	*Teucrium chamaedrys*
4	0.5	5	late flowering	*Aster spectabilis*
7	0.8	8	slow to develop	*Sedum telephium* 'Emperor's Waves'
4	0.5	5	attractive foliage	*Sesleria autumnalis*
3	0.4	4	suckers, may dominate	*Zauschneria cana*
100	12.0	120		

Two-layer communities

Whereas a single-layer community is composed of species that are relatively alike in growth rates and the volumes of space that their canopies occupy, this will not be so in a two-layer community. Using difference in these characteristics provides additional creative opportunities, and the vegetation will have more varied surface topography due to the two distinctive layers present. These communities have much more potential for line contrast between a mounded or horizontal ground layer and the erect stems of the taller emergent layer. The value of the resulting habitat to invertebrates, different guilds of which are likely to use different layers to live or feed in, may be increased as well.

Shade-intolerant lower layer and taller emergent layer

The base layer, which covers the ground, has both utilitarian and aesthetic roles. By shading the ground from spring to autumn—and for much longer in the case of evergreen species—weed establishment in the plantings is greatly reduced. The base layer is also important in providing display events, particularly in spring and early summer, as many of the taller emergent species tend to flower from early summer on.

As the plant density, mass, and height of the upper layer increases, the shade cast on the base layer increases. The emergents in the upper layer that cast the least shade are those that have leafless flowering stems, that is, typically basal foliage within the space occupied by the base layer, and then naked flowering stems that cast moderate to little shade. Many of the plants that do this are monocots, such as *Agapanthus*, *Dierama*, *Eremurus*, *Galtonia candicans*, *Kniphofia*, *Watsonia*, and *Yucca*. Quite a few of these species are prone to winter kill in areas colder than USDA Hardiness Zones 6 and 7. There are also some dicots with similar growth habits, but which are much more cold tolerant, including *Echinacea pallida*, *Echinacea paradoxa*, *Eryngium yuccifolium*, and *Rudbeckia maxima*. Another alternative is to use emergents that are more mound-like and not much taller than ground-layer species, such as *Aster amellus*, *Aster oblongifolius*, and *Euphorbia epithymoides*.

For both taller erect and mound-like emergents, the most powerful way to minimize the negative effect of the emergents on the base layer is to keep the former at wide spacing, by having a low target density for sowing or planting of emergents. This also maintains a sense of transparency through the emergent stems and allows the designer to counterpoint different views and structural form within the emergent stems. So just how low should the densities of sown emergent species be? There is no hard and fast right answer to this question; it's a design judgement depending largely on the effects to be generated and the shade intolerance of the understorey species. As a crude rule of thumb, however, emergent density should generally not exceed 10 per cent of the total seeding or planting density, and it will often be much lower than this. An example of this is given in the table of the two-layer system using the relatively shade intolerant base layer previously shown in the table of the single-layer system.

Two-layer South African planting which Sarah Price and I designed in the Queen Elizabeth Olympic Park gardens, with the upper emergent layer formed by *Agapanthus*, *Galtonia*, and *Gladiolus*.

Two-layer systems can be successfully applied to large- and small-scale schemes, here created through planting in my home garden with *Kniphofia* 'Jane Henry' and others at a diversity of heights.

A two-layer system using planted, nonmassive emergents, with the base layer established by sowing seed over the top of the widely spaced planted emergents, or, if preferred, entirely by planting at 12 plants/m²

The community is suitable for well-drained moist to dryish soils. The orange areas show when the species flower, and the grey areas represent species whose main contribution is attractive foliage or form.

FLOWERING SEASON

SPECIES	FLOWER COLOUR	JAN	FEB	MAR	APR	MAY	JUN	JUL	AUG	SEP	OCT	NOV	DEC
Base layer													
Euphorbia epithymoides	acid yellow				▓	▓							
Primula veris	yellow				▓	▓							
Pulsatilla vulgaris	violet or red			▓	▓								
Buphthalmum salicifolium 'Alpengold'	yellow						▓	▓					
Dianthus carthusianorum	cerise pink					▓	▓	▓					
Dracocephalum peregrinum	violet						▓	▓					
Galium verum	acid yellow						▓	▓					
Oenothera tetragona	yellow						▓	▓					
Salvia ×sylvestris 'Blaukönigin'	violet						▓	▓					
Anaphalis triplinervis	white								▓	▓			
Aster amellus	mauve-violet								▓	▓	▓		
Hyssopus officinalis subsp. aristatus	dark blue								▓	▓			
Inula ensifolia	yellow							▓	▓				
Limonium platyphyllum	mauve							▓	▓				
Origanum vulgare	pink-purple							▓	▓				
Teucrium chamaedrys	pink							▓	▓	▓			
Aster spectabilis	violet									▓	▓		
Sedum telephium 'Emperor's Waves'	purple-red									▓	▓		
Sesleria autumnalis	pale green							▓	▓	▓	▓	▓	
Zauschneria cana	orange-red												
Emergent layer													
Echinacea pallida	pink						▓	▓	▓				
Eremurus stenophyllus	yellow						▓	▓					
Echinacea paradoxa	yellow							▓	▓	▓			
Solidago speciosa	yellow								▓	▓			
Kniphofia uvaria	orange-red									▓	▓		

IF SEEDED: 100 SEEDLINGS/M²	IF PLANTED: 12 PLANTS/M²	IF PLANTED: 120 PLANTS/10 M²	RATIONALE FOR NUMBERS, ESPECIALLY WHEN LARGE OR SMALL
2	0.2	2	plants large
14	1.7	17	plants small
6	0.7	7	very attractive
3	0.4	4	
10	1.2	12	plants small, long flowered
3	0.4	4	
5	0.6	6	visually exciting with salvia
3	0.4	4	evergreen basal leaves
3	0.4	4	relatively large, not too many
7	0.8	8	long flowering, silver leaf contrast
3	0.4	4	
3	0.4	4	
5	0.6	6	good structural hummock
3	0.4	4	good evergreen leaves
5	0.6	6	long flowering, very attractive to bees
7	0.8	8	relative small, evergreen
4	0.5	5	late flowering
7	0.8	8	slow to develop
4	0.5	5	attractive foliage
3	0.4	4	suckers, may dominate
100	12.0	120	
	0.5	5	
	0.4	4	
	1	10	long flowering and compact
	0.5	5	
	0.2	2	large foliage clumps
0	2.6	26	

Two- and three-layer structures do not generally emerge visually until later in the growing season. Here in the University of Oxford Botanic Garden in June 2015, the large emergents are beginning to do that, but the planting is still essentially at this time just a single layer. By August all will change, with the 3-m naked stems of *Silphium* towering above.

The type of structure the two-layer sowing and planting mix in the table on pages 152–153 would create.

Because the number of emergents per square metre should normally be kept very low, it becomes economic to plant these into a sown base layer. This removes the risk of emergent species sown at very low densities (say less than 1 seedling/m²) failing to establish and resulting in no emergents at all. Planting the emergents also gives you the capacity to use species that are not practical to establish from sowing seed, because their germination biology is too difficult in situ (such as *Actaea* species), the time to get sufficiently mature to flower is so long (for example, *Eremurus*), or the seed is just too expensive to broadcast sow (for example, the heavy and rather erratically germinating seed of the larger *Stipa* species). Planting also gives you access to cultivars, which cannot be established by seeding, to achieve highly specific design effects. Even when used at very low densities, planting provides a sense of success. There are some plants physically present from the outset, and these often flower in the first year, when the sown material doesn't. Integrating planting with seeding is discussed in detail in the next chapter, and examples of doing this in practice are given in the case studies.

Shade-tolerant lower layer and taller emergent layer

This approach recognizes the difficulty of using taller species, which expand over time vegetatively and by self-seeding; at lower levels of maintenance, they gradually eliminate the shade-intolerant base layer. To address this problem, a base-layer palette is required which can persist in heavy shade under a herbaceous overstorey. Most of the plants for this base-layer palette occur naturally in woodland or on woodland edges. In effect, this design model creates a miniature herbaceous version of a woodland. Woodland understorey species mainly flower in spring, before or just as deciduous trees are coming into leaf. In mild winter climates, many are winter evergreen or often come into growth in winter and are able to photosynthesize sufficiently before the light levels drop under the tree canopy. Foliage retention aside, there are also quite a number of summer- or autumn-flowering species that can be used, particularly in eastern North America (*Aster divaricatus* and *Heuchera villosa*) and China (*Begonia* and *Impatiens* species, *Saxifraga fortunei*), although these are generally less able to thrive in very dense shade than some of the species that go quiescent or even completely dormant by mid summer.

In any case, summer- or autumn-flowering species are very difficult to appreciate as a flower spectacle in these sorts of plantings except on the edges. The wintergreen, or at least partly wintergreen, lower layer is very functional when used with winter-deciduous emergent layers as it inhibits winter weed invasion and provides welcome winter greenery.

Because the base layer is highly shade tolerant, the density of the taller emergent species and their capacity to extinguish light reaching the ground below is less critical, although clearly there is a need to compensate for high-density emergent layers by selecting the most shade-tolerant understories. To extend the season of interest beyond the spring-flowering understorey layer, the emergents are normally chosen to flower from early summer to late autumn. Where the emergent layer is kept relatively open and not too densely packed, there are more opportunities to use a greater diversity of species in the ground layer, including moderately shade tolerant, late-flowering species such as *Aster divaricatus* and *Rudbeckia fulgida*.

In regions where slugs are numerous, a critical factor in selecting a palette for the emergent layer is that the species need to be unpalatable. The presence of a relatively dense ground layer that may shelter large slug populations often results in serious damage or death to the emerging shoots of palatable plants. Species with high shoot thrust (for example, *Baptisia alba*) to push through the layer as quickly as possible is also a desirable characteristic for the emergent species.

In the table showing the two-layer system with a shade-tolerant base layer, the species are substantially more moisture demanding than those used to create the base layer in the single-layer table and the subsequent variants thereof. If desired to reduce cost, some of the base-layer species can be established by sowing over the top post planting, which is also true of some of the emergents.

A two-layer system using a shade-tolerant base layer that is partly planted (for species not possible from seeding) and a planted emergent layer

The community is suitable for well-drained moist soils. The orange areas show when the species flower.

SPECIES	FLOWER COLOUR	JAN	FEB	MAR	APR	MAY	JUN	JUL	AUG	SEP	OCT	NOV	DEC
Shade-tolerant base layer													
Primula vulgaris	acid yellow			■	■								
Primula elatior	yellow			■	■								
Ajuga reptans	dark blue			■	■								
Omphalodes cappadocica	sky blue				■	■							
Polemonium reptans	pale blue					■	■						
Phlox stolonifera 'Blue Ridge'	pale blue					■	■						
Geum coccineum	orange					■	■						
Aster divaricatus	white								■	■			
Heuchera villosa	white								■	■			
Emergent layer													
Leucanthemum ×superbum	white						■	■					
Veronica longifolia	purple blue						■	■					
Silene chalcedonica	red							■	■				
Malva alcea var. *fastigiata*	pink							■	■				
Rudbeckia fulgida var. *sullivantii* 'Goldsturm'	yellow								■	■	■		
Solidago rugosa 'Fireworks'	yellow									■	■		
Miscanthus sinensis 'Flamingo'	purple red									■	■		
Aster 'Little Carlow'	lavender blue									■	■		
Aster novae-angliae 'September-rubin'	garnet-cerise									■	■		
Aster novae-angliae 'Purple Dome'	purple									■	■	■	

FLOWERING SEASON

IF SEEDED: 100 SEEDLINGS/M²	IF PLANTED: 12 PLANTS/M²	IF PLANTED: 120 PLANTS/10 M²	RATIONALE FOR NUMBERS, ESPECIALLY WHEN LARGE OR SMALL
30	2.0	20	good for ground cover, very attractive
30	2.0	20	good for ground cover, very attractive
	1.0	10	
	1.0	10	
5	0.3	3	larger, self seeds
	1.0	10	
15	1.0	10	good for evergreen ground cover
5	0.3	3	larger
5			larger
90	8.6	86	
5	0.5	5	
5	0.5	5	relatively thin tall species
10	0.5	5	relatively thin tall species
3	0.1	1	spreads widely
10	0.5	5	long-flowering workhorse
	0.5	5	
	0.05	1	tall, very occasional accent
	0.1	1	large foliage clumps
5	0.3	3	
	0.3	3	
38	3.4	34	

Two-layer communities with a shade-tolerant base layer have very different flowering displays and structure in spring versus summer and autumn. Here, the underlying woodland shade layer is dominated by *Primula elatior* and *Primula vulgaris* in spring.

The same vegetation in August. The spring-flowering primulas are still present, but they are obscured by the foliage of the predominantly North American prairie species. The primulas go semi-dormant in summer but come into leaf again in winter.

The same vegetation flowering at 1.2–1.5 m tall in autumn, with the dormant primula beneath.

The planting and sowing mix in the table on pages 156–157 for the two-layer system using a shade-tolerant base layer creates a community with a structure like this. Because the emergents need not be separated from one another, this allows many more species to be packed into the upper layer, potentially leading to a more flat-topped appearance with reduced layer definition.

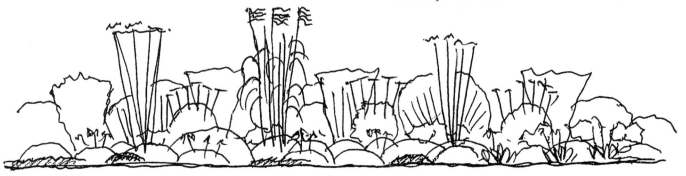

Three-layer communities

These communities are essentially the previously discussed two-layer systems but with an extra layer, often involving really gigantic mega forbs, such as *Eupatorium fistulosum*, *Ferula* species, and *Silphium* species. The addition of these species is valuable when designing vegetation for really large spaces where height and scale are important. An alternative, of course, is to use large shrubs and small trees for the same purpose.

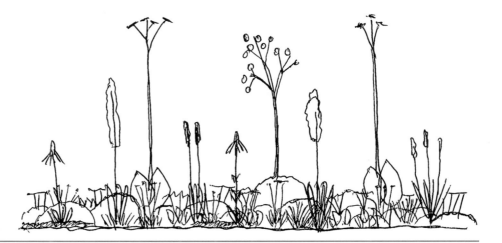

A three-layer system using plants suitable for well-drained moist to dryish soils created by the mix in the table on pages 162–163.

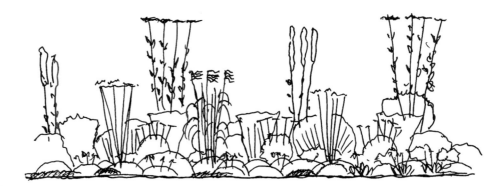

The planting structure generated by the mix in the second three-layer table on pages 164–165 is almost identical to that of the two-layer system using a shade-tolerant base layer, with the exception that the taller emergents create more layer definition.

A three-layer system at RHS Garden Wisley, with the upper layer being created by *Silphium laciniatum* and *Silphium terebinthinaceum*.

Almost the ultimate in three-layered sowing and planting at the Queen Elizabeth Olympic Park in London, with *Verbascum olympicum* as the large visually dominant species.

A three-layer system using planted emergents and relatively massive, taller emergents with the shade-intolerant base layer established by sowing seed over the top or by planting at 12 plants/m²

The community is suitable for well-drained moist to dryish soils. The orange areas show when the species flower, and the grey areas represent species whose main contribution is attractive foliage or form.

SPECIES	FLOWER COLOUR	JAN	FEB	MAR	APR	MAY	JUN	JUL	AUG	SEP	OCT	NOV	DEC
Base layer													
Euphorbia epithymoides	acid yellow				■	■							
Primula veris	yellow				■	■							
Pulsatilla vulgaris	violet or red			■	■								
Buphthalmum salicifolium 'Alpengold'	yellow					■	■	■	■				
Dianthus carthusianorum	cerise pink						■	■					
Dracocephalum peregrinum	violet						■	■					
Galium verum	acid yellow						■	■					
Oenothera tetragona	yellow						■	■					
Salvia ×sylvestris 'Blaukönigin'	violet						■						
Anaphalis triplinervis	white								■	■			
Aster amellus	mauve-violet								■	■	■		
Hyssopus officinalis subsp. *aristatus*	dark blue							■	■				
Inula ensifolia	yellow							■	■				
Limonium platyphyllum	mauve							■					
Origanum vulgare	pink-purple							■	■				
Teucrium chamaedrys	pink							■	■				
Aster spectabilis	violet									■	■		
Sedum telephium 'Emperor's Waves'	purple red									■	■	■	
Sesleria autumnalis	pale green							■	■	■	■	■	■
Zauschneria cana	orange-red									■	■		
Emergent layer													
Echinacea pallida	pink						■	■	■				
Eremurus stenophyllus	yellow						■	■					
Echinacea paradoxa	yellow							■	■				
Solidago speciosa	yellow									■	■		
Kniphofia uvaria	orange-red										■		
Tall emergent layer													
Ferula communis	yellow					■	■						
Stipa gigantea	bronze-gold							■	■				
Silphium terebinthinaceum	yellow								■				

IF SEEDED: 100 SEEDLINGS/M²	IF PLANTED: 12 PLANTS/M²	IF PLANTED: 120 PLANTS/10 M²	RATIONALE FOR NUMBERS, ESPECIALLY WHEN LARGE OR SMALL
2	0.2	2	plants large
14	1.7	17	plants small
6	0.7	7	very attractive
3	0.4	4	
10	1.2	12	plants small, long flowered
3	0.4	4	
5	0.6	6	visually exciting with salvia
3	0.4	4	evergreen basal leaves
3	0.4	4	relatively large, not too many
7	0.8	8	long flowering, silver leaf contrast
3	0.4	4	
3	0.4	4	
5	0.6	6	good structural hummock
3	0.4	4	good evergreen leaves
5	0.6	6	long flowering, very attractive to bees
7	0.8	8	relative small, evergreen
4	0.5	5	late flowering
7	0.8	8	slow to develop
4	0.5	5	attractive foliage
3	0.4	4	suckers, may dominate
100	12	120	
	0.3	3	
	0.4	4	
	0.5	5	long flowering and compact
	0.4	4	
	0.1	1	large foliage clumps
0	1.7	17	
	0.05	0.5	large and massive, very occasional
	0.05	0.5	large and massive, very occasional
	0.05	0.5	large and massive, very occasional
0	0.15	1.5	

DESIGNING NATURALISTIC HERBACEOUS PLANT COMMUNITIES

A three-layer system using planted nonmassive and massive emergents with a shade-tolerant but relatively moisture demanding base layer. The base- and emergent-layer species available as commercial seed are established by sowing seed over the top post planting.

The community is suitable for well-drained moist soils. The orange areas show when the species flower.

SPECIES	FLOWER COLOUR	JAN	FEB	MAR	APR	MAY	JUN	JUL	AUG	SEP	OCT	NOV	DEC
Shade-tolerant base layer													
Primula vulgaris	acid yellow			■	■								
Primula elatior	yellow			■	■								
Ajuga reptans	dark blue			■	■								
Omphalodes cappadocica	sky blue				■	■							
Polemonium reptans	pale blue					■	■						
Phlox stolonifera 'Blue Ridge'	pale blue					■	■						
Geum coccineum	orange					■	■						
Aster divaricatus	white								■	■			
Heuchera villosa	white								■	■			
Emergent layer													
Leucanthemum ×superbum	white						■	■	■				
Veronica longifolia	purple blue						■	■	■				
Silene chalcedonica	red							■	■				
Malva alcea var. *fastigiata*	pink								■	■			
Rudbeckia fulgida var. *sullivantii* 'Goldsturm'	yellow								■	■	■		
Solidago rugosa 'Fireworks'	yellow									■	■		
Aster 'Little Carlow'	lavender blue									■	■		
Aster novae-angliae 'September-rubin'	garnet-cerise									■	■	■	
Aster novae-angliae 'Purple Dome'	purple									■	■	■	
Tall emergent layer													
Eupatorium fistulosum	purple									■	■		
Aconitum carmichaelii	lavender blue									■	■	■	
Leucanthemella serotina	white									■	■	■	
Miscanthus sinensis 'Malepartus'	purple									■	■		

Header spanning: FLOWERING SEASON covers JAN–DEC.

IF SEEDED: 100 SEEDLINGS/M²	IF PLANTED: 12 PLANTS/M²	IF PLANTED: 120 PLANTS/10 M²	RATIONALE FOR NUMBERS, ESPECIALLY WHEN LARGE OR SMALL
30	2.0	20	good for ground cover, very attractive
30	2.0	20	good for ground cover, very attractive
	1.0	10	
	1.0	10	
5	0.3	3	larger, self seeds
	1.0	10	
15	1.0	10	good for evergreen ground cover
5	0.3	3	larger
5			larger
90	8.6	86	
5	0.5	5	
5	0.5	5	relatively thin tall species
10	0.5	5	relatively thin tall species
3	0.1	1	widely spreading
10	0.5	5	long flowering workhorse
	0.5	5	
	0.1	1	large foliage clumps
5	0.3	3	
	0.3	3	
38	3.3	33	
	0.05	0.5	
	0.1	1.0	not so massive, very erect
	0.05	0.5	
	0.05	0.5	
0	0.25	2.5	

SEED MIX DESIGN, IMPLEMENTATION, AND INITIAL ESTABLISHMENT

The seed mix is the vehicle through which all of the ecological and design principles that underlie the creation of attractive and sustainable naturalistic vegetation are united in practice. The seed mix is where you make your final decisions on the palette of plants to be used, and hence the structure and flowering characteristics, as well as maximizing the long-term capacity of species to coexist within the community and to fit the site into which they are to be sown.

In many parts of the world, it is possible to purchase ready-made seed mixes to create a variety of herbaceous plant communities. These mainly comprise plant communities of annual species drawn from across the world (that is, mainly exotic to any given region), communities of perennial species native to the geographic region in question, or communities of perennial species drawn from across the world.

Commercial annual seed mixes generally work quite reliably and deliver on our expectations of them. This is true for several reasons. Firstly, it is easy for the vendors to trial and evaluate their products. They sow their mixes, observe them over a 6-month period, and then amend the seed mix by adding more seed of species which are absent or present at too low a density. Conversely species that are present at too high a density can have their seed rates reduced. In addition, the seed of annual species is normally highly germinable; this is an essential evolved biological trait, as failure to germinate leads to a risk of local extinction. Most annuals have little or no seed dormancy, and so as long as it is warm enough and the soil is adequately moist, germination is successful. Dormancy is the situation in seeds when the sowing environment is appropriate for germination to occur but this does not happen, due to an internal (to the seed) or external factor.

Seed mixes for perennial plant species, whether native or non-native, are potentially an entirely different proposition. It's more difficult for the companies formulating the mixes to refine their seed mixes because the species involved are more unpredictable, and using trials to improve seed mix design requires more time and money. Even under optimal conditions, seed of perennial species tends to have intrinsically lower germinability than that of annuals, and this worsens as seed ages in storage. Perennial species are also much more likely to experience dormancy of some sort, so that when sown, many fewer seeds actually develop into seedlings. In practice, for some species these characteristics typically lead to low densities of seedlings per square metre, resulting in a chain of events leading to poorer performance in both the short and longer term. How to successfully overcome these issues is a major focus of this chapter.

One of the fundamental goals of the design process is to identify solutions to specific problems. With generic seed mixes formulated by other people, who don't know your conditions or aesthetic expectations, buying ready-made mixes potentially has a relatively high likelihood of disappointing. These mixes are generally ok when establishing meadows on the sides of motorways which will only be seen from afar at high speed. But what about busy urban places where you need to inspire the public or in private gardens where you want to express your creative persona, your likes and dislikes, what is meaningful to you? Seed mix design gives you the opportunity to create something truly original, extraordinary, never seen before. The purpose of this chapter is to help you understand the processes that allow you to create extraordinary naturalistic vegetation, whatever the context.

ENVISAGING THE APPEARANCE AND PERFORMANCE OF THE COMMUNITY YOU WISH TO CREATE

You can't logically develop a sensible seed mix—or for that matter a planting mix—unless you are first capable of projecting a vision of the vegetation you wish to create. This involves beginning to develop thoughts on form and character and an outline list of species to fit the environmental conditions to deliver the aesthetic and functional performance required.

Which species are suitable for sowing in situ and why?

Not all species that you might want to use are available commercially. The total pool of herbaceous plant species currently available as commercial seed in bulk (that is, by weight) is probably in the region of 5000 species and seed strains. This is less than 2 per cent of the species making up the world's flora, but it includes many of the most attractive and useful species. In any geographic region, only a small percentage of species are hyper-attractive, the plant equivalent of the Hollywood A-lister. Then there is a slightly larger group of B-listers, and then the rest, which while possessing some useful properties are aesthetically or functionally limited in some ways. You can parallel this idea with those regarding how to score aesthetic impact.

These perennial plant species generally come from two sources: the seed industry associated with restoration ecology (normally supplying seed of species native to a particular country to people living there) and the horticultural seed industry supplying seed to nursery growers. In contrast to agricultural and horticultural crops and turf grass, generally there is no legislation that imposes quality standards on minimum seed germinability of flower seed in these industries.

The price of seed tends to be substantially lower in the restoration ecology seed industry than for the same species sold in the horticultural equivalent, but so too is the quality. While it is difficult to generalize, as there are companies who are much more focused on seed quality than others, typically seed in the restoration ecology industry is a lower cost, lower quality product. By quality, I am referring to the capacity of 100 seeds of a given species to produce seedlings when sown in the field under conditions appropriate for its germination. This notion of quality says nothing about genetic fitness for a location, which can also be a very important quality notion, but is all for naught if the seed is not capable of germinating and emerging in the first place.

Irrespective of the complexity of the specific germination biology of a species, germinability is typically lowest for species that are more obscure or relatively difficult to produce. Demand for more obscure species tends to be more episodic and hence this seed potentially sits much longer in storage. Where this storage is relatively unsophisticated (that is, not involving subzero temperature and reduced humidity), germinability declines year by year. Some companies manage their inventory more effectively than others and throw away seed after a certain number of years, whereas others clearly do not. Within Europe (and I assume the United States, too), there is a large internal market in wildflower

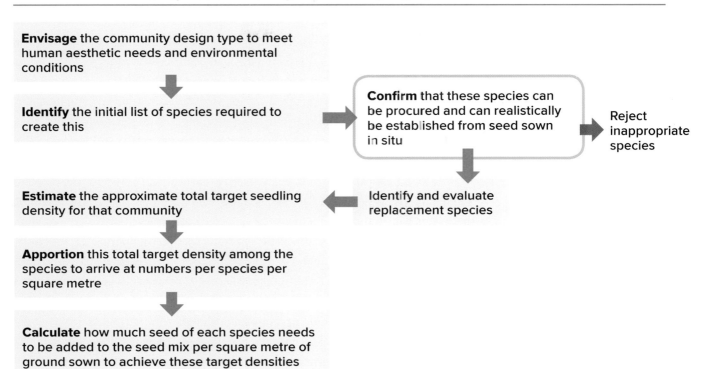

Envisage the community design type to meet human aesthetic needs and environmental conditions

Identify the initial list of species required to create this

Confirm that these species can be procured and can realistically be established from seed sown in situ

Reject inappropriate species

Identify and evaluate replacement species

Estimate the approximate total target seedling density for that community

Apportion this total target density among the species to arrive at numbers per species per square metre

Calculate how much seed of each species needs to be added to the seed mix per square metre of ground sown to achieve these target densities

seed for restoration projects, and seed is often bought from third parties to make up orders without intermediate or final purchasers having any guarantees of germinability. While working on the Queen Elizabeth Olympic Park in London, we bought 1 kg of *Salvia pratensis* seed from a well-known seed merchant that on testing proved to be almost 100 per cent dead. This vendor had bought it in good faith from someone else; the chain can be protracted.

This situation prevails because most seed from the restoration seed industry is traditionally purchased by landscape architects or landscape contractors working on infrastructure type projects who don't really understand the sowing and germination process very well and are unclear as to what to expect post sowing. In the main, the people in these groups struggle to reliably identify seedlings to species level, and therefore confirming the presence or absence of species as small seedlings within the typically 12-month contractual period is difficult. Hence, there is rarely a complaint about seed quality.

Species whose seed is relatively short lived in dry storage are most badly affected by poor storage conditions and lax inventory management. There is nothing fundamentally problematic about using seed that has low germinability other than you need to know this is the case. If you knew germinability was low, then you could add more seed of that species to compensate in order to achieve the target number of seedlings per square metre. This would increase the cost, sometimes very substantially, of establishing each seedling of that species, highlighting that seed that seemed a good value was not. Unless you have the time and money to have seed tested—which is only likely to happen on large, high-profile projects with a long schedule—you will never know how good or bad the germinability is. It is this unpredictability that bedevils the creation of meadows by landscape architects and others and is often the reason why many sowings are not very effective. How can you improve practice if the seed you are using may respond differently each time you use it? Even if there is time to allow seed tests, it is rather difficult to interpret the results of such tests when dealing with species that are subject to marked seed dormancy.

The seed companies who primarily sell seed to horticultural nurseries, such as Jelitto Perennial Seeds in Germany, have much higher seed quality standards, as it would be more immediately apparent to their better-informed customers if seed quality was low. As a result, they have to invest in much higher quality seed cleaning, testing, inventory, and storage facilities. When these companies buy seed from large-scale native seed producers whose main business is restoration ecology and infrastructure projects, they clean it to remove all of the lighter seed, which is less viable or nonviable, to arrive at a higher quality product with minimum test germination. For Jelitto Seeds this value is typically 70 per cent, and they constantly test their inventory to ensure that their seeds are this germinable. As a result, their seed is more expensive per gram or kilogram because they have to throw more seed away. The seed may, however, actually be cheaper per seedling germinated because it typically has higher viability and more importantly less variability.

This horticultural seed is of little interest to restoration ecology, because it is generally many generations removed from its wild-occurring antecedents. With widespread species, it is generally unclear where in the natural distribution the seed originally came from. The latter point is a strong consideration in restoration ecology, and rather paradoxically more attention is paid to this in project specification than to whether the seed is actually capable of germination.

Irrespective of where you buy seed, there are often large differences in the cost of seed of different species depending on the ease of production. Some species readily produce large amounts of seed of high viability that is easily harvested, whereas others have very small amounts of seed per plant or seed that is very slow or difficult to harvest. Compared to many other European native species, *Primula vulgaris*, because the seed pods are at ground level, is an example of a more challenging species to harvest. This is reflected in prices and availability. As a general principle, species with big heavy seed are more expensive per seed than those with very small seed. But these notions of cost per seed (calculated by dividing the cost of a gram of seed by the number of seed in each gram) are a bit of a red herring.

The cost per seedling established is the real cost to be concerned about in making comparisons. This will depend primarily on the viability of the seed batch and the intrinsic capacity of those seeds to establish seedlings when sown in the field. This latter characteristic is known as field emergence and is a hugely important factor in establishing plant communities from sowing.

Field emergence

Germination is the initial steps by which seeds produce a root and seed leaves, and seed laboratory germination tests are conducted to establish the viability of a batch of seed. The percentage germination is not, however, the same as percentage field emergence. Indeed, outside the sterile world of seeds sown on moist filter papers in Petri dishes, field emergence is nearly always much lower than percentage germination. Many seeds germinate but do not progress to emerge from the soil as seedlings. Some seedlings die because roots are malformed due to embryo damage, while others do not make it into the light because of being buried too deeply in the soil or too shallowly, drying out, and dying. Some germinating seeds are killed by pathogens or predators before they emerge. Field emergence is what you can see as seedlings. When seed is broadcast, field emergence is rarely more than 30–40 per cent, even when seed is sown into standardized sowing mulches which are irrigated to keep them moist during the germination window (generally early April to the beginning of June in the northern hemisphere). For many desirable species, field emergence is much lower than this. Exactly the same seed sown in a Petri dish may give 70–90 per cent germination. Given equal viability, in general, grasses tend regularly to have higher field emergence than forbs.

When sowing into loose sowing mulches such as sand, broadcasting followed by raking in places seeds at a range of depths, from being on the surface down to perhaps 50–70 mm. Small-seeded species (>5000 seed/g) emerge best when sown no deeper than 25 mm, but with tiny-seeded species, say with 20,000+ seed/g, few seeds below 10 mm are likely to emerge. Conversely, with large-seeded species, such as *Silphium laciniatum* with 40 seeds/g, emergence is probably possible from a depth of at least 75 mm; here, the problem is drying out of the seed on or close to the surface. In a random process such as broadcasting and raking in, there are inevitably winners and losers simply due to random chance of the depth at which seeds are placed in the sowing mulch. All this contributes to field emergence being substantially less than test germinability.

Irrespective of depth of placement, different species also exhibit markedly different field emergence values. It's possible to identify four broad response groups: plants with high emergence rates typically show 40 per cent plus emergence (for example, *Dianthus carthusianorum*), average 20–30 per cent, low 10–20 per cent, and very low less than 10 per cent. The tables at the end of this chapter categorize more than 600 species in terms of these emergence groups, derived from comparative field research undertaken by me and my students over the past 20 years on seed that in laboratory tests has a minimum of 70 per cent germination.

Having some idea what likely field emergence is going to be is really helpful when developing sowing mixes. If you have a species that shows high emergence, then you need to put less seed in the mix than a species with low emergence to get the number of seedlings per square metre that you need. Species with low emergence have high establishment cost per seedling. Sowing is an expensive means of establishing species that have large, highly priced seed that typically shows low field emergence. Some examples are *Baptisia* species, *Ferula communis*, *Phlox pilosa*, and *Stipa gigantea*.

Where these species are being included to act as occasional emergents, such as *Ferula* and *Stipa* species, then it is probably more cost effective to plant these as 9-cm-diameter pots either immediately before sowing or in the first year post sowing. When for some reason emergence of a species is spectacularly high, this also avoids the potentially embarrassing situation of ending up having to pull out lots of expensive surplus seedlings.

The values for field emergence in the tables at the end of this chapter are based on scientific research in which seed was sown across a number of different sowing mulches and irrigated at various frequencies to produce germination conditions from the relatively dry to almost constantly wet. In most cases, emergence was only assessed in the year of sowing. Some species have pulsed emergence, in which most of the seedlings that are able to germinate and emerge do so within a relatively short period of time, as occurs in *Dianthus carthusianorum*. This behaviour tends to be common in the high emerging groups. Other species have a much more conservative reproductive behaviour in order to increase the likelihood of survival in their wild habitats, with emergence typically involving far fewer seedlings per unit time. Emergence occurs spasmodically over a period of months and in some cases years. While the advantage of this staggered germination is clear in the wild habitat, with fluctuating conditions over time, in designed vegetation from sowing, these second-year emergers are often eliminated by competition with the relatively dense, year-old established vegetation. Many of these erratically emerging species have seed dormancy that affects some individual seeds more than others.

In addition to dormancy, another major factor determining emergence patterns is how moist the soil is during the typical emergence period. Nearly all species that we have investigated scientifically, even when they naturally occur in very dry habitats, show the best emergence when they are not subject to moisture stress during the germination and emergence period. Seed near or on the surface of well-drained sowing mulch, such as sand, is clearly going to be subjected to rapid drying on sunny days from mid morning on. As this seed will already have absorbed water and initiated the biochemical chain of events that lead to germination, if there are then long periods when the substrate is dry, several outcomes are possible. Where germination has started and the critical biochemical point of no return has been passed, then the seed may die under these dry conditions. If this point has not yet been reached, the seed may enter a period of enforced dormancy (quiescence) from which it may germinate at some point in the future when moisture is once again available. Either way, it is unlikely that seed exposed to prolonged periods of drought stress will lead to the target number of emerged seedlings during the desired period.

Seed dormancy

Dormancy is when a seed, while capable of germinating and emerging, does not do so. Many scientific studies have examined seed dormancy, with the focus on the biochemical and physiological mechanisms that underpin dormancy. Our interest in dormancy is how to avoid this phenomenon greatly reducing field emergence of species in designed sowing mixes. Dormancy is driven by factors operating within the seed and in the sowing environment, plus complex interactions between both.

Environmental factors preventing the onset of germination or reinforcing within-seed dormancy might include insufficient moisture, temperatures that are too low or high, a lack of light (particularly necessary to stimulate germination in small seed), too much water (really a lack of oxygen or excessive carbon dioxide), or seed being buried too deeply to experience diurnal (day–night) temperature fluctuations that occur at the soil surface and cue germination in some species. Some of these potential dormancy-inducing factors can be avoided simply by sowing at the appropriate time of the year.

Within-seed dormancy is much more intractable. Both mechanical and physiological factors within the seed control dormancy.

Mechanical factors

The most common mechanical factor controlling seed dormancy is a seed coat that is impermeable to the passage of water and air, often known as hard-seededness. This state is the norm within many genera within the pea family, but is also a problematic factor in efforts to germinate some plants that are not legumes, such as *Convolvulus*, *Euphorbia*, *Hypoxis*, *Lanaria*, and *Onosma*. The seed coat can also physically restrict the expansion of the embryo, thus inhibiting germination. In nature these mechanical factors are overcome by the seed being exposed to fire or to digestive acids during the passage of the seed through the gut of an animal. These processes damage the seed coat, permitting water and oxygen ingress.

This is an easy type of dormancy to overcome prior to sowing, with mechanical scarification the most widely used technique. This can be done by a variety of approaches depending on the volume of seed that needs to be treated. On a small scale, batches of seed can be rubbed between two sheets of 100–120 grit abrasive paper to scratch the often extremely resilient outer layer of the seed. The duration of abrasion is normally between 10 and 30 seconds depending on the hardness of the seed coat. You can increase or reduce the degree of seed coat damage by varying time and pressure applied during scarification. Stopping the circular grinding action and observing the state of the seed every 5–10 seconds will reveal whether any are showing creamy white embryo or endosperm. Stopping abrasion before this is widely evident is desirable. In genera that are really difficult to germinate, such as *Hypoxis*, abrading until a few seeds in the batch are beginning to disintegrate is warranted. On a larger scale, seed can be mixed with sharp sand in a blender or put into a coffee grinder, although I have to confess I have never done this. It's probably best to avoid species with the need for seed coat abrasion if sowing on a very large scale.

An alternative to mechanical abrasion is the use of heat, normally as boiling water treatment. This typically involves placing batches of dry seed in a sieve in boiling water for approximately 20 seconds, after which the seed is removed and dried off ready for mixing and sowing. For large volumes of seed, boiling water treatment is more convenient than scarification, but it is also a rather unpredictable treatment in terms of potentially seriously damaging the seed.

Physiological factors

Physiological dormancy is controlled by chemical inhibitors within the seed that prevent the onset of germination or the development of embryos that are immature at the point of seed dispersal. This type of dormancy operates across a spectrum from superficial ("non-deep" in dormancy speak) to extreme or deep. Non-deep dormancy is common in many temperate species, as a means to ensure that seedlings germinate at the best time of year (mostly spring, occasionally autumn) to avoid being damaged or killed by environmental stresses such as drought or winter cold.

Non-deep dormancy is most readily broken by exposing the seed to a period of cool moist chilling before or after sowing. This need for chilling is very common in many European, Asian, and North American temperate species. Many prairie forbs, for example, are subject to dormancy of this sort to some degree. To do this before sowing, seed is mixed with moist sand in a sealed polythene bag in a refrigerator for 6–15 weeks. The seed must have absorbed water and be imbibed for the chilling message to be received, and chilling has no effect on dormancy in dry seed. The thermostats in most domestic refrigerators do not maintain constant temperatures but allow the temperature to oscillate between 1 and 6°C (34 and 43°F), depending on the dial setting, and this chilling works reasonably well for most species. As a general principle, however, prechilling seed in refrigerators is best avoided except in situations where the opportunities for natural chilling have been missed, for example, when sowing must take place in spring or summer. The potential problem with artificial chilling, especially when dealing with mixes of many species, is that some species germinate within the bag of sand once a threshold period of chilling has been experienced (10 weeks in many superficially dormant temperate species). A better option is to chill species separately, but this becomes a bit of a logistical nightmare on a large scale, and you still have the risk of germination within the bag. Plus, will the chilled seed ever be reconciled with the nonchilled seed at sowing time? You have to have inordinate confidence in landscape contractors to do this when working on really large scale projects.

Where the sowing site can be prepared in time, a more straightforward and satisfactory method is to sow between mid autumn and early winter to expose seed to natural chilling. Due to the more variable temperature range and the combination of drying and rewetting cycles in the field, this is generally more successful than artificial chilling in promoting germination and emergence and avoids the risk of germination occurring in the refrigerator.

The next step on the dormancy ladder involves species which require longer periods of cold, lower temperatures, or more cycles of this. The genera in which this is most common are within the Ranunculaceae, for example, *Anemone*, *Caltha*, *Delphinium*, *Pulsatilla*, *Ranunculus*, and *Trollius*. It is also common in hemi-parasites such as *Pedicularis*. Species with this type of dormancy commonly show low levels of emergence over a number of years and are often unreliable for use in designed sowings. These plants are better added to schemes as plugs or 9-cm-diameter pots, because by the time germination occurs (sometimes in the second year) the community is too dense for most seedlings to survive. There are exceptions to this, however. For example, many *Pulsatilla* species typically show excellent emergence from a late-autumn sowing, but it is generally sensible to expect relatively low emergence with species in this group.

Deep dormancy is the final and most intractable dormancy to overcome in sown seed. In species with these mechanisms, the seed needs to be first exposed to a warm period of moist seed storage, mirroring what happens post seed shedding in late summer or autumn in the habitat. The seed then needs to be exposed to an often quite lengthy chilling period, of 14 weeks plus, and then another warm period to finally germinate. In nurseries it is relatively easy to organize these processes, but when sowing in gardens and landscapes this is more difficult, as it requires sowing in late summer, and even then emergence of these species may be very low in the following year. Classic examples of genera with these mechanisms are *Aconitum*, *Actaea*, *Helleborus*, *Paeonia*, and *Trillium*.

The problem with this early sowing in cool to cold temperate climates is that many of the nondormant species will germinate in early autumn and will then be subject to potential frost heave and death as small seedlings. Hence, allowing a small number of species with these deep dormancies to determine the overall sowing strategy is not a good idea. Many of these species are better established by planting out as 9-cm-diameter pots prior to spreading the sowing mulch in preparation for late-autumn sowing.

APPORTIONING THE TOTAL SEEDLING TARGET TO INDIVIDUAL SPECIES IN THE MIX

For many small to medium herbaceous plants, a sown target of approximately 100 seedlings/m² is a reasonable starting point. Where maintenance will be limited, you might want to go to 200 seedlings/m², but that will result in the loss of many of the slower growing species through increased competition. Where there is maintenance and the aim is to develop sown communities that have the much more varied surface topography associated with planted vegetation, you might go as low as 60–70 seedlings/m². Assuming that for argument's sake you decide on approximately 20 species in total, how do you decide how many seedlings of species A versus B and so on you want to aim for? The simplest approach would be to divide the overall target of 100 seedlings by 20 to arrive at 5 seedlings per species. This might work reasonably well for a single-layer community, where all of the species are similar in terms of their size, tolerance of shade, flowering duration, drama, ease of establishment, longevity, and dominance potential. In most cases, however, the species you pick will be rather different in terms of these characteristics, rather individual, in fact. Idiosyncrasy is the norm in plant species, as in individual human beings. Some will be much larger than other species and will have different capacities to generate and tolerate shade, plus the other properties listed above.

The design intention will often be to arrange the species in two or even three layers. Hence, dividing total seedling target density by the number of species simply doesn't work very effectively. It's fine with annuals because they only live for 6–9 months, so the impact of differences between the species is much less important, and there are no consequences down the track because there is no second or third year.

With perennial species it is necessary to make a decision on target seedlings per species for every species in the mix. In essence, this is the essential design decision, because it influences both short- and long-term appearance and performance. A spreadsheet is the ideal tool to undertake this part of the design process. The names of the species under consideration are put in column A. In column B and subsequent columns, the headings for the key design factors to be considered are entered. These factors might then be given a numerical ranking for each species if that helps make the final judgement on what the target density should be for that species.

Some rules of thumb can generally be applied to help in this decision-making. Species that grow very slowly or are small (not always the same thing) or are less shade tolerant, highly attractive, or long flowering are put at higher densities, whereas species that are fast growing or large, flower for a shorter time period, or are less attractive are put in at lower densities.

The two closely related genera *Knautia* and *Scabiosa* can provide a useful example of this decision-making process in practice. If you didn't want to have complete dominance by the largest readily available species, *Knautia arvensis*, the maximum target of this species in a mixed community would probably be about 3 seedlings/m². *Knautia macedonica* would have a similar density. It is less tall, but typically more wide-spreading, so 3 seedlings/m² would also be the maximum to avoid elimination of most of the slowly growing neighbours. At the other end of the spectrum, *Scabiosa columbaria* and *Scabiosa ochroleuca* are much smaller, less leafy, essentially rosette-forming species, with very low capacity to dominate species other than those that have prostrate foliage or are smaller. They could probably coexist with similar-sized species at densities up to 10 seedlings/m². Dropping down further in scale, there is the carpet-forming *Scabiosa graminifolia* and the small rosette-forming *Scabiosa silenifolia* that could have a target of more than 10 seedlings/m² without threatening other species. With really large plants, the target per square metre will be less than 1, perhaps as low as 0.1, which equates to one seedling for every 10 m², an area of approximately 3.3 × 3.3 m, the size of a typical domestic bedroom.

In the example just given, the emphasis was on physical size and growth rate, but it is also necessary to include aesthetic factors such as how close or far apart species need to be to maximize their aesthetic contribution. As you increase the target number for one species, you inevitably have to accept that the floral impact of the other species will be correspondingly reduced, because there is a fixed total seedling target. With emergent species, it is often important to reduce the numbers per square metre so as to avoid the spaces between the emergents becoming too clogged, in essence inserting spaces into the composition.

Your best guess target values are placed in the spreadsheet next to the name of each species in the mix so that as you play round with different scenarios it is easy to check whether the overall target has been under- or overshot.

Calculating the weight of seed of each species to be included in the mix to achieve the target density

Thus far we have dealt with seed mix design in largely qualitative terms, but this final quantitative stage is necessary to realize the design aims. What might seem like a relatively mysterious connection between a target number of seedlings per species and the amount of seed you add to get close to this in a sowing is actually quite simple to achieve. As I began in the late 1990s to apply my research to creating sown herbaceous plant communities in practice, I needed to find a way to effectively control the composition of the resulting vegetation. To use this method, a spreadsheet is required, plus three pieces of information and a simple paste-in formula which does the math.

The first piece of information is the seedling target per square metre, which you decide upon as discussed above. The impact of this on seed required should be obvious to everyone once they think about it. If you double the number of seedlings per square metre in the target, you will inevitably have to double the amount of seed you sow per square metre.

The second piece of information needed is the approximate number of seeds in a gram (or ounce) of seed. This information is provided for more than 600 species in the tables at the end of this chapter. As the number of seeds per gram increases (that is, seeds get smaller), then the weight of seed required to achieve the same seedling target per square metre will decrease. The bigger the seeds, the more grams you have to put in the mix.

The final piece of information required is the approximate field emergence value for each species. A species with a field emergence of 30 per cent, for example, will require only one-third the amount of seed of a species with 10 per cent field emergence to achieve the same seedling density.

The final step is to integrate these three pieces of information using a formula that when pasted into a spreadsheet will automatically calculate how many grams of seed are required to achieve an approximate target density per square metre. The spreadsheet then uses the grams of seed per square metre to calculate the grams per total area to be sown. If for a certain species you need 0.1 g/m² to achieve the target seedling density, then for a sowing area of 1000 m² you will need 0.1 × 1000, that is, 100 g of seed of that species.

In terms of the reliability of this approach, the greatest uncertainty in the process comes from the estimate of per cent field emergence, but this is mitigated by the fact that this value typically only involves at most a three-fold difference, for example, 10 to 30 per cent. This is small compared to the differences in the individual target densities, which frequently involve up to 100-fold differences (for example, 10 seedlings/m^2 compared with 0.1 seedling/m^2). So even if the field emergence estimates turn out to be unreliable, the net result is normally still broadly acceptable.

As shown in the table, the spreadsheet steps are as follows:
- Column B: identify the number of seeds per gram and insert
- Column C: estimate and insert field emergence value
- Column D: enter the number of target seedlings per square metre
- Column E: paste in the formula =SUM(1/(B2*C2/100)*D2) into the second row of the spreadsheet (the headings shown in the table occupy the first row) in column E and drag down to calculate the gram of seed per square metre for each species in the rows below this
- Column F: enter a formula to multiply the calculated value in column E for grams of seed by the total area to be sown (in this case, multiply by 288).

Making the mixes

The easiest way to do this is to order the seed in grams or fractions of grams that are closest to the calculated amount of each species required. Jelitto Perennial Seeds allow you to order most species in quantities of 0.25 g, 0.5 g, and multiples of grams. This means you only have to mix the contents of the ordered seed packets together and you have your mix.

Mixing gets more complicated when you have a number of sub-areas that are to be sown with the same mix. One option is to make up the mix separately for each sub-area, but this becomes very labour intensive, not to say laborious, as the number of sub-areas increases. What I normally do in practice is to make up a mix for the total of all of the sub-areas where that mix is to be sown. I then divide up this master mix into the sub-areas on the basis of the weight required for each sub-area as a percentage of the total weight for all of the areas. For example, the total area to be sown with Mix A is 1000 m^2 divided into five sub-areas of 200 m^2 each. The mix is sown at 1 g/m^2, and hence the total weight of Mix A is 1000 g, and this is divided up into five 200-g lots in preparation for sowing. I have picked a very simple example (if only real life was so simple), but the principle is the same no matter how complicated the areas.

The possible disadvantage of subdividing a master mix is that you don't get exactly the same composition of species in each subdivision you weigh out, no matter how careful you are about continuously stirring or otherwise mixing the master mix. In most projects this level of heterogeneity is simply not perceivable after establishment.

An example of how to calculate the weight of seed needed for each species to make up a designed seed mix for a 288-m² plot

The example used is for the base layer in the Eurasian community at the University of Oxford Botanic Garden.

A SPECIES	B NUMBER OF SEEDS/G	C TYPICAL PER CENT FIELD EMERGENCE	D TARGET SEEDLINGS/M²	E GRAM OF SEED/ M² TO ACHIEVE THIS	F GRAM(S) OF SEED FOR 288 M²
Allium senescens	300	15	8	0.178	51.26
Campanula persicifolia 'Grandiflora'	16000	10	2	0.001	0.29
Dianthus carthusianorum	1000	25	2	0.008	2.30
Dianthus carthusianorum 'Rupert's Pink'	1100	20	5	0.023	6.62
Dracocephalum argunense 'Fuji Blue'	250	20	2	0.040	11.52
Eryngium maritimum	40	15	1	0.167	48.09
Eryngium planum 'Blaukappe'	340	20	1	0.015	4.32
Euphorbia epithymoides	290	10	0.5	0.017	4.90
Euphorbia nicaeensis	330	15	3	0.061	17.56
Galium verum	2100	30	3	0.005	1.44
Hyssopus officinalis subsp. *aristatus*	1064	20	3	0.014	4.03
Incarvillea delavayi 'Bees Pink'	200	15	1	0.033	9.50
Incarvillea zhongdianensis	200	20	3	0.025	7.20
Inula ensifolia	2400	10	3	0.013	3.74
Limonium platyphyllum	1000	20	3	0.015	4.32
Linum narbonense	253	15	3	0.079	22.75
Marrubium supinum	950	15	1	0.007	2.01
Pulsatilla vulgaris	400	15	2	0.033	9.50
Salvia ×*sylvestris* 'Blaukönigin'	900	20	1	0.006	1.72
Scabiosa comosa	660	20	2	0.015	4.32
Scabiosa ochroleuca 'Moon Dance'	660	25	3	0.018	5.18
Scutellaria baicalensis	690	25	3	0.017	4.89
Sedum telephium 'Emperor's Waves'	16600	15	3	0.002	0.58
Silene schafta 'Persian Carpet'	2632	20	5	0.009	2.59
Teucrium chamaedrys	550	20	2	0.018	5.18
Veronica spicata subsp. *incana*	14000	20	5	0.002	0.58

At some point in the mixing process, you will need to weigh out seed, necessitating access to a reasonably accurate digital balance. Robust and sufficiently accurate portable scientific balances that weigh up to 100 or 200 g with two decimal places of precision and run off mains and batteries can be bought relatively cheaply on the internet. Where you are dealing with relatively large weights of seed, better quality digital kitchen scales are probably good enough, but these have less precision so are no good for seed lots of less than a gram.

AVOIDING ALL OF THE CALCULATION AND WEIGHING NEEDED FOR SELF-DESIGNED SEED MIXES

If the idea of designing your own seed mix is just too daunting, then you will have to rely on commercially available seed mixes. Even with these there is often some capacity to exercise some control over the mix, with many suppliers of perennial meadow or prairie mixes offering the opportunity to purchase either a mix of grasses and forbs or a forb-only mix. If you want to maximize the floweriness of the resulting vegetation, go for the forb-only mix. If you want to close the surface as quickly as possible and floweriness or diversity is less important, go for the grasses and forbs mix. It's important, however, not to see the grasses as some kind of benign ecological angel looking out for the well-being of your forbs. Despite all of the media-driven desire to believe in synergistic relationships as opposed to out and out competition with winners and losers in ecological systems, understand that grasses tend to be aggressive competitors.

In terms of the number of seeds sown, the grasses plus forbs mixes are primarily grasses—in European meadow mixes, it is common to have ten to fifty times more grass seeds than forb seeds—and this results in major skewing of competition in favour of the grasses from the outset. Many grasses are readily established post the establishment of the forbs by oversowing, and I would recommend this strategy in many cases. Adding grasses at a later date is much easier than taking them away when too dominant.

Variants of some of the plant community mixes that I have developed over the years through my research are now offered by Pictorial Meadows (see Resources), who fully understand the issues about seed quality and who have an ongoing programme of testing and evaluating the perennial mixes that they offer.

DESIGNING AND IMPLEMENTING PLANTING MIXES

Although designing planting mixes requires ecological, design, and horticultural knowledge, in many ways it is less technically demanding than designing seed mixes. You don't need to understand about seed dormancy and establishment requirements. Instead, the plants already exist, and they simply need to be planted at the site and kept weed free. If you picked the right plants, it generally more or less works. Because planting takes place at much lower densities per square metre than sowing, it is much easier to conceptualize the spatial relationships between the different species, both laterally and vertically among the different layer structures.

Much of the challenge in establishing naturalistic vegetation by planting is in laying out the plants prior to planting to reflect the design in practice. This succulent meadow planting in northern Spain has about 10 plants/m². We calculated how many plants of each species were required per 10-m run of planting bed, and then laid out the emergent layer first and filled in with the ground-layer species. The planting staff got their heads around this quite quickly.

The critical design issue to focus on is how many planting spaces you intend to have per square metre. (Often it is better to think about the number of plants per 10 m² to get around the problems of having, say, half a plant in one square metre and the other half in another.) This density issue is strongly related to the mature size of the plants in the palette you have chosen to work with. The bigger the ultimate dimensions of the plants, typically the fewer the planting spaces per unit area. For large species with dense basal foliage, for example, plants suitable for semi-shade such as *Actaea* species, *Anemone* ×*hybrida*, larger *Hemerocallis,* and *Persicaria amplexicaulis*, 4 plants/m² would be satisfactory. However, if this planting was made as a single layer of just these species, there would be much empty space from winter to late spring; the space would be better utilized as a sown ground layer of *Primula elatior* or *Primula vulgaris* to fill in the space during the dormant season.

When using plants of drier, sunnier habitats, you should increase the number of plants per square metre, because the plants are smaller; the same is true with plants of erect structure, as in many prairie species. A community of *Aster amellus* 'Violet Queen', *Dianthus carthusianorum*, *Eryngium planum*, *Galium verum*, *Inula ensifolia* 'Compacta', *Origanum laevigatum*, *Pulsatilla subslavica*, and *Salvia* ×*sylvestris* 'Mainacht' might be associated with 9 plants/m². Again, between early winter and late spring the planting will be very open even at the increased density, so an undersowing of a shade- and drought-tolerant species such as *Primula veris* would improve manageability (and provide good contrast with the purple *Pulsatilla*).

The decisions on what percentages of those nine species occur within the planting mix are undertaken in exactly the same way as for sowing. You should give more spaces to base-layer species such as *Pulsatilla* and *Galium* because these are the smallest elements, and then diminish the percentage as the plants get larger. You also, however, must factor in the flowering period of each species: a long time, increase the percentage; a short time, decrease the percentage. Larger, taller emergents are given the lowest percentage of the

The rain gardens and drainage swales at Burgess Park in London are surfaced with a minimum 150-mm depth of 8- to 12-mm pea gravel. Because the surface dries out very quickly, weed invasion is greatly reduced. No weeds have established in this garden (June) in a park that is elsewhere struggling to stay on top of weed management.

planting spaces so their negative impact on sun-demanding species is minimized or at least localized.

Instead of using a primula or similar shade-tolerant layer, another way to handle the lack of plant density between early winter and late spring and reduce the invasion of weeds during this period is to use deep surface mulches. This is particularly feasible where the existing soil has been stripped off in the course of site development and can be replaced with a 150- to 300-mm layer of sand, crushed limestone (8- to 15-mm diameter, with as few fines as possible), or similar sized pea gravel. This technique is widely used in Germany as part of the Silbersommer random mix planting system and works well for many relatively drought tolerant herbaceous plants. Very low productivity substrates such as pea gravel reduce the growth rate and standing growth, meaning that there will often be substantial areas of bare mulch; however, the dry surface and low nutrient content of these materials do effectively mitigate against weed establishment. This system even works well in rain gardens, where the surface of the gravel mulch is frequently wet, but dries out very quickly once rain or water levels subside.

The alternative to deep mineral mulches is the standard sterile surface mulch of at least 75-mm depth of a mineral aggregate or composted bark or woody chip. These mulches greatly assist managing weed invasion, although the chip has to be applied every 2 years, as it becomes a better germination surface for incoming weed seeds as it decomposes.

SOWING AND PLANTING PRACTICE

This chain of activities includes the entire process from site preparation to the completion of seedling emergence and coordinating sowing with planting where this is also to be used. Although the aim of these activities is to maximize success and minimize risk of failure, what is successful is a relative rather than absolute notion.

In highly urban locations such as Queen Elizabeth Olympic Park in London, with high pedestrian traffic and expectations to match, vegetation that does not seem to be performing as expected is likely to be judged very harshly.

The most demanding notions of success are associated with urban sites that are very closely viewed, often by many people, who are likely to have relatively clear images in their minds of what they are going to see and particular expectations of the level of drama generated by the sowing. Satisfying these aspirations often requires the establishment of a dense and uniform sown plant community without large gaps or the presence of many weeds. This requires the most stringent control over the sowing process. This approach is often associated with private gardens (large or small) or high-profile, prestigious public or commercial greenspace. There is a strong political constituency to satisfy, who are very product oriented, and the product must be delivered and perform as it says on the tin.

Contrast this with the restoration ecology or green infrastructure scenario on, for example, a motorway embankment. Here timescales are much more elongated, because meadow establishment is seen as part of eternal ecological processes. If the meadow doesn't seem very successful now, perhaps it will be in the future. Expectations are process rather than product driven, and it is unlikely that the client will be unhappy as long as you can provide evidence that the seed was actually sown and some sort of coherent approach was employed. These sites normally don't have large numbers of people viewing them from close by, and detailed perception is difficult when driving past at high speed.

The critical thing is to be clear in your own mind which of these games you are playing from the outset; otherwise you will either disappoint the client or use a lot of resources that were not really necessary. In practice, many scenarios lie between these two polar opposites, and hence thought is required on how to approach landscape site works.

I have developed the process described in this chapter when dealing with sites in which expectations of success are high to very high. If you are working on a project where this is not the case, then you will be able to use your judgement to cut some corners and still in many cases achieve acceptable outcomes.

The nature of the site, past management, and existing flora have a major impact on developing the weed control strategy that precedes site development. This area has been long but only occasionally mown, and it contains a mixture of perennial grasses but few really problematic weedy forbs such as creeping thistle and bindweed. The site preparation weed control strategy needs to address what is actually there.

Site preparation

Seedlings cannot generally establish successfully in the presence of adult plants, especially on moderately to highly productive soils. Thus, on sites with an existing herbaceous plant cover, the first activity is to kill this plant cover. Don't think that this fundamental ecological requirement to reset the site dominance clock is negated by using native species.

We created a range of large-scale native wildflower meadows in a Sheffield park as part of a Ph.D. study. In autumn 2006, an area of mown grass was sprayed by local authority staff with a glyphosate herbicide and then sown with various native wildflower mixes. When we undertook the first assessment in May 2007 the emergence of the sown seed mix was excellent; however, we noted that many of the roots of the perennial grasses (particularly creeping bent grass, *Agrostis stolonifera*) had not been killed, presumably because the concentration of herbicide used was too low or rain fell soon afterwards, reducing absorption through the leaves. By September 2007, the once promising meadow was a tall lawn of *Agrostis*, and almost all of the native meadow seedlings had been eliminated by its competition. This is the inevitable outcome on productive soils if you can't completely kill the original vegetation cover.

The big question is how you eliminate existing vegetation. The answer to this depends on your own philosophical preferences, the legislative framework where the site is, project timescale, the resources available, and the nature of the plant species present that need to be killed. Sometimes in commercial landscape architecture practice there is no existing vegetation to get rid of, because the original soil and its normally weedy flora has long since been stripped off, necessitating a new soil to be imported. I will describe working with the existing soil and plant cover first.

If you have only a very short timescale prior to sowing, say it is June and sowing has to occur by November, the only practical approach that does not involve soil stripping is to spray the vegetation at least twice at 4- to 6-week intervals with a translocated herbicide that contains glyphosate. The actual products differ depending on whether the people applying the herbicide have been professionally trained in how to do this safely and effectively, or whether they are home gardeners who have not. Many readers are likely to see this approach as highly un-ecological, for a variety of philosophical reasons; the irony of using a biocide to create a rich biodiverse habitat is a challenging idea to the ecocentric people who are most likely to be interested in designed naturalistic vegetation in the first place. In some parts of the world, legislation may not permit the use of this otherwise very widely used herbicide.

Cultivation will rarely achieve sufficient levels of control in this time period, unless the weed flora is dominated by annuals only (this is rare) or the site is in a garden, relatively small, and free of weeds in the first instance. Even if the site is very weedy, if it is small, it can be done, but on most public landscape sites this is not the case. Another aspect to consider is that cultivation equipment uses large quantities of highly toxic, carbon dioxide–emitting fossil fuels.

If you have more time than June to November, say at least a year, the possibility of cultivation being successful increases, although if you have infestations of creeping thistle and docks that resprout from even small root fragments, a year or even 2 years makes little difference. A better option is to shade the weed vegetation by two layers of engineering fabric or weed mat. This works very well, but with weeds like docks and creeping thistle takes a long time, probably up to 2 years for the latter species. It's often difficult to do this in public spaces because the weed mat often disappears (probably to suppress weeds on private vegetable-growing allotments). In private gardens and more controlled public spaces, shading is potentially a highly effective means of killing weeds.

In climates with hot summers, using solarization—placing a clear polythene sheet over the vegetation to use the heat build-up within the glasshouse created to kill the vegetation—might seem attractive. Annuals are quick to die, but perennials will resprout from deeply placed roots unaffected by the surface-layer heat. Only the temperature of the top 100 mm is significantly raised.

Irrespective of philosophical perspectives, it is easy to see why glyphosate-based herbicides are widely used for control of perennial weeds in site preparation.

Where the soil has already been removed during prior site work, making it possible to import a nonweedy alternative soil, short timescales are much less of a problem. At the Queen Elizabeth Olympic Park in London, all of the meadow sowings were made on a sandy substrate quarried nearby from deep deposits initially free of weed fragments and weed seeds. This material was also very unproductive due to low nutrient levels, an ideal substrate for the meadows we wanted to make.

An excavator may be used to strip off the top 600 mm of weedy topsoil and then bury this under the underlying weed-free subsoil. This is assuming the underlying subsoil is granular and capable of drainage; plastic clay subsoils are not really appropriate for this treatment. In addition, you can't do this where there are trees close by, as it is catastrophic for the tree roots. Burying topsoil containing docks and creeping thistle does not, however, kill the roots of these plants; sooner or later new shoots emerge into your sown vegetation. Alternatively, weedy topsoil can be used elsewhere on site where it is less of a problem, for example, for lawns and tree planting. At the stripped planting site, the soil levels can be made up with sand or ameliorated crushed building material or other low-nutrient substrates. An example of this strategy in practice is given in the Fidelity International case study. Generally speaking, soil stripping is not done in home gardens, where you might instead think about using deep sowing mulches in certain areas.

The advantage of changing at least the soil surface is that this allows for a range of different soil conditions to be created that can support a diversity of interesting plant communities, while removing the need to incur the additional costs and problems of covering the meadow areas with a sowing mulch.

Soil cultivation

The preference with sown perennial vegetation is often to use soil types of low to moderate productivity. Cultivation (other than when this is the preferred means of weed control) is often only necessary where the existing soil type is significantly compacted and impenetrable to seedling roots. Unless the compaction is severe, the roots of species gradually penetrate when seed is sown into 75–100 mm of sowing mulch laid on top of the soil; however, highly sensitive species may be lost before this happens. Where sowing mulches cannot be used for economic or other reasons, soil compaction is much more problematic. If seedling roots cannot punch through the compaction layer, they have no where to go, and seedlings simply die.

The most troublesome surface compaction is usually created by the trucks and tractors delivering or spreading sowing mulch materials. This is especially so when the underlying soil is wet. Ideally sowing mulches should be spread when the soil is not really wet (that is, at least a couple of days after a heavy rain) and preferably in early autumn for standard sowing done in late autumn to winter. Soil compaction can be further reduced by thinking about how these materials are transported and spread across the sowing area. On a large-scale project, instead of using tractors and trailers moving back and forward from a central loading point, sowing mulches should be spread from multiple points from the edge of the site into the middle, trafficking the previously laid sowing mulch rather than the soil surface. This dissipates the compactive forces of the machinery into the mulch and provides some protection to the underlying, highly compaction-prone soil. The sowing mulches themselves, with the exception of subsoil, are not generally damaged by compaction because they do not contain clay particles and the surface is broken up by raking in seed post sowing.

Prior to spreading sowing mulch, the degree to which the soil surface is smeared or compacted, thus warranting cultivation, can be gauged by the resistance posed when trying to push a garden fork into the soil. If you tried to do this in a garden border (a typical noncompacted situation), the fork would readily enter the soil to the full depth of the

Even in the second year, this project shows the impact of underlying soil compaction created by spreading sand sowing mulch when the soil was too wet. Note the openness due to the low density of seedlings and their small size in the middle foreground, compared to the surrounding less compacted edges.

prongs when you stood on it. If you cannot get the fork to enter the soil at all even when you stand on it, the soil is significantly compacted. The resistance the soil poses to pushing in a fork is inversely related to how dry the soil is. When very wet (say, post heavy rain), the fork is relatively easy to push into even a heavily compacted soil, because the water acts as a lubricant. You have to use your judgement on this.

On small-scale projects, if the soil surface does seem compacted, surface cultivation using fork digging or a rotavator needs to be undertaken prior to spreading sowing mulch. Rotavators are better than nothing—but not much better—where the compaction is not just restricted to the surface. A series of ripping tines on the back or a small Caterpillar tractor is better still, but few projects have this type of equipment on hand. The site needs to be carefully levelled afterwards to produce a uniform, flat surface, so a constant depth of sowing mulch can be achieved. Where the surface is really rough, soil mounds occur close to the surface of the spread sowing mulch. Weed seedlings emerge en masse at these points, and you have the beginnings of a potential disaster.

Sowing mulches

A sowing mulch is a layer of weed-seed-free mineral or organic debris material spread on top of the soil to inhibit the generally massive weed seed bank (up to 50,000 viable seeds/m² in the top 100 mm of soil) from germinating and emerging among the sown seed. When the firmed sowing mulch layer is a minimum of 75 mm deep, very few of these weed seeds are able to emerge and compete with the sown species. Those that do are mainly large-seeded grasses like false oat grass, *Arrhenatherum elatius*, and generally numerically few. A layer of sowing mulch shallower than 50 mm has very little effect on inhibiting the emergence of species other than those with very small seeds. Sowing mulches have a significant cost but also a huge positive effect on making sowing a

In my home garden, 25-kg bags of sand are laid on the surface as a mulch, awaiting slitting and bag removal. Stan the dog is in a state of shock.

relatively low risk means of establishing vegetation by greatly reducing weed competition in the first year. Sowing mulches may sometimes contain some weed seeds, especially when they have been stored prior to purchase on sites with masses of weeds raining seed onto them from adjacent vegetation.

For large projects, visiting the sand supplier's storage yard is highly recommended to get a sense of what is likely to happen. Sometimes just asking the supplier to scrape off the top 100 mm of the heap onto which most seeds will have fallen is hugely beneficial. In addition to precontamination of the mulch with weed seeds, some species establish from wind-blown seeds during the establishment irrigation period (in Europe, particularly dandelions, whose seed dispersal occurs in May).

Another potent source of weeds is the pots of plants. When planting is integrated with sowing, you should always remove the top 25–40 mm of the growing compost, which generally contains both vegetative weeds and weed seeds, prior to moving plants to the planting area. This was a major source of weed colonization at a project in Burgess Park, London, which led to part of the project spiralling out of control and ultimately failing.

As a result of these sources of weed seedling establishment, even with sowing mulches, where high-quality outcomes are required a capacity for hand weeding is essential in the first year. On a smaller garden scale, suitable sowing mulch materials like sand can be purchased either in bulk 1-tonne bags or in 25-kg bags. This sand has usually been recently quarried and the problems of weed seed contamination are normally hugely reduced.

After years of experience working with a variety of sowing mulch materials, on balance, my preference is generally to use a sharp sand where this is readily available at low cost. Sand is nutrient free and normally relatively consistent. When irrigated at intervals of 1 to 3 days (depending on the weather) between April and the beginning of June, sand mulch results in excellent germination in a wide range of species. In general, sand-mulched sowings typically have the lowest levels of weed seedlings.

Another affordable mineral option is crushed building rubble, which is particularly useful for species hailing from dry, lime-rich soils. Where it contains a high percentage of fines (normally crushed mortar or concrete dust), crushed rubble tends to pack together, making it resistant to seedling root penetration. The packing is worst on finely crushed rubbles, but when the maximum particle size is about 15 mm this is sometimes less problematic. This packing is most associated with the surface layer and can be reduced by shallowly rotavating in a 50-mm layer of sand or composted green waste. Given that building rubble is often highly alkaline (pH 9+) and may inhibit root penetration, seedling growth is often very slow on rubble sowing mulches. Hence, these are most appropriate for less-prestigious situations where this will be acceptable to the client.

For species that prefer moister conditions, excavated subsoil is a good material, although it must have a granular (that is, gritty) texture rather than the soapy plastic texture of many clay subsoils. The latter stay wet and give good germination but often poorer establishment, due to issues of root penetration and low soil oxygen levels. It is a good choice for species of wetter habitats.

The final option is various types of decomposed organic debris, of which PAS100 composted green waste is most widely available in Britain and other European countries. This material is meant to have been subjected to sufficient heat generated by the composting process to be weed seed free (that is, seeds present should be killed), but this is not always done and some samples can contain large numbers of weed seeds. Decomposed organic debris is generally excellent for germination and emergence, as it stays wet for long periods of time. Sometimes it contains relatively few nutrients, whereas in other cases it is nutrient rich and excessively productive.

This range of materials varies substantially in their suitability as a germination substrate when not irrigated in the absence of rainfall. When irrigated regularly and with a jute erosion mat used on the surface (to provide 50 per cent shading of the sowing mulch), some of the differences in capacity for seedling emergence disappear. As a general principle, however, emergence tends to be highest for many species on the organic debris or subsoil sowing mulches, because they stay wetter for longer.

The flip side of this is that with sowing mulches based, for example, on composted green waste, any seedlings present that self-seed after the cessation of irrigation tend to create a huge second-generation weed population from mid summer onwards in the first growing season. This is further fuelled by the relatively high nutrient loadings in some composted green waste. The same process simply does not occur on sand-based sowing mixes once irrigation ceases. Despite these problems, there is a lot of green waste around, so there is often pressure to use it. Composted green waste is much less heavy than sand to move across sites, and it gives more reliable germination if you have to rely on rainfall only. The Green Estate (an impressive plant- and landscape-based social enterprise) in Sheffield has done much experimentation on green waste for near-native meadow establishment, and it works very well, particularly when the resulting vegetation is dense and closes canopy quickly.

My experiments conducted at Shenyang Jianzhu University in north-eastern China tested the effect of a sowing mulch's capacity to dry out quickly on the emergence of *Perovskia atriplicifolia* and *Dalea purpurea* (rear). All sowing mulches were sown with 100 seeds of these species in July. The sowing mulch on the left is subsoil, the one in the middle sharp sand, and the one on the right composted green waste. These results show how critical irrigation is for good emergence, especially in summer sowings under high temperatures, and how sowing mulch type mediates success.

Candelabra *Primula* species in northern England show excellent emergence on a 1:1 mix of subsoil and composted green waste, from an unirrigated (it did rain heavily the day after sowing) early-August sowing, but in a much cooler summer climate than the one in north-eastern China.

Some sowing mulches have significant effects on the developing sown plant community beyond the emergence period. Sand mulches, for example, greatly reduce spring slug grazing in both the short and long term. They also facilitate the success of species from more arid climates that often need a highly oxygenated soil surface to succeed in temperate, frequent-rainfall climates. Coarse, highly alkaline mineral mulches such as crushed building material favour the development of sustainable low-nitrogen calcareous plant communities. For plants that are highly palatable to slugs, such as many North American prairie forbs, sand sowing mulches should always be used. These allow species to persist in the long term that are quickly eaten out on subsoil or composted green waste surfaces.

Sowing mulch is the skin that seals in weed seeds present in the millions in the soil below. It's important that the edges of sites to be sown are fully resolved before sowing mulches are applied. It is all too common to arrive on a site to undertake a sowing to find this has not been done. When the location of the edge is an unknown, this usually means a difficult to manage weedy edge which will lead to invasion into the sowings.

Sowing

Pretreatments are available to increase germination and emergence. These are most readily undertaken in garden projects on a small scale when extra effort can be made to establish desired species. On a larger scale, the mechanics of doing this are often just too difficult. With large, very expensive seed, such as that of *Baptisia*, there is a strong economic argument for pretreatment. In this case, without mechanical scarification, you have to sow ten seeds to get one seedling, whereas with scarification two or three seeds result in one seedling.

Scarification can be undertaken prior to sowing to improve the emergence of many legumes and other hard-seeded species. Not all legumes require this, with the European *Lotus corniculatus* and North American *Dalea purpurea* being two examples.

Prechilling entails mixing seed with moist sand and storing it in a refrigerator at around 4°C. It is important not to start chilling the seed until you are absolutely sure that the sowing date will be within 12 weeks, to reduce the risk of germination in the refrigerator. Likewise, the risk of germination occurring within the bag after removing seed from the refrigerator is very real, if this gap is more than a day or so.

Smoke treatment is very helpful with some Mediterranean plant communities, including many South African members of the daisy family, such as *Arctotis* and *Gazania*. Smoke-impregnated disks can be purchased (from Silverhill Seeds, see Resources) that are then soaked in water to liberate the active chemical constituents. Seed is soaked in this solution for 12–24 hours, dried on paper towels, and sown with untreated species. As with all presowing treatments, you are unlikely to be able to do smoke treatment on a large scale, but you can use this to germinate seedlings to grow on as plugs for future planting out.

Finally, soaking in water is simple and successful for some hard-seeded species that are not legumes, such as *Geranium* and *Euphorbia* species. Seed is simply floated in water for 24 hours, dried off on paper towels, and sown with other species.

Species best sown between mid autumn and early winter

For most plant species and communities discussed in this book, the period from mid autumn to early winter is the optimal sowing time to ensure that the species with nondeep dormancy can germinate adequately in spring. It also seems to be reasonably satisfactory for species that do not have any marked dormancy. I have no scientific evidence from experimentation, but my experience from practice suggests that by the time spring arrives, seed sown in autumn is, as a result of winter rainfall and snow, well bedded into the sowing mulch and in contact with soil moisture films, maximizing germination and emergence.

Species best sown in spring

In Britain and Europe, most warm-season (C4) grasses, including most North American prairie grasses, regularly show very poor emergence when sown with forbs from the same plant community prior to mid winter. The same behaviour has been observed in North America. Although it is unclear precisely why this occurs, the assumption is that the seed is damaged in cool moist conditions by fungal pathogens. In *Andropogon gerardii*, *Schizachyrium scoparium*, *Sorghastrum nutans*, and *Sporobolus heterolepis* emergence is much higher when sown in mid spring as temperatures rise, and it is probably optimal in late spring or early summer. This raises a conundrum about when to sow North American prairie communities including grasses and forbs. A compromise for prairie forb and C4 grass sowings is to sow in late winter or early spring in the hope of getting sufficient forbs that require some chilling to emerge without seriously depressing emergence of the prairie grasses.

Another group that establishes best from sowing within the growing season are glamorous candelabra *Primula* of wet meadows, such as *Primula bulleyana*, *Primula prolifera*, and *Primula pulverulenta*. These meadow species are problematic because they have the somewhat contradictory behaviour of establishing best when sown when air temperatures are above 15°C, but also have a chilling requirement as dry seed. These species are plants of wet boggy soils, and in their habitat they shed their seeds after the summer monsoon, when soils are still wet. These germinate immediately en masse because the seed is initially not dormant, and the seedlings are protected from overwintering frost heave by deep snow. When sown in winter to overcome their dormancy as dry stored seed, these species typically show very poor emergence in spring. When sown as fresh (that is, recently collected), nondormant seed in late summer or as seed treated to be nondormant (cool moist chilling in the refrigerator or chemically treated with gibberellic acid), emergence occurs within 2 weeks and seedling growth is rapid. The problem, however, is that these seedlings are too small to avoid very heavy overwintering mortality due to frost heave in climates with winter frosts but without reliable winter snow cover. Although we never tested this in our experimental program, these *Primula* species are probably best sown in late spring as temperatures rise, using either moist refrigerator-chilled (for 12 weeks) seed or seed treated chemically with gibberellic acid, such as Jelitto Perennial Seeds' Gold Nugget seeds.

A final group of species that are best sown in spring are dicots and monocots associated with the grasslands of eastern South Africa. These species occur from the Drakensberg Mountains down into the eastern Cape and typically have little or no dormancy, with the conspicuous exception of hard-seeded genera such as *Hypoxis*. In Britain, we have sown these communities between November and January in practice without any obvious

Gazania krebsiana and many other South African Mediterranean composites are reluctant to germinate unless soaked in smoke water presowing and sown in late summer or early autumn. (Ye Hang's Ph.D. research, Department of Landscape, University of Sheffield)

evidence of reduced performance, but they certainly do not require sowing at this time of year. Most of the grasses of this community (such as *Cymbopogon*) are classic warm-season grasses (like prairie grasses) and are likely to germinate poorly following winter sowing. Some of the geophyte species found in these communities (such as *Dierama* and *Watsonia*) produce seed in which the embryos are immature at seed dispersal. This means that there is a long lag (up to 90 days) between sowing and seedling emergence while the embryo develops. This is the case even at high soil temperatures. It seems unlikely that embryo development can take place at the low temperatures experienced following winter sowing and, hence, that there is any benefit to be gained by sowing earlier than spring, in terms of speeding up emergence.

Species best sown in late summer

South African species from the western, Mediterranean (cool wet winters, warm dry summers) half of the country are best suited to sowing in late summer. Many species can only germinate when they experience the progressive decline in air temperature (and probably particularly nocturnal minima) as summer moves into autumn. Sowing at this time of year is problematic in climates that are marginal for these species in terms of winter cold (such as the United Kingdom), as seedlings are potentially exposed to lethal temperatures when very small and most sensitive to this stress and the related problem of frost heave.

Species best sown in early and mid autumn

With communities that contain species with deep dormancy, sowing in early autumn is likely to improve emergence in spring, especially if the winter turns out to be very mild. Exposure to warm conditions, then cold, and then warm is the cycle required for germination of many woodland and woodland edge genera, such as *Aconitum* and *Actaea*. Many hemi-parasites within *Rhinanthus* and *Pedicularis* have very long chilling requirements, typically in excess of 190 days, and early autumn sowing assists in overcoming this. Many temperate woodland species such as *Primula elatior* naturally germinate very early in the spring, and, given their often long chilling requirements for reliable germination, they also emerge best from these early-autumn sowings.

In an ideal world, no species present in mixed communities sown at this time of year would emerge until spring, thus avoiding a mix of very large (autumn emergers) and very small (spring emergers) seedlings in which the prognosis for the latter is poor due to the size disparity. The other potential issue is that autumn germinators are often very small when exposed to winter freeze-thaw cycles, leading to high mortality due to uprooting via frost heave.

Sowing at other than optimal times

When it is impossible to sow a desired community at the optimal time, what are the options and consequences? In species that have a chilling requirement, it is possible to pretreat using refrigerator chilling. This works reasonably well for many species, but it complicates the sowing process of logistically reconciling these seeds with the unchilled dry seed with less dormancy.

When species need some chilling but artificial chilling is not practicable, then leaving these species out and adding more species with zero or much reduced chilling requirements is a sensible strategy. Data on the chilling requirements of species are given in the tables at the end of this chapter.

The net effect of sowing at the wrong time is to reduce likely field emergence of some individual species, and hence overall target density may not be met. When I am confronted by these situations in practice, I reduce my estimates of field emergence in the spreadsheet. If both funds and extra seed are available, you can always just add more seed to achieve the original target.

The logistics of sowing in practice

If you are undertaking sowing on a relatively small scale or by yourself, then the logistics are not too complicated. If you are working with others or doing it on a large scale, much more attention needs to be given to this process.

The area(s) to be sown will have been confirmed long before the day of sowing, as this information will have been needed for where to lay the sowing mulches. A planting plan of the site usually exists, showing the boundary of each sown area. Where there is more than one area to sow and more than one seed mix, it is essential to have a plan of the site which clearly shows the margin of each sowing unit/mix. Each of these will generally correspond to a bag of premixed seed, which has been weighed out for the number of square metres of that sowing unit. Each sowing unit on the planting plan should have a code that is also present on the seed bag so that the two can be reconciled easily to make sure the right bag is sown into the correct area. Each of these areas needs to be marked out on the sowing mulch the day before, with either canes or spray marker, to avoid uncertainty on the sowing day. What follows is a description of the process I use in my own sowings, and which can be used as a basis for improvisation as required.

MIXING THE SEED WITH A CARRIER-BULKING AGENT

Because most perennial seed mixes (minus grasses) only involve 1–2 g seed/m², the seed must be mixed with an inert carrier or bulking agent to make it easier to distribute evenly onto the surface of the sowing mulch. Where the area of the sowing units are large, it is sometimes necessary to divide the unit into two or more subunits, and then to divide the seed between these proportionately in relation to the area of these subunits. The reason for this subdivision is purely practical: the seed carrier containing the seed mix is sown as two passes over the area to be sown, at one handful per square metre at each pass. This means that for each square metre of sowing unit you need two handfuls of carrier. A 15-L (3-gallon) builder's bucket contains about 100 handfuls of carrier, enough for two passes on 50 m² of sowing mulch surface. You can comfortably get about three buckets of carrier in a builder's wheel barrow, enough to sow at two passes over 150 m² of surface. If you have a sowing area of 1000 m², this means you need 1000 m²/150 m² or 6.6 wheel barrows to mix the carrier and seed together.

Most landscape contractors don't have anything bigger than barrows to mix in, and so hence the need for subdividing sowing mixes for big areas into smaller subunits. It's much easier and accurate to do this subdivision work before you get to the site, so you don't have to guess when dividing a bag of seed into subunits.

Although this process is relatively simple and requires only very basic arithmetic, I will recap because it seems rather more complex in writing than in practice. Let's assume that you have two different mixes to sow, one for full sun and one for semi-shady areas under and around trees. There are three areas to sow with the full sun mix, and three areas in semi-shade. In our example each of these sub-areas are 300 m², so the carrier for each area will fit in two wheel barrows: 300 handfuls in the first sowing pass followed by 300 handfuls in the second pass, that is, 600 handfuls (six builder's buckets) in total. The most pleasant carrier to work with is damp sawdust, because it is light and you can easily see its distribution pattern on the ground. You put three buckets of sawdust in the first barrow, and three buckets in the second. You then take the bag of seed with the code for that area and evenly split the seed between the barrows. (I normally take one handful at a time of the seed mix and put it in one barrow, then another into the other barrow until all the seed is evenly distributed.) The seed in each barrow is then mixed thoroughly with the sawdust, for between 3 and 5 minutes, and two parallel string lines 1 m apart are then placed across the area to be sown.

Seed is mixed with sawdust in a very unsatisfactory wheel barrow in Kaixian, western China. Plastic barrows with no corners are much nicer for your fingers.

Previously planted slopes at Burgess Park in London are oversown.

With a builder's bucket of the sawdust and seed mix in one hand, the sower walks between the lines using a sowing action that involves the arm moving rapidly from left to right (if right handed) to evenly distribute one handful of mix over approximately 1 m² of sowing mulch. Different individuals vary in the energy they put into this sowing action; as long as one is consistent, the results are normally satisfactory. When the sower reaches the end of the sowing channel, one of the string lines is moved 1 m over the other to create the next channel to be sown. The process is continued until the entire area as been sown with one pass, and all of the sawdust and seed mix in the first barrow used. The process is then repeated for the second barrow. By using two passes, a very uniform distribution of seed is achieved, even with sowers who have no previous experience of this process.

The seed is then raked into the surface of the sowing mulch using a 900-mm-wide wood or plastic toothed landscape rake. The technique entails not moving the sowing mulch but swimming the pegs of the rake in two directions at right angles to one another through the top 25 mm of the mulch until the seed is incorporated. Incorporation is easiest when sand is used as the sowing mulch and most difficult with materials such as wet subsoil or rubble sowing mulches.

INTEGRATING SOWING AND PLANTING

Because planting involves excavating soil containing many weed seeds, it is best undertaken before sowing mulches are spread. This approach is essential for plants in 1-L pots and bigger, if major weed seed contamination of the sowing mulch is to be avoided. Once covered by the sowing mulch, the crown of the planted material is largely protected from damage from subsequent foot traffic during over-sowing.

Landscape rakes are used to incorporate the seed post sowing. The shoots of the planted material can be seen in the foreground.

Where this is not possible, small plants (plugs and 9-cm-diameter pots) can be planted after spreading the sowing mulch, but before sowing. The best technique is to drag the sowing mulch (easiest with sand) to one side and plant so the crown of each plant is below the finished sowing mulch level (to protect it from damage in subsequent sowing activities). When dragging the sowing mulch back over the crown of the inserted plant, care must be taken to ensure the soil spoil is covered by a 75-mm-deep layer of the sowing mulch. When working with contractors, you need to demonstrate the process to make sure this is completely understood.

It is only sensible to plant plugs post sowing, using a stainless steel bulb dibble, which allows the plugs to be inserted with the base of the plug in contact with the underlying soil with minimal disturbance of the seeded sowing mulch. This activity is best carried out prior to late winter.

JUTE MATTING AS A SURFACE STABILIZER

On projects where expectations of quality are high or on sites that are steeply sloping, we normally wrap the site with an open-weave jute matting (Soil Saver brand, see Resources) immediately after raking the seed in. The matting comes in folded bundles, 1.2 m wide, and is held in place by U-shaped steel staples (200 mm long) at approximately 1.5 m intervals. This has a number of benefits: it creates a stable surface, preventing digging by foxes and cats (potentially a significant cause of disturbance); greatly reduces seed wash on steep slopes; and shades the surface, extending the time the sowing mulch stays moist between irrigations. The matting changes colour as the sowing mulch below dries out. When the sowing mulch is dry it is beige, when wet it is a much darker grey-beige. This

At Merton Borders, University of Oxford Botanic Garden, jute erosion mat is being laid and pegged down, post raking the seed in.

is a useful guide to staff managing the irrigation, as you can clearly see the patches that are wet and dry. This prevents having to water the entire surface and making the bits that were already wet anaerobic. The jute matting lasts for about 2 years; it decomposes in situ and does not have to be removed.

EMERGENCE DATA TO USE IN DESIGNING SEED MIXES

The data in the eight tables in this section are the results of our research performed over many years in Sheffield, United Kingdom. Seed weight estimates are generally based on counting and weighing three samples of twenty or thirty seeds. Using more or less standardized techniques, 100 seeds (mostly from Jelitto Perennial Seeds) of each species were sown into 9-cm-diameter pots containing a 1:1 mix of sharp sand and composted green waste. Seeds were raked into the surface using a mini rake to simulate the seed distribution into the profile that is typical when raking in seed during field sowing. This meant there were often some seeds exposed on the surface, and this obviously reduced emergence success, but we wanted to mirror practice as much as possible. There were generally a minimum of four replicates for each species sown, that is, the emergence values in the tables are the average of four pots. The pots were then placed under transparent plastic screens to prevent them from being wetted by rain, and they were irrigated either once or twice a week. Pots were thoroughly soaked at each irrigation event. Our previous research had shown that what happened emergence-wise in a 9-cm pot was very similar to what happened in a sowing mulch of the same material sown in practice on the same day; that is, the estimates are realistic.

In terms of interpreting the data for sowings in practice, if you are sowing into a material that is quicker to dry out, such as sand mulch, the emergence you see in the field will be at least 10 per cent less than the tables suggest. If you are sowing into a composted green waste mulch, it will be similar or a little higher.

Another factor to consider is the depth of raking in. In the field, small-seeded species in particular are often buried too deeply to emerge, whereas in a pot they tend to be buried at shallower depths. Thus, when undertaking your seed mix calculations, I would allow for this by reducing the emergence rate by up to 10 per cent.

In the experiments we only watered twice a week, but in practice we often water every 2 days, that is, three times per week. As irrigation frequency is the major factor determining field emergence, if you irrigate three times a week it is likely to push the emergence rate towards the data in the table even on sand sowing mulch, and potentially more on more moisture retentive sowing mulches.

Species with very small seeds (more than 4000 seeds/g) tend to be the most adversely affected in terms of emergence percentages when subject to moisture stress on sand mulches. If you are using sand mulch, then I would allow for this in the sowing rates for very small-seeded species. Really small-seeded species, such as *Heuchera villosa* (25,000 seeds/g), generally show very low to no emergence on sand mulches even when frequently irrigated. It's very useful to compare the emergence of small-seeded species at the once per week irrigation regime with the twice per week results. In the most sensitive species, these values are very different. In species that are not so sensitive to moisture stress, the differentials between once and twice per week are much less pronounced.

The species showing less than 10 per cent emergence when irrigated twice per week are the problematic ones in that their emergence is potentially very low, although as suggested in the final column of the table, the actual emergence of these species in field sowings can often be increased simply through sowing in autumn so there is a longer period of winter chilling. This is particularly true of many of the species showing less than 10, 10–20, or 20–30 per cent emergence when irrigated twice per week.

Species showing less than 10 per cent emergence when irrigated twice per week

FIELD EMERGENCE <10% WHEN WATERED TWICE PER WEEK	APPROXIMATE NUMBER OF SEEDS PER GRAM	PER CENT FIELD EMERGENCE WHEN IRRIGATED ONCE PER WEEK	PER CENT FIELD EMERGENCE WHEN IRRIGATED TWICE PER WEEK	CONVENTIONAL SEED OR TREATED TO BE NON-DORMANT JELITTO 'GOLD NUGGET' (GN)	SOWING TIME CORRESPONDING TO THESE EMERGENCE VALUES	PALATABLE TO SLUGS AS ADULTS	SPECIFIC MEANS OF INCREASING EMERGENCE *
Adenophora takedae	2500	7	4		mid February	?	1
Ajuga genevensis	600	7	6		mid February	no	1
Ajuga reptans	600	1	0		mid February	no	1
Alcea rosea subsp. ficifolia	150	6	5		mid February	?	1
Alcea pallida	150	7	8		mid February	yes	1
Alchemilla mollis	3400	8	9	GN	mid April	no	1
Alstroemeria aurea	50	0	0		mid February	no	1
Alstroemeria ligtu hybrids	50	7	4		mid February	no	1
Anaphalis triplinervis	2500	2	3		mid April	no	1
Anemone narcissiflora	150	0	1		mid February	no	1
Aquilegia flabellata	1000	1	3		mid February	no	1
Arnica chamissonis	1800	13	8		mid February	yes	1
Artemisia lactiflora	6000	0	7		mid June	?	1
Aruncus dioicus var. aethusifolius	12000	0	5	GN	mid June	no	1
Aruncus dioicus	7000	0	1		mid February	no	1
Asphodeline liburnica	100	1	1		mid February	no	1
Asphodeline lutea	60	5	7		mid February	yes	1
Aster laevis	2000	3	6		mid April	yes	1
Aster linosyris	600	0	1		mid June	?	1
Astilbe chinensis var. pumila	24000	0	3		mid February	no	1
Astilbe chinensis var. taquetii	16000	3	1		mid February	no	1
Astilbe thunbergii hybrids	24000	0	0		mid February	no	1
Baptisia alba	70	5	5		mid February	yes	1, 2
Boltonia asteroides var. latisquama 'Nana'	1200	0	0		mid February	?	1
Bulbinella hookeri	400	1	1		mid February	no	1
Callirhoe involucrata	180	3	5		mid February	?	1
Camassia quamash	300	1	4		mid February	no	1
Campanula cochleariifolia	20000	3	5		mid February	yes	1
Campanula patula	4000	2	3		mid February	yes	1
Campanula portenschlagiana	12000	0	8	GN	mid June	no	1
Cardamine pratensis	2700	1	7		mid February	yes	1
Carex flacca	1200	1	3		mid February	no	1

* 1, sow in October; 2, scarify pre-sowing; 3, soak in water pre-sowing; 4, sow in April.

FIELD EMERGENCE <10% WHEN WATERED TWICE PER WEEK	APPROXIMATE NUMBER OF SEEDS PER GRAM	PER CENT FIELD EMERGENCE WHEN IRRIGATED ONCE PER WEEK	PER CENT FIELD EMERGENCE WHEN IRRIGATED TWICE PER WEEK	CONVENTIONAL SEED OR TREATED TO BE NON-DORMANT JELITTO 'GOLD NUGGET' (GN)	SOWING TIME CORRESPONDING TO THESE EMERGENCE VALUES	PALATABLE TO SLUGS AS ADULTS	SPECIFIC MEANS OF INCREASING EMERGENCE *
Chamaenerion angustifolium	1200	0	1		mid February	no	1
Chasmanthium latifolium	200	0	0		mid February	no	1
Chelone obliqua	2000	0	10	GN	mid June	no	1
Chiastophyllum oppositifolium	50000	0	0	GN	mid June	no	1
Chionochloa conspicua	1300	1	1		mid February	no	1
Chionochloa flavicans	1500	1	1		mid February	no	1
Cirsium heterophyllum	500	12	9		mid February	no	1
Crambe tatarica	30	9	4		mid February	?	1
Delosperma congestum	3000	3	5		mid April	no	1
Delosperma cooperi	12000	11	3		mid April	no	1
Dodecatheon jeffreyi 'Rotlicht'	2800	7	5		mid February	no	1
Dracocephalum austriacum	350	7	5		mid February	no	1
Dracocephalum grandiflorum	180	9	9		mid February	yes	1
Duchesnea indica	2500	9	9		mid February	no	1
Echinacea paradoxa	200	14	9		mid February	yes	1
Eryngium amethystinum	400	0	2		mid February	no	1
Eryngium campestre	650	3	1		mid February	no	1
Eryngium maritimum	40	5	9		mid February	no	1
Euphorbia wallichii	250	3	1		mid February	no	1, 2
Genista sagittalis	300	0	1		mid June	no	1, 2
Gentiana asclepiadea	800	0	0	GN	mid April	no	1
Gentiana dinarica	2500	0	2	GN	mid June	?	1
Gentiana makinoi 'Royal Blue'	12000	0	1	GN	mid June	no	1
Gentiana septemfida	12000	0	5	GN	mid April	no	1
Gentiana triflora subsp. *japonica*	8000	0	0	GN	mid June	no	1
Geranium ibericum	100	0	1		mid February	no	1, 2
Geranium maculatum	200	2	4		mid February	no	1, 2
Geranium sylvaticum	150	0	1	GN	mid April	no	1, 2
Geum coccineum	650	3	3		mid February	no	1
Geum rivale 'Album'	900	10	6		mid February	no	1
Helenium autumnale	2500	1	6		mid February	no	1
Helianthemum nummularium subsp. grandiflorum	600	9	7		mid February	no	1

* 1, sow in October; 2, scarify pre-sowing; 3, soak in water pre-sowing; 4, sow in April.

FIELD EMERGENCE <10% WHEN WATERED TWICE PER WEEK	APPROXIMATE NUMBER OF SEEDS PER GRAM	PER CENT FIELD EMERGENCE WHEN IRRIGATED ONCE PER WEEK	PER CENT FIELD EMERGENCE WHEN IRRIGATED TWICE PER WEEK	CONVENTIONAL SEED OR TREATED TO BE NON-DORMANT JELITTO 'GOLD NUGGET' (GN)	SOWING TIME CORRESPONDING TO THESE EMERGENCE VALUES	PALATABLE TO SLUGS AS ADULTS	SPECIFIC MEANS OF INCREASING EMERGENCE *
Helianthus ×*laetiflorus*	200	3	1		mid February	no	1
Helianthus maximiliani	300	2	2		mid February	no	1
Helianthus mollis	300	0	1		mid February	no	1
Hemerocallis minor	80	1	1		mid June	no	1
Heuchera americana 'Palace Purple'	1500	1	5	GN	mid April	no	1
Heuchera sanguinea Bressingham hybrids	20000	1	1	GN	mid April	no	1
Heuchera villosa 'Autumn Bride'	25000	1	7	GN	mid June	no	1
Hierochloe odorata	1600	0	9		mid June	?	1
Horminum pyrenaicum	1100	3	5		mid April	?	1
Hypericum coris	6200	0	2		mid February	no	1
Incarvillea olgae	1200	1	9		mid June	no	1
Iris setosa	100	1	4	GN	mid April	no	1
Iris setosa subsp. *canadensis*	100	0	6	GN	mid June	no	1
Lathyrus aureus	30	13	8		mid February	?	1, 2
Lathyrus vernus 'Rosenelfe'	50	0	7	GN	mid June	no	1, 2
Leontodon rigens	2000	10	3		mid February	no	1
Libertia grandiflora	500	0	4		mid June	no	1
Libertia ixioides	450	0	1		mid February	no	1
Lobelia siphilitica 'Blaue Auslese'	15000	0	1		mid February	no	1
Lobelia tupa	9000	0	1		mid June	no	1
Luzula nivea	3000	6	9		mid February	no	1
Lychnis ×*haageana* 'Molten Lava'	750	0	8		mid June	no	1
Lysimachia clethroides	3000	1	0		mid February	no	1
Lythrum salicaria	20000	1	1		mid February	no	1
Meconopsis ×*sheldonii* 'Lingholm'	800	0	3	GN	mid April	no	1
Melica ciliata	1700	11	7		mid April	no	1
Morina longifolia	50	12	7		mid April	no	1
Nardus stricta	1500	17	8		mid February	no	1
Nepeta cataria	1300	7	9		mid February	no	1
Oenothera fruticosa 'Youngii'	8000	0	3		mid June	no	1
Oenothera pilosella 'Yella Fella'	6500	0	8		mid June	no	1
Oenothera tetragona	8000	1	7		mid April	no	1
Origanum vulgare	1500	1	5		mid April	no	1

* 1, sow in October; 2, scarify pre-sowing; 3, soak in water pre-sowing; 4, sow in April.

FIELD EMERGENCE <10% WHEN WATERED TWICE PER WEEK

	APPROXIMATE NUMBER OF SEEDS PER GRAM	PER CENT FIELD EMERGENCE WHEN IRRIGATED ONCE PER WEEK	PER CENT FIELD EMERGENCE WHEN IRRIGATED TWICE PER WEEK	CONVENTIONAL SEED OR TREATED TO BE NON-DORMANT JELITTO 'GOLD NUGGET' (GN)	SOWING TIME CORRESPONDING TO THESE EMERGENCE VALUES	PALATABLE TO SLUGS AS ADULTS	SPECIFIC MEANS OF INCREASING EMERGENCE *
Pelargonium endlicherianum	60	7	8		mid February	no	1
Penstemon cyananthus	650	0	5		mid February	no	1
Penstemon richardsonii	8000	1	1		mid February	no	1
Penstemon venustus	4500	7	6		mid February	no	1
Persicaria capitata	1500	1	6		mid June	?	1
Phlomis russeliana	100	8	8		mid February	no	1
Phygelius aequalis	10000	0	8		mid June	no	1
Phyteuma spicatum	40000	1	0		mid February	yes	1
Pimpinella major	700	1	1		mid February	no	1
Pimpinella saxifraga	3000	2	5		mid June	no	1
Polemonium caeruleum 'Cashmerianum'	650	0	0		mid June	no	1
Potentilla recta	1400	9	4		mid February	no	1
Primula chionantha	6100	0	7	GN	mid June	no	1
Primula denticulata	12000	0	1		mid April	no	1
Primula elatior	1100	2	9	GN	mid April	no	1
Primula japonica 'Carminea'	4000	1	8	GN	mid April	yes	1
Primula pulverulenta	5000	0	7	GN	mid June	no	1
Primula rosea 'Gigas'	8000	0	0	GN	mid April	no	1
Pycnanthemum tenuifolium	15000	0	1		mid June	?	1
Ratibida pinnata	1300	1	7		mid June	yes	1
Rodgersia aesculifolia var. *henricii*	8000	1	0		mid April	no	1
Rudbeckia fulgida var. *speciosa*	1300	3	9	GN	mid April	yes	1
Rudbeckia fulgida var. *sullivantii* 'Goldsturm'	1000	2	3	GN	mid April	yes	1
Rudbeckia subtomentosa	1500	2	2		mid February	no	1
Salvia verticillata	1000	3	3		mid June	yes	1
Sanguisorba menziesii	300	11	3		mid February	no	1
Saxifraga ×*arendsii* 'Blütenteppich'	16000	0	9		mid June	no	1
Scabiosa graminifolia	150	0	2		mid February	no	1
Scutellaria baicalensis	700	21	9		mid February	no	1
Scutellaria incana	950	6	8		mid February	no	1
Sedum album	40000	4	7		mid February	no	1
Sedum sexangulare	35000	3	3		mid February	no	1
Sempervivum arachnoideum	40000	11	2		mid February	no	1

* 1, sow in October; 2, scarify pre-sowing; 3, soak in water pre-sowing; 4, sow in April.

FIELD EMERGENCE <10% WHEN WATERED TWICE PER WEEK	APPROXIMATE NUMBER OF SEEDS PER GRAM	PER CENT FIELD EMERGENCE WHEN IRRIGATED ONCE PER WEEK	PER CENT FIELD EMERGENCE WHEN IRRIGATED TWICE PER WEEK	CONVENTIONAL SEED OR TREATED TO BE NON-DORMANT JELITTO 'GOLD NUGGET' (GN)	SOWING TIME CORRESPONDING TO THESE EMERGENCE VALUES	PALATABLE TO SLUGS AS ADULTS	SPECIFIC MEANS OF INCREASING EMERGENCE *
Senecio aureus	3900	0	1		mid February	?	1
Silene flos-cuculi	6500	2	3		mid February	no	1
Silene regia	700	1	1		mid February	no	1
Silphium laciniatum	30	11	7		mid February	no	1
Sisyrinchium idahoense	800	0	1		mid February	?	1
Solidago speciosa	6000	0	1		mid February	yes	1
Sphaeralcea coccinea	320	2	1		mid February	no	1, 2
Sporobolus heterolepis	500	1	1		mid February	no	4
Stachys monieri	800	1	4		mid February	no	1
Stachys officinalis	800	13	9		mid February	no	1
Stipa gigantea	70	2	6		mid February	no	1, 2
Stipa pennata	50	5	3		mid February	no	1, 2
Stipa pulcherrima	50	1	1		mid February	no	1, 2
Tellima grandiflora	15000	7	9		mid February	no	1
Teucrium hircanicum	2200	3	3		mid February	?	1
Teucrium polium	1200	6	8		mid April	?	1
Uncinia rubra	550	0	1		mid February	no	1
Verbena hastata	3200	9	9		mid February	?	1
Viola cornuta 'Minor'	800	0	0		mid April	no	1
Viola pedatifida	800	15	9		mid February	no	1
Zizia aptera	530	7	4		mid February	yes	1

* 1, sow in October; 2, scarify pre-sowing; 3, soak in water pre-sowing; 4, sow in April.

Species showing 10–20 per cent emergence when irrigated twice per week

FIELD EMERGENCE 10–20% WHEN WATERED TWICE PER WEEK	APPROXIMATE NUMBER OF SEEDS PER GRAM	PER CENT FIELD EMERGENCE WHEN IRRIGATED ONCE PER WEEK	PER CENT FIELD EMERGENCE WHEN IRRIGATED TWICE PER WEEK	CONVENTIONAL SEED OR TREATED TO BE NON-DORMANT JELITTO 'GOLD NUGGET' (GN)	SOWING TIME CORRESPONDING TO THESE EMERGENCE VALUES	PALATABLE TO SLUGS AS ADULTS	SPECIFIC MEANS OF INCREASING EMERGENCE *
Aconitum napellus	450	4	17	GN	mid April	no	1
Aethionema grandiflorum	900	16	17		mid February	no	1
Agastache foeniculum	2000	7	13		mid April	no	1
Allium senescens	300	9	18		mid February	no	1
Ammophila arenaria	250	13	13		mid February	no	1
Amorpha canescens	400	24	17		mid February	no	1
Amsonia hubrichtii	100	9	13	GN	mid April	no	1
Anaphalis alpicola	1600	16	17		mid February	no	1
Andropogon gerardii	600	7	16		mid April	no	4
Aquilegia flabellata	1000	1	14	GN	mid June	no	1
Asclepias incarnata	200	18	18		mid February	yes	1
Aster divaricatus	1500	9	11		mid February	no	1
Aster novae-angliae	2500	2	13		mid April	no	1
Aster turbinellus	1500	17	18		mid February	no	1
Baptisia australis var. *minor*	50	19	17		mid February	no	1, 2
Baptisia bracteata var. *glabrescens*	70	7	17		mid February	no	1, 2
Brachypodium sylvaticum	250	5	16		mid June	no	1
Campanula latifolia var. *macrantha*	2500	3	14	GN	mid April	yes	1
Campanula pendula	10000	3	15		mid April	?	1
Campanula poscharskyana	12000	11	18		mid February	no	1
Campanula poscharskyana	12000	1	14	GN	mid June	no	1
Centaurea ruthenica	60	7	16		mid June	yes	1
Chelone obliqua	1900	11	17		mid February	no	1
Chionochloa rubra	850	0	11		mid June	no	1
Chrysopogon gryllus	350	16	11		mid February	no	1
Coreopsis major	600	12	16		mid February	no	1
Coreopsis palmata	350	24	19		mid February	no	1
Coreopsis tripteris	300	17	13		mid February	yes	1
Crocosmia masoniorum	300	7	15		mid April	no	1
Cynoglossum officinale	50	13	17		mid February	no	1
Dierama pulcherrimum	70	3	10		mid April	no	1

* 1, sow in October; 2, scarify pre-sowing; 3, soak in water pre-sowing; 4, sow in April.

FIELD EMERGENCE 10–20% WHEN WATERED TWICE PER WEEK	APPROXIMATE NUMBER OF SEEDS PER GRAM	PER CENT FIELD EMERGENCE WHEN IRRIGATED ONCE PER WEEK	PER CENT FIELD EMERGENCE WHEN IRRIGATED TWICE PER WEEK	CONVENTIONAL SEED OR TREATED TO BE NON-DORMANT JELITTO 'GOLD NUGGET' (GN)	SOWING TIME CORRESPONDING TO THESE EMERGENCE VALUES	PALATABLE TO SLUGS AS ADULTS	SPECIFIC MEANS OF INCREASING EMERGENCE *
Digitalis grandiflora	5000	0	**14**		mid June	no	1
Dodecatheon meadia 'Goliath'	1600	1	**17**	GN	mid April	no	1
Doronicum orientale	1000	4	**12**		mid June	no	1
Dracocephalum ruyschiana	300	17	**17**		mid February	no	1
Echinacea tennesseensis	250	10	**11**		mid February	?	1
Erysimum helveticum	1000	4	**12**		mid June	no	1
Euphorbia characias subsp. *wulfenii*	100	8	**11**		mid February	no	1, 2
Euphorbia corollata	300	17	**11**		mid February	no	1, 2
Euphorbia dulcis 'Chameleon'	400	7	**15**	GN	mid April	no	1, 2
Filipendula ulmaria	1500	16	**13**		mid February	no	1
Filipendula vulgaris	700	9	**15**		mid April	no	1
Gazania linearis	400	3	**16**		mid June	no	1
Gentiana lutea	700	1	**19**	GN	mid June	no	1, 3
Geranium pratense	100	11	**17**	GN	mid April	no	1, 3
Geranium sanguineum	100	8	**14**	GN	mid April	no	1, 3
Geum coccineum Borisii Strain	650	1	**10**	GN	mid April	no	1
Geum triflorum	1700	19	**17**		mid February	no	1
Helenium autumnale 'Rotgold-Hybriden'	5500	7	**11**		mid April	yes	1
Helichrysum italicum	20000	17	**19**		mid April	no	1
Hibiscus moscheutos	80	8	**11**	GN	mid April	no	1
Iberis sempervirens	270	3	**13**		mid June	no	1
Incarvillea delavayi	200	13	**19**		mid April	no	1
Inula ensifolia	2500	7	**10**		mid April	no	1
Iris ensata	70	0	**17**	GN	mid June	no	1
Knautia arvensis	250	11	**11**		mid February	no	1
Kniphofia caulescens	450	1	**15**	GN	mid June	no	1
Kniphofia uvaria 'Flamenco'	350	10	**14**		mid February	no	1
Leontopodium nivale subsp. *alpinum*	800	1	**15**		mid June	?	1
Liatris ligulistylis	500	3	**19**		mid June	?	1
Liatris pycnostachya	300	3	**15**		mid April	no	1
Ligularia stenocephala hybrid	400	9	**16**		mid April	no	1

* 1, sow in October; 2, scarify pre-sowing; 3, soak in water pre-sowing; 4, sow in April.

FIELD EMERGENCE 10–20% WHEN WATERED TWICE PER WEEK	APPROXIMATE NUMBER OF SEEDS PER GRAM	PER CENT FIELD EMERGENCE WHEN IRRIGATED ONCE PER WEEK	PER CENT FIELD EMERGENCE WHEN IRRIGATED TWICE PER WEEK	CONVENTIONAL SEED OR TREATED TO BE NON-DORMANT JELITTO 'GOLD NUGGET' (GN)	SOWING TIME CORRESPONDING TO THESE EMERGENCE VALUES	PALATABLE TO SLUGS AS ADULTS	SPECIFIC MEANS OF INCREASING EMERGENCE *
Luzula sylvatica 'Auslese'	1500	7	15		mid February	no	1
Lysimachia punctata	2700	9	13		mid February	no	1
Lysimachia vulgaris	3000	12	10		mid February	no	1
Macleaya microcarpa	750	23	17		mid February	no	1
Milium effusum 'Aureum'	1500	1	13		mid June	no	1
Mimulus luteus	25000	0	17		mid June	no	1
Mimulus cupreus 'Red Emperor'	40000	0	19		mid June	no	1
Monarda citriodora	2400	27	17		mid February	?	1
Monarda didyma 'Red Colors'	1600	0	15		mid June	?	1
Monarda fistulosa	2000	13	19		mid April	yes	1
Nepeta clarkei	1700	0	13		mid June	no	1
Oenothera biennis	1800	12	14		mid February	no	1
Parthenium integrifolium	300	5	17		mid April	no	1
Pennisetum orientale	700	3	13		mid June	no	4
Penstemon cobaea	550	12	12		mid February	no	1
Penstemon serrulatus	6000	9	11		mid February	no	1
Phlomis cashmeriana	200	24	16		mid February	no	1
Phygelius capensis	8000	0	14		mid June	no	1
Polemonium foliosissimum	1300	5	11		mid February	no	1
Polemonium reptans	600	5	15		mid April	no	1
Primula veris	1000	3	11	GN	mid April	no	1
Primula vulgaris	1000	0	19	GN	mid June	no	1
Ranunculus gramineus	350	5	10	GN	mid April	no	1
Sanguisorba officinalis	300	24	17		mid February	no	1
Santolina chamaecyparissus	3000	25	15		mid February	no	1
Scabiosa columbaria	700	17	18		mid February	no	1
Scabiosa ochroleuca	700	14	13		mid February	no	1
Schizachyrium scoparium	850	8	11		mid April	no	4
Scutellaria orientalis subsp. *pinnatifida*	1000	11	10		mid February	no	1
Sedum hybridum 'Czar's Gold'	20000	7	12		mid June	no	1
Sedum kamtschaticum	20000	15	17		mid June	no	1
Sedum spurium 'Voodoo'	22000	16	18		mid February	no	1

* 1, sow in October; 2, scarify pre-sowing; 3, soak in water pre-sowing; 4, sow in April.

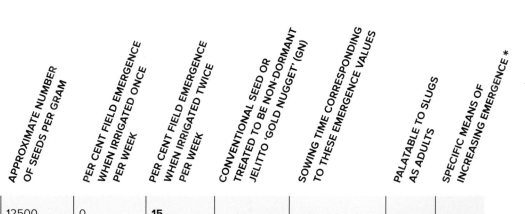

FIELD EMERGENCE 10–20% WHEN WATERED TWICE PER WEEK	APPROXIMATE NUMBER OF SEEDS PER GRAM	PER CENT FIELD EMERGENCE WHEN IRRIGATED ONCE PER WEEK	PER CENT FIELD EMERGENCE WHEN IRRIGATED TWICE PER WEEK	CONVENTIONAL SEED OR TREATED TO BE NON-DORMANT JELITTO 'GOLD NUGGET' (GN)	SOWING TIME CORRESPONDING TO THESE EMERGENCE VALUES	PALATABLE TO SLUGS AS ADULTS	SPECIFIC MEANS OF INCREASING EMERGENCE *
Sedum telephium 'Emperor's Waves'	12500	0	15		mid February	no	1
Sempervivum tectorum	15000	16	13		mid February	no	1
Sesleria heufleriana	320	11	15		mid February	no	1
Silphium perfoliatum	40	26	12		mid February	no	1
Sisyrinchium striatum	550	11	17		mid February	no	1
Solidago ohioensis	3300	3	10		mid February	?	1
Thalictrum aquilegiifolium	400	11	13		mid February	no	1
Thalictrum lucidum	900	19	15		mid February	no	1
Themeda triandra	130	3	14		mid April	no	4
Thermopsis villosa	100	11	17		mid June	no	1, 2
Thymus serpyllum 'Magic Carpet'	5500	22	19		mid April	no	1
Tradescantia ohiensis	250	17	19		mid February	?	1
Tradescantia ×andersoniana	250	14	17		mid February	no	1
Tricyrtis hirta	400	0	17	GN	mid June	yes	1
Verbena bonariensis	4500	22	15		mid February	no	1
Vernonia fasciculata	1000	32	18		mid February	no	1
Veronica longifolia	20000	7	15		mid April	no	1
Veronicastrum sibiricum	10000	5	10		mid February	no	1
Zizia aurea	350	14	12		mid February	?	1

* 1, sow in October; 2, scarify pre-sowing; 3, soak in water pre-sowing; 4, sow in April.

Species showing 20–30 per cent emergence when irrigated twice per week

FIELD EMERGENCE 20–30% WHEN WATERED TWICE PER WEEK	APPROXIMATE NUMBER OF SEEDS PER GRAM	PER CENT FIELD EMERGENCE WHEN IRRIGATED ONCE PER WEEK	PER CENT FIELD EMERGENCE WHEN IRRIGATED TWICE PER WEEK	CONVENTIONAL SEED OR TREATED TO BE NON-DORMANT JELITTO 'GOLD NUGGET' (GN)	SOWING TIME CORRESPONDING TO THESE EMERGENCE VALUES	PALATABLE TO SLUGS AS ADULTS	SPECIFIC MEANS OF INCREASING EMERGENCE *
Acaena microphylla	650	0	**27**	GN	mid June	no	1
Aconitum anthora	350	5	**25**	GN	mid June	no	1
Adenophora khasiana	3000	29	**21**		mid February	yes	1
Agapanthus campanulatus 'Headbourne Blue'	200	4	**21**		mid June	no	5
Allium senescens subsp. *montanum*	180	17	**29**		mid February	no	1
Amsonia tabernaemontana	70	3	**23**	GN	mid April	no	1
Anemone hupehensis	3000	1	**21**	GN	mid April	no	1
Anemone sylvestris	2500	11	**21**		mid April	no	1
Antennaria dioica	24000	20	**23**		mid February	no	1
Aquilegia caerulea hybrids	1000	5	**27**		mid June	no	1
Aquilegia caerulea	800	1	**28**		mid June	no	1
Asphodeline lutea	60	16	**22**	GN	mid April	yes	1
Aster amellus 'Rudolf Goethe'	540	23	**23**		mid April	no	1
Aster azureus	3200	23	**28**		mid February	yes	1
Aster ericoides	7000	24	**27**		mid February	?	1
Aster oblongifolius	3000	14	**29**		mid February	no	1
Baptisia australis	70	13	**24**	GN	mid April	no	1, 2
Buphthalmum salicifolium	1000	17	**28**		mid April	no	1
Calamagrostis brachytricha	1700	26	**29**		mid February	no	1
Calamintha grandiflora	1000	3	**28**	GN	mid June	no	1
Campanula alliariifolia	3200	19	**21**		mid April	no	1
Campanula garganica	16000	16	**24**		mid February	no	1
Campanula lactiflora	4000	0	**29**		mid June	no	1
Campanula persicifolia 'Grandiflora'	16000	10	**26**		mid April	no	1
Campanula portenschlagiana	12000	15	**21**		mid February	no	1
Campanula rapunculus	50000	0	**25**		mid June	no	1
Campanula rotundifolia	16000	22	**29**		mid April	no	1
Centaurea montana	60	16	**21**		mid April	no	1
Centaurea orientalis	2000	9	**22**		mid June	yes	1
Centaurea scabiosa	150	7	**25**		mid April	no	1
Coreopsis auriculata 'Elfin Gold'	540	1	**21**		mid June	no	1

* 1, sow in October; 2, scarify pre-sowing; 3, soak in water pre-sowing; 4, sow in April.

FIELD EMERGENCE 20–30% WHEN WATERED TWICE PER WEEK	APPROXIMATE NUMBER OF SEEDS PER GRAM	PER CENT FIELD EMERGENCE WHEN IRRIGATED ONCE PER WEEK	PER CENT FIELD EMERGENCE WHEN IRRIGATED TWICE PER WEEK	CONVENTIONAL SEED OR TREATED TO BE NON-DORMANT JELITTO 'GOLD NUGGET' (GN)	SOWING TIME CORRESPONDING TO THESE EMERGENCE VALUES	PALATABLE TO SLUGS AS ADULTS	SPECIFIC MEANS OF INCREASING EMERGENCE *
Cortaderia selloana 'Pumila' hybrids	6000	0	**27**		mid June	no	1
Delphinium elatum Pacific hybrids	450	5	**23**		mid June	yes	1
Deschampsia cespitosa	5500	19	**23**		mid April	no	1
Deschampsia flexuosa	2000	3	**29**		mid June	no	1
Dianthus superbus	1400	3	**24**		mid June	no	1
Dodecatheon jeffreyi 'Rotlicht'	2800	0	**21**	GN	mid June	no	1
Doronicum orientale 'Magnificum'	1400	3	**22**		mid June	no	1
Dorycnium hirsutum	200	31	**27**		mid February	no	1
Echinacea pallida 'Hula Dancer'	200	18	**24**	GN	mid April	yes	1
Echinacea purpurea 'Magnus'	250	13	**29**		mid April	yes	1
Echinops ritro	60	18	**21**		mid April	no	1
Echinops sphaerocephalus 'Arctic Glow'	90	9	**20**		mid June	no	1
Eriogonum umbellatum	250	14	**21**		mid February	no	1
Ferula communis	20	24	**21**		mid February	no	1
Foeniculum vulgare 'Purpureum'	350	15	**25**		mid February	no	1
Fragaria vesca	2500	8	**25**		mid February	no	1
Galega officinalis	100	13	**21**		mid June	no	1
Galium mollugo	1600	24	**25**		mid February	no	1
Galtonia candicans	150	10	**28**		mid June	yes	1
Geum chiloense 'Feuerball'	500	7	**29**		mid April	no	1
Gypsophila repens 'Rosea'	1300	29	**24**		mid April	no	1
Helianthus occidentalis	550	17	**20**		mid February	no	1
Hibiscus moscheutos 'Galaxy'	80	5	**20**		mid June	no	1
Hypericum perforatum	8000	1	**25**		mid June	no	1
Hypochoeris uniflora	350	1	**27**		mid June	?	1
Jasione laevis 'Blaulicht'	18000	21	**25**		mid April	no	1
Knautia macedonica	250	45	**29**		mid February	no	1
Kniphofia hirsuta 'Fire Dance'	350	2	**20**	GN	mid June	no	1
Koeleria cristata	4000	17	**24**		mid April	no	1
Lathyrus vernus	50	7	**21**	GN	mid April	no	1
Leymus arenarius	80	11	**25**		mid February	no	1
Linum flavum 'Compactum'	800	7	**25**		mid April	no	1

* 1, sow in October; 2, scarify pre-sowing; 3, soak in water pre-sowing; 4, sow in April.

FIELD EMERGENCE 20–30% WHEN WATERED TWICE PER WEEK	APPROXIMATE NUMBER OF SEEDS PER GRAM	PER CENT FIELD EMERGENCE WHEN IRRIGATED ONCE PER WEEK	PER CENT FIELD EMERGENCE WHEN IRRIGATED TWICE PER WEEK	CONVENTIONAL SEED OR TREATED TO BE NON-DORMANT JELITTO 'GOLD NUGGET' (GN)	SOWING TIME CORRESPONDING TO THESE EMERGENCE VALUES	PALATABLE TO SLUGS AS ADULTS	SPECIFIC MEANS OF INCREASING EMERGENCE *
Lunaria annua	50	20	**26**		mid February	no	1
Miscanthus sinensis	1000	28	**27**		mid February	no	4
Monarda bradburiana	1700	5	**27**		mid June	no	1
Monardella odoratissima	3000	24	**25**		mid February	?	1
Papaver orientale 'Brilliant'	3500	11	**29**		mid April	no	1
Patrinia scabiosifolia	1000	34	**28**		mid February	no	1
Pennisetum setaceum	800	13	**29**		mid June	no	4
Penstemon ovatus	5500	0	**28**	GN	mid June	no	1
Penstemon ×mexicanus 'Sunburst Ruby'	2000	3	**21**		mid June	no	1
Phlomoides tuberosa	380	23	**23**		mid February	no	1
Platycodon grandiflorus 'Mariesii'	1000	33	**27**		mid April	no	1
Primula beesiana	4500	3	**20**	GN	mid April	no	5
Primula chionantha	4500	0	**28**	GN	mid June	no	5
Primula florindae	2500	0	**23**		mid June	no	5
Primula ×bulleesiana	2700	17	**22**		mid February	no	5
Primula ×bulleesiana	2700	1	**27**	GN	mid June	no	5
Prunella vulgaris	1200	28	**27**		mid February	no	1
Pulsatilla vulgaris	400	12	**27**	GN	mid April	no	1
Rhaponticum scariosum subsp. *rhaponticum*	30	18	**23**		mid February	?	1
Rudbeckia maxima	100	31	**23**		mid February	yes	1
Sagina subulata	36000	0	**26**		mid June	no	1
Salvia officinalis subsp. *lavandulifolia*	110	25	**21**		mid February	no	1
Scutellaria alpina 'Moonbeam'	1100	38	**22**		mid February	no	1
Scutellaria pontica	1300	29	**27**		mid February	no	1
Sedum montanum	25000	5	**23**		mid June	no	1
Sedum roseum	5000	19	**22**	GN	mid April	no	1
Seseli gummiferum	500	27	**27**		mid February	no	1
Sidalcea malviflora	350	14	**24**		mid February	no	1
Silene uniflora	1200	9	**28**		mid June	no	1
Silene vulgaris	1000	9	**21**		mid June	no	1
Solidago rigida	1100	18	**27**		mid April	no	1

* 1, sow in October; 2, scarify pre-sowing; 3, soak in water pre-sowing; 4 sow in April.

FIELD EMERGENCE 20–30% WHEN WATERED TWICE PER WEEK	APPROXIMATE NUMBER OF SEEDS PER GRAM	PER CENT FIELD EMERGENCE WHEN IRRIGATED ONCE PER WEEK	PER CENT FIELD EMERGENCE WHEN IRRIGATED TWICE PER WEEK	CONVENTIONAL SEED OR TREATED TO BE NON-DORMANT JELITTO 'GOLD NUGGET' (GN)	SOWING TIME CORRESPONDING TO THESE EMERGENCE VALUES	PALATABLE TO SLUGS AS ADULTS	SPECIFIC MEANS OF INCREASING EMERGENCE *
Sorghastrum nutans	600	17	**22**		mid February	no	4
Spodiopogon sibiricus	500	17	**27**		mid April	no	4
Stachys byzantina	700	15	**22**		mid February	no	1
Stachys macrantha	150	13	**29**	GN	mid April	no	1
Stokesia laevis	110	6	**21**		mid April	no	1
Succisella inflexa 'Frosted Pearls'	500	14	**21**		mid February	no	1
Talinum calycinum	3400	15	**21**		mid February	no	1
Teucrium chamaedrys hort.	550	16	**25**		mid April	no	1
Thalictrum rochebrunnianum	400	7	**23**	GN	mid June	no	1
Thermopsis chinensis	100	5	**26**		mid June	no	1, 2
Thermopsis montana	100	3	**23**		mid June	?	1, 2
Thymus praecox	7000	1	**26**		mid June	no	1
Trollius europaeus	1400	0	**22**	GN	mid June	no	1
Verbascum chaixii	7000	19	**29**		mid April	no	1
Verbena rigida	1300	31	**26**		mid February	no	1
Vernonia noveboracensis	750	8	**26**	GN	mid April	no	1
Veronica gentianoides	1300	19	**25**		mid February	no	1
Veronica spicata subsp. *incana*	1400	2	**24**		mid June	no	1

* 1, sow in October; 2, scarify pre-sowing; 3, soak in water pre-sowing; 4, sow in April.

Species showing 30–40 per cent emergence when irrigated twice per week

FIELD EMERGENCE 30–40% WHEN WATERED TWICE PER WEEK	APPROXIMATE NUMBER OF SEEDS PER GRAM	PER CENT FIELD EMERGENCE WHEN IRRIGATED ONCE PER WEEK	PER CENT FIELD EMERGENCE WHEN IRRIGATED TWICE PER WEEK	CONVENTIONAL SEED OR TREATED TO BE NON-DORMANT JELITTO 'GOLD NUGGET' (GN)	SOWING TIME CORRESPONDING TO THESE EMERGENCE VALUES	PALATABLE TO SLUGS AS ADULTS	SPECIFIC MEANS OF INCREASING EMERGENCE *
Achillea filipendulina 'Parkers Variety'	8800	27	33		mid April	no	1
Acinos alpinus	3000	46	39		mid February	no	1
Aethionema grandiflorum	900	12	37	GN	mid June	no	1
Althaea officinalis	370	25	32		mid February	?	1
Aquilegia canadensis	1000	35	35		mid February	no	1
Aquilegia vulgaris 'Clementine Blue'	1100	0	30		mid June	no	1
Aquilegia vulgaris 'Grandmother's Garden'	1000	33	37		mid February	no	1
Armeria maritima 'Splendens'	1100	33	39		mid February	no	1
Arnica montana	700	37	35		mid February	yes	1
Artemisia ludoviciana	12000	18	32		mid February	no	1
Asclepias tuberosa	150	27	35		mid February	yes	4
Aster alpinus 'Goliath'	700	18	39		mid April	no	1
Aster tongolensis 'Wartburgstern'	700	23	33		mid April	no	1
Aubrieta ×cultorum 'Cascade Blau'	2000	3	33		mid June	no	1
Bergenia purpurascens 'Winterglut'	4000	0	35		mid June	no	1
Berkheya purpurea	250	21	37		mid April	no	1
Briza media	2500	3	34		mid June	no	1
Centaurea dealbata	110	28	39		mid April	no	1
Centaurea jacea	450	21	39		mid April	?	1
Centaurea macrocephala	40	32	37		mid April	no	1
Centranthus ruber var. coccineus	450	27	37		mid April	no	1
Cephalaria alpina	30	35	33		mid February	no	1
Cichorium intybus	450	12	38		mid June	no	1
Codonopsis clematidea	1500	25	31		mid February	yes	1
Codonopsis clematidea	1500	5	37	GN	mid June	yes	1
Coronilla varia	300	14	36		mid June	no	1
Dalea purpurea	600	29	34		mid April	yes	1
Delphinium elatum	300	8	37		mid June	yes	1
Digitalis obscura	2300	4	37		mid June	no	1
Digitalis mariana subsp. heywoodii	12500	0	33		mid June	no	1

* 1, sow in October; 2, scarify pre-sowing; 3, soak in water pre-sowing; 4, sow in April.

FIELD EMERGENCE 30–40% WHEN WATERED TWICE PER WEEK	APPROXIMATE NUMBER OF SEEDS PER GRAM	PER CENT FIELD EMERGENCE WHEN IRRIGATED ONCE PER WEEK	PER CENT FIELD EMERGENCE WHEN IRRIGATED TWICE PER WEEK	CONVENTIONAL SEED OR TREATED TO BE NON-DORMANT JELITTO 'GOLD NUGGET' (GN)	SOWING TIME CORRESPONDING TO THESE EMERGENCE VALUES	PALATABLE TO SLUGS AS ADULTS	SPECIFIC MEANS OF INCREASING EMERGENCE *
Dracocephalum argunense 'Fuji Blue'	300	19	**35**	GN	mid April	no	1
Echinacea angustifolia	200	23	**36**	GN	mid April	yes	1
Erigeron karvinskianus 'Blütenmeer'	13000	5	**31**		mid June	no	1
Erinus alpinus	12000	1	**39**		mid June	no	1
Eryngium yuccifolium	250	26	**32**		mid February	no	1
Eupatorium maculatum	3500	1	**38**	GN	mid June	yes	1
Eupatorium maculatum 'Atropurpureum'	2000	1	**34**	GN	mid June	yes	1
Euphorbia characias	130	33	**33**		mid February	no	1, 2
Euphorbia characias	130	6	**32**	GN	mid June	no	1, 2
Euphorbia palustris	100	9	**35**	GN	mid June	no	1, 2
Euphorbia epithymoides	300	38	**39**	GN	mid April	no	1, 2
Euphorbia rigida	100	32	**33**		mid February	no	1, 2
Glaucium flavum	800	30	**37**	GN	mid April	no	1
Globularia cordifolia	2500	13	**31**		mid February	no	1
Hedysarum hedysaroides	150	33	**35**		mid February	yes	1
Helianthemum nummularium	750	15	**34**		mid June	no	1
Hypericum cerastioides	3000	3	**35**	GN	mid June	no	1
Hypericum polyphyllum 'Grandiflorum'	4000	27	**33**		mid February	no	1
Hyssopus officinalis	1000	16	**38**		mid June	no	1
Inula helenium	550	22	**37**		mid April	no	1
Inula magnifica	40	1	**33**		mid June	no	1
Inula orientalis	1500	2	**36**		mid June	no	1
Jurinea mollis	150	23	**36**		mid February	?	1
Lathyrus latifolius	20	12	**36**	GN	mid June	no	1
Lavandula angustifolia	950	10	**30**		mid February	no	1
Lavandula angustifolia	950	13	**38**	GN	mid June	no	1
Leucanthemum graminifolium	1300	9	**30**		mid June	no	1
Liatris punctata	200	15	**38**		mid June	yes	1
Liatris spicata	350	27	**37**		mid April	no	1
Ligularia altaica	180	33	**31**		mid February	yes	1
Limonium platyphyllum	1000	27	**35**		mid April	no	1

* 1, sow in October; 2, scarify pre-sowing; 3, soak in water pre-sowing; 4, sow in April.

FIELD EMERGENCE 30–40% WHEN WATERED TWICE PER WEEK

	APPROXIMATE NUMBER OF SEEDS PER GRAM	PER CENT FIELD EMERGENCE WHEN IRRIGATED ONCE PER WEEK	PER CENT FIELD EMERGENCE WHEN IRRIGATED TWICE PER WEEK	CONVENTIONAL SEED OR TREATED TO BE NON-DORMANT JELITTO 'GOLD NUGGET' (GN)	SOWING TIME CORRESPONDING TO THESE EMERGENCE VALUES	PALATABLE TO SLUGS AS ADULTS	SPECIFIC MEANS OF INCREASING EMERGENCE *
Lupinus perennis	50	20	**37**		mid June	?	1
Lychnis ×arkwrightii 'Vesuvius'	850	17	**35**		mid April	no	1
Lysimachia punctata	2700	0	**31**	GN	mid June	no	1
Malva moschata	400	25	**33**		mid February	no	1
Malva sylvestris	250	34	**35**		mid February	no	1
Nepeta subsessilis 'Blue Dreams'	1100	0	**30**		mid June	no	1
Oenothera macrocarpa subsp. *incana*	170	9	**36**	GN	mid June	no	1
Ononis spinosa	160	52	**31**		mid February	no	1
Panicum virgatum	500	32	**36**		mid February	no	1
Papaver nudicaule	5500	6	**33**		mid June	no	1
Papaver rupifragum	12000	5	**30**		mid June	no	1
Penstemon barbatus 'Coccineus'	950	29	**31**		mid February	no	1
Penstemon barbatus 'Rondo'	1100	15	**36**		mid June	no	1
Penstemon digitalis 'Husker Red Strain'	3000	17	**37**	GN	mid April	no	1
Penstemon grandiflorus	500	3	**39**	GN	mid June	no	1
Physalis alkekengi var. *franchetii* 'Gigantea'	650	13	**31**	GN	mid April	no	1
Physostegia virginiana 'Rosea'	400	13	**30**	GN	mid April	no	1
Polemonium caeruleum	900	21	**31**		mid April	no	1
Polemonium yezoense 'Purple Rain Strain'	800	15	**34**		mid June	no	1
Potentilla aurea	3000	23	**37**		mid February	no	1
Potentilla nepalensis 'Ron McBeath'	3000	9	**35**		mid June	no	1
Potentilla thurberi	2400	25	**35**		mid February	no	1
Prunella grandiflora	500	26	**33**		mid February	no	1
Ruellia humilis	180	24	**33**	GN	mid April	no	1
Salvia nemorosa	850	31	**32**		mid April	yes	1
Salvia pratensis	500	17	**37**		mid April	yes	1
Salvia transsylvanica 'Blue Spires'	80	11	**35**		mid June	?	1
Saponaria officinalis	450	3	**35**	GN	mid June	no	1
Satureja montana	1700	9	**31**		mid June	no	1
Scabiosa japonica var. *alpina*	750	27	**35**		mid February	no	1

* 1, sow in October; 2, scarify pre-sowing; 3, soak in water pre-sowing; 4, sow in April.

FIELD EMERGENCE 30–40% WHEN WATERED TWICE PER WEEK	APPROXIMATE NUMBER OF SEEDS PER GRAM	PER CENT FIELD EMERGENCE WHEN IRRIGATED ONCE PER WEEK	PER CENT FIELD EMERGENCE WHEN IRRIGATED TWICE PER WEEK	CONVENTIONAL SEED OR TREATED TO BE NON-DORMANT JELITTO 'GOLD NUGGET' (GN)	SOWING TIME CORRESPONDING TO THESE EMERGENCE VALUES	PALATABLE TO SLUGS AS ADULTS	SPECIFIC MEANS OF INCREASING EMERGENCE *
Sedum acre	20000	30	35		mid April	no	1
Sedum kamtschaticum	10000	6	34		mid June	no	1
Sedum hispanicum	50000	14	30		mid June	no	1
Sedum selskianum 'Goldilocks'	25000	16	36		mid June	no	1
Sedum spurium 'Coccineum'	15000	25	34		mid February	no	1
Silene coronaria	1800	32	38		mid April	no	1
Silene viscaria	8000	0	30		mid June	no	1
Stipa capillata	250	23	35		mid June	no	1, 2
Telekia speciosa	1700	25	36		mid April	no	1
Trifolium ochroleucon	220	15	33		mid April	no	1
Verbena hastata	3200	0	39	GN	mid June	?	1
Veronica spicata	13000	17	32		mid April	no	1
Viola cornuta 'Ulla'	1000	12	36		mid April	no	1
Viola labradorica 'Purpurea'	1200	10	37	GN	mid April	no	1

* 1, sow in October; 2, scarify pre-sowing; 3, soak in water pre-sowing; 4, sow in April.

Species showing 40–50 per cent emergence when irrigated twice per week

FIELD EMERGENCE 40–50% WHEN WATERED TWICE PER WEEK	APPROXIMATE NUMBER OF SEEDS PER GRAM	PER CENT FIELD EMERGENCE WHEN IRRIGATED ONCE PER WEEK	PER CENT FIELD EMERGENCE WHEN IRRIGATED TWICE PER WEEK	CONVENTIONAL SEED OR TREATED TO BE NON-DORMANT JELITTO 'GOLD NUGGET' (GN)	SOWING TIME CORRESPONDING TO THESE EMERGENCE VALUES	PALATABLE TO SLUGS AS ADULTS	SPECIFIC MEANS OF INCREASING EMERGENCE *
Adenophora liliifolia	6000	37	43		mid February	yes	5
Allium tuberosum	300	17	42		mid June	no	5
Anchusa azurea	50	17	40		mid June	no	5
Aquilegia alpina	700	33	47		mid February	no	5
Aquilegia chrysantha 'Yellow Queen'	900	34	48		mid February	no	5
Berkheya multijuga	350	13	40		mid June	no	5
Bouteloua curtipendula	950	25	42		mid April	no	5
Bouteloua gracilis	2200	29	49		mid April	no	5
Buchloe dactyloides	70	35	47		mid June	no	5
Calamintha nepeta	3000	33	41		mid February	no	5
Callirhoe involucrata	180	12	47	GN	mid June	?	5
Campanula carpatica	15000	5	41		mid June	no	5
Campanula garganica	16000	1	47	GN	mid June	no	5
Campanula trachelium	6500	9	49		mid June	no	5
Catananche caerulea	300	40	47		mid April	no	5
Centaurea atropurpurea	150	23	43		mid June	yes	5
Chaenorhinum origanifolium 'Blue Dreams'	14500	8	47		mid June	no	5
Chamaemelum nobile	6000	1	47		mid June	no	5
Claytonia sibirica	1000	43	46		mid February	no	5
Claytonia sibirica	1000	11	49	GN	mid June	no	5
Dianthus carthusianorum	1000	48	45		mid April	no	5
Digitalis purpurea 'Gloxiniaeflora'	8000	1	47		mid June	no	5
Dracocephalum rupestre	400	53	44		mid February	no	5
Echium vulgare	300	40	46		mid February	no	5
Erigeron speciosus 'Rosa Juwel'	2300	42	43		mid April	no	5
Eryngium planum 'Blaukappe'	340	45	45		mid February	no	5
Euphorbia myrsinites	100	52	41	GN	mid April	no	2
Gaura lindheimeri 'The Bride'	60	46	46		mid April	no	5
Geranium wallichianum 'Buxton's Variety'	100	9	40	GN	mid June	no	5
Glandularia aristigera	750	15	47		mid June	no	5

* 1, sow in October; 2, scarify pre-sowing; 3, soak in water pre-sowing; 4, sow in April; 5, no specific treatment required.

FIELD EMERGENCE 40–50% WHEN WATERED TWICE PER WEEK	APPROXIMATE NUMBER OF SEEDS PER GRAM	PER CENT FIELD EMERGENCE WHEN IRRIGATED ONCE PER WEEK	PER CENT FIELD EMERGENCE WHEN IRRIGATED TWICE PER WEEK	CONVENTIONAL SEED OR TREATED TO BE NON-DORMANT JELITTO 'GOLD NUGGET' (GN)	SOWING TIME CORRESPONDING TO THESE EMERGENCE VALUES	PALATABLE TO SLUGS AS ADULTS	SPECIFIC MEANS OF INCREASING EMERGENCE *
Helenium hoopesii	450	28	45		mid April	yes	5
Heliopsis helianthoides 'Sommersonne'	250	10	49		mid June	no	5
Hesperis matronalis	550	13	40		mid June	no	5
Hibiscus moscheutos 'Galaxy'	80	11	43	GN	mid June	no	5
Hieracium pilosella	5500	4	45		mid June	no	5
Hieracium villosum	1500	33	41		mid February	no	5
Hyssopus officinalis subsp. *aristatus*	1050	11	40		mid June	no	5
Kalimeris incisa	1000	1	49		mid June	?	5
Koeleria glauca	5000	24	48		mid April	no	5
Lathyrus latifolius	20	21	41		mid June	no	5
Ligularia dentata 'Dark Beauty'	100	2	43		mid June	?	5
Linum capitatum	630	8	43	GN	mid June	no	5
Linum narbonense	250	22	45	GN	mid June	no	5
Lotus corniculatus	850	13	48		mid June	no	5
Lupinus Russell hybrids	40	19	43		mid June	no	5
Malvaviscus arboreus	60	4	40	GN	mid June	no	5
Nepeta racemosa	1100	18	49		mid June	no	5
Papaver alpinum	9000	3	44		mid June	no	5
Penstemon grandiflorus	500	23	46		mid February	no	5
Penstemon heterophyllus 'Züriblau'	700	46	42		mid February	no	5
Penstemon smallii	7000	4	43	GN	mid June	no	5
Penstemon strictus	1100	32	49	GN	mid April	no	5
Perovskia atriplicifolia	1100	41	49		mid February	no	5
Pilosella aurantiaca	5500	1	48		mid June	no	5
Potentilla atrosanguinea 'Red'	3100	6	41		mid June	no	5
Primula bulleyana	2900	0	48	GN	mid June	no	5
Rudbeckia fulgida var. *deamii*	1000	3	43	GN	mid June	yes	5
Rudbeckia occidentalis	350	5	41		mid June	yes	5
Rumex acetosa	2100	9	44		mid June	no	5
Ruta graveolens	400	11	49		mid June	no	5
Saccharum ravennae	1900	2	40		mid June	no	5
Salvia farinacea 'Victoria Blue'	1000	9	46		mid June	no	5

* 1, sow in October; 2, scarify pre-sowing; 3, soak in water pre-sowing; 4, sow in April; 5, no specific treatment required.

FIELD EMERGENCE 40–50% WHEN WATERED TWICE PER WEEK	APPROXIMATE NUMBER OF SEEDS PER GRAM	PER CENT FIELD EMERGENCE WHEN IRRIGATED ONCE PER WEEK	PER CENT FIELD EMERGENCE WHEN IRRIGATED TWICE PER WEEK	CONVENTIONAL SEED OR TREATED TO BE NON-DORMANT JELITTO 'GOLD NUGGET' (GN)	SOWING TIME CORRESPONDING TO THESE EMERGENCE VALUES	PALATABLE TO SLUGS AS ADULTS	SPECIFIC MEANS OF INCREASING EMERGENCE *
Salvia nemorosa subsp. *pseudosylvestris*	600	24	**45**		mid June	yes	5
Scabiosa caucasica 'Perfecta'	70	31	**40**		mid June	no	5
Sedum pulchellum	8000	23	**43**		mid June	no	5
Sedum rupestre	15000	28	**40**		mid April	no	5
Silene chalcedonica	2100	20	**42**		mid April	no	5
Solidago virgaurea	2200	6	**49**		mid June	no	5
Tanacetum niveum 'Jackpot'	9000	8	**45**		mid June	no	5
Thalictrum flavum subsp. *glaucum*	750	17	**49**		mid February	no	5
Thermopsis villosa	130	13	**49**	GN	mid June	no	5
Thymus pulegioides	5500	8	**40**		mid June	no	5
Trifolium rubens	350	43	**49**		mid April	no	5
Trollius chinensis 'Golden Queen'	850	1	**44**	GN	mid June	no	5
Veronica austriaca subsp. *teucrium* 'Royal Blue'	3100	31	**40**		mid April	no	5

* 1, sow in October; 2, scarify pre-sowing; 3, soak in water pre-sowing; 4, sow in April; 5, no specific treatment required.

Species showing 50–60 per cent emergence when irrigated twice per week

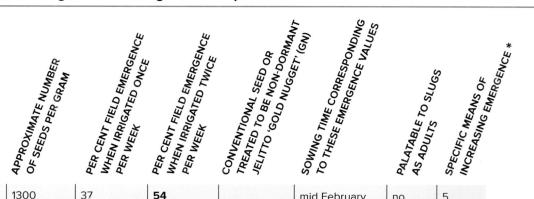

FIELD EMERGENCE 50–60% WHEN WATERED TWICE PER WEEK	APPROXIMATE NUMBER OF SEEDS PER GRAM	PER CENT FIELD EMERGENCE WHEN IRRIGATED ONCE PER WEEK	PER CENT FIELD EMERGENCE WHEN IRRIGATED TWICE PER WEEK	CONVENTIONAL SEED OR TREATED TO BE NON-DORMANT JELITTO 'GOLD NUGGET' (GN)	SOWING TIME CORRESPONDING TO THESE EMERGENCE VALUES	PALATABLE TO SLUGS AS ADULTS	SPECIFIC MEANS OF INCREASING EMERGENCE *
Achnatherum calamagrostis	1300	37	**54**		mid February	no	5
Alchemilla erythropoda	1800	7	**50**	GN	mid June	no	5
Anacyclus pyrethrum	1700	12	**51**		mid June	no	5
Arabis caucasica 'Compacta'	3400	11	**53**		mid June	no	5
Armeria pseudarmeria	950	17	**57**		mid June	no	5
Cerastium tomentosum	2400	54	**57**		mid April	no	5
Chasmanthium latifolium	220	13	**57**		mid June	no	5
Chrysanthemum coccineum	350	25	**57**		mid June	yes	5
Coreopsis lanceolata 'Sterntaler'	500	20	**53**		mid June	no	5
Delosperma sutherlandii	4500	25	**56**		mid June	no	5
Dianthus pinifolius	1800	20	**59**		mid June	no	5
Echinacea tennesseensis 'Rocky Top' hybrids	250	19	**51**	GN	mid June	?	5
Erigeron glaucus	4500	1	**57**		mid June	no	5
Euphorbia characias subsp. wulfenii	130	23	**58**	GN	mid June	no	5
Festuca glauca	1000	38	**57**		mid April	no	5
Festuca ovina	1300	39	**50**		mid April	no	5
Gaillardia aristata 'Burgunder'	200	15	**57**		mid June	yes	5
Gaillardia aristata wild form	350	17	**51**		mid June	yes	5
Galium verum	2000	34	**55**		mid April	no	5
Leucanthemum vulgare	2500	7	**51**		mid June	no	5
Linaria purpurea	7500	42	**51**		mid February	no	5
Linaria purpurea	7500	6	**56**	GN	mid June	no	5
Mirabilis jalapa	10	33	**57**		mid June	no	5
Oenothera macrocarpa	200	25	**51**	GN	mid April	no	5
Pennisetum alopecuroides	400	5	**59**		mid June	no	5
Penstemon heterophyllus 'Züriblau'	700	5	**50**	GN	mid June	no	5
Phalaris arundinacea	1300	57	**51**		mid February	no	5
Ratibida columnifera	1200	19	**57**		mid June	yes	5
Salvia sclarea	250	32	**58**		mid June	no	5
Saponaria ocymoides	500	41	**50**		mid February	no	5

* 1, sow in October; 2, scarify pre-sowing; 3, soak in water pre-sowing; 4, sow in April; 5, no specific treatment required.

FIELD EMERGENCE 50–60% WHEN WATERED TWICE PER WEEK	APPROXIMATE NUMBER OF SEEDS PER GRAM	PER CENT FIELD EMERGENCE WHEN IRRIGATED ONCE PER WEEK	PER CENT FIELD EMERGENCE WHEN IRRIGATED TWICE PER WEEK	CONVENTIONAL SEED OR TREATED TO BE NON-DORMANT JELITTO 'GOLD NUGGET' (GN)	SOWING TIME CORRESPONDING TO THESE EMERGENCE VALUES	PALATABLE TO SLUGS AS ADULTS	SPECIFIC MEANS OF INCREASING EMERGENCE *
Silene dioica	1200	38	**50**		mid April	no	5
Taraxacum officinale	1500	12	**53**		mid June	no	5
Valeriana officinalis	1400	3	**55**		mid June	no	5
Verbena bonariensis	4500	6	**57**	GN	mid June	no	5
Viola sororia 'Freckles'	680	8	**53**	GN	mid June	no	5

* 1, sow in October; 2, scarify pre-sowing; 3, soak in water pre-sowing; 4, sow in April; 5, no specific treatment required.

Species showing 60–70 per cent emergence when irrigated twice per week

FIELD EMERGENCE 60–70% WHEN WATERED TWICE PER WEEK	APPROXIMATE NUMBER OF SEEDS PER GRAM	PER CENT FIELD EMERGENCE WHEN IRRIGATED ONCE PER WEEK	PER CENT FIELD EMERGENCE WHEN IRRIGATED TWICE PER WEEK	CONVENTIONAL SEED OR TREATED TO BE NON-DORMANT JELITTO 'GOLD NUGGET' (GN)	SOWING TIME CORRESPONDING TO THESE EMERGENCE VALUES	PALATABLE TO SLUGS AS ADULTS	SPECIFIC MEANS OF INCREASING EMERGENCE *
Aethionema cordifolium	2500	32	**66**		mid June	no	5
Agastache aurantiaca	1600	15	**65**		mid June	no	5
Anthemis tinctoria 'Kelwayi'	2000	27	**61**		mid June	no	5
Anthyllis vulneraria	300	27	**64**		mid June	no	5
Cymbalaria muralis	7000	17	**63**		mid June	no	5
Dianthus arenarius	1400	23	**68**		mid June	no	5
Dianthus deltoides 'Erectus'	4500	11	**67**		mid June	no	5
Eragrostis curvula	3300	45	**68**		mid June	no	5
Eriophyllum lanatum	2400	67	**66**		mid February	no	5
Festuca mairei	1200	15	**63**		mid June	no	5
Gonolirion tataricum hort.	900	16	**61**		mid June	no	5
Heliopsis helianthoides var. scabra 'Summer Nights'	250	16	**62**		mid June	no	5
Isatis tinctoria	150	38	**66**		mid June	no	5
Leucanthemum maximum 'Alaska'	700	11	**61**		mid June	no	5
Leucanthemum vulgare	2500	5	**62**		mid June	no	5
Liatris scariosa 'Alba'	460	6	**62**		mid June	no	5
Lychnis viscaria 'Feuer'	12500	2	**62**		mid June	no	5
Lysimachia vulgaris	3000	1	**61**	GN	mid June	no	5
Malva alcea var. fastigiata	350	31	**61**	GN	mid June	no	5
Nassella tenuissima	3100	47	**61**		mid February	no	5
Nepeta nervosa	1700	41	**60**		mid April	no	5
Penstemon pinifolius	1800	39	**61**		mid February	no	5
Phuopsis stylosa	1000	51	**67**		mid April	no	5
Salvia officinalis	120	28	**62**		mid June	no	5
Sidalcea malviflora 'Rosanna'	350	3	**62**	GN	mid June	no	5
Silene caroliniana subsp. wherryi	1100	56	**69**		mid February	?	5
Silene schafta 'Splendens'	3000	13	**69**		mid June	no	5
Verbascum phoeniceum	8000	7	**60**		mid June	?	5

* 1, sow in October; 2, scarify pre-sowing; 3, soak in water pre-sowing; 4, sow in April; 5, no specific treatment required.

Species showing more than 70 per cent emergence when irrigated twice per week

FIELD EMERGENCE >70% WHEN WATERED TWICE PER WEEK	APPROXIMATE NUMBER OF SEEDS PER GRAM	PER CENT FIELD EMERGENCE WHEN IRRIGATED ONCE PER WEEK	PER CENT FIELD EMERGENCE WHEN IRRIGATED TWICE PER WEEK	CONVENTIONAL SEED OR TREATED TO BE NON-DORMANT JELITTO 'GOLD NUGGET' (GN)	SOWING TIME CORRESPONDING TO THESE EMERGENCE VALUES	PALATABLE TO SLUGS AS ADULTS	SPECIFIC MEANS OF INCREASING EMERGENCE *
Alyssum montanum 'Mountain Gold'	600	35	**73**		mid June	no	5
Anthyllis vulneraria	300	39	**83**	GN	mid June	no	5
Bellis perennis	8000	12	**77**		mid June	no	5
Dianthus plumarius	700	21	**77**		mid June	no	5
Festuca punctoria	950	80	**82**		mid February	no	5
Linum perenne	600	19	**75**		mid June	no	5
Petrorhagia saxifraga	4800	24	**75**		mid June	no	5
Plantago lanceolata	600	61	**73**		mid February	no	5

* 1, sow in October; 2, scarify pre-sowing; 3, soak in water pre-sowing; 4, sow in April; 5, no specific treatment required.

ESTABLISHMENT AND MANAGEMENT

As with all designed landscape vegetation, the long-term success of sown and planted meadow-like vegetation relies heavily on the availability of thoughtful management. These types of vegetation are often easier to maintain compared with conventional horticultural vegetation, but they are by no means management free. In his own sown prairie garden, Tom Stuart-Smith, one of my design collaborators, has calculated that the management is about 10 per cent of the time required to manage the same area of conventional mixed herbaceous planting—and this is for a prairie to die for, not a rather rough version in a public park. This long-term management, however, can only deliver the

intended benefits and experiences when the establishment period is managed to ensure that enough plants are established to form the basis of a viable plant community.

If the sowing targets are not achieved, then it is almost inevitable that the plant community will close together less quickly and contain more weeds and a larger total weed biomass. Large weed biomasses increase the competitive pressure on the sown species, leading to increased mortality often through competition for light, potentially leading to a tipping point when the sown community begins to decline. The first year of a sown naturalistic community is therefore necessarily the most management intensive of that plant community's life. You can sometimes cut corners in subsequent management phases, but doing this during the first year is likely to be disastrous in the longer term.

KEY ESTABLISHMENT ACTIVITIES IN THE FIRST YEAR

In order to establish a successful community for the long term, in the first year it is important to irrigate to achieve target field emergence and manage herbivory by slugs and snails and weed invasion of the site to reduce mortality among seedlings. If this is undertaken successfully, it will encourage satisfactory growth of the community and in particular canopy closure by the end of the first growing season.

Irrigation to achieve target field emergence

Among the factors you can readily influence in a sown community, the one that has the greatest effect on achieving adequate levels of seedling emergence is avoiding exposing germinating seed to moisture stress. If you can irrigate every couple of days during the typical emergence window from early spring to early summer, the risk of below-target seedling numbers is largely removed. If you have to rely on natural rainfall, the risk of very low emergence or even complete failure, particularly on potentially dry sowing mulches such as sand, is much higher. This is very much the case in the United Kingdom and Western Europe, where spring rainfall is often highly unpredictable.

The perennial native wildflower meadow sowings at the Queen Elizabeth Olympic Park in London undertaken from January to March 2011 came perilously close to failing due to problems in connecting the temporary irrigation system to the mains network. The dependence on irrigation is potentially much reduced in continental climates where rainfall in late spring to summer is often both reliable and heavy, despite the high summer temperatures. This seems to be true in, for example, western China (see Kaixian case study). The need for irrigation is also reduced when sowing onto subsoil clay, composted green waste, and other sowing mulches with high moisture-holding capacity.

If irrigation is not available during the germination and emergence period, it is a risky business to propose to clients a high-quality, flower-rich end point. Under such circumstances, I would be actively lowering expectations in line with the likely much reduced emergence. As a consultant, I generally decline to be involved in projects where short-term expectations are very high but irrigation is not available.

Temporary first-year (from early spring to early summer) but fixed-position impact drive sprinklers are an ideal means of irrigation on medium to large projects, as in Tom Stuart-Smith's prairie garden. Removing the need to drag hosepipes across emerging seedlings greatly reduces trafficking damage.

At sites that are not closely viewed (and hence not so heavily politically contested) with very infertile soils, it is possible that even with a failure of germination in a dry spring, weed colonization will be so slow that many of the seedlings that emerge in the second year will actually survive and eventually create a successful plant community. The visually stunning native wildflower meadows on chalk cuttings around the London orbital M25 motorway share elements of this history, with *Centaurea scabiosa*, *Galium verum*, and *Origanum vulgare* in particular driving the drama.

The frequency of irrigation in high-profile prestige settings depends heavily on the climatic characteristics of the region (solar radiation and the frequency and intensity of rainfall). On sloping sites, aspect and slope angle, which markedly affects solar gain and therefore evaporation potential, as well as the moisture-holding capacity of the underlying soil type have a great influence on how frequent irrigation needs to be. Steep slopes are particularly problematic because the upper portions of the slopes is always much drier than the lower portions due to gravity. This requires judgement as to how much water to apply to the upper slope to prevent making the lower slopes anaerobic. Where jute matting is employed in sowings, its changing colour in response to the wetness of the underlying sowing mulch helps in this irrigation decision-making process.

In the absence of rainfall, irrigation is required at least every 2 days to rewet the top 100 mm of the sowing mulch–soil profile. Irrigation on a daily basis maximizes emergence, especially if undertaken in the late afternoon or early evening. This latter practice maximizes the number of hours the sowing mulch stays wet. If irrigated at say 5:00 p.m., due to rapidly falling evaporation the sowing mulch will typically remain as wet as it possibly can be (known as field capacity) until 10:00 a.m. the next morning or longer if it is a cloudy day. Irrigation in the morning as evaporation is rapidly increasing often means that the sowing mulch will be dry by lunchtime, giving a wet period of 2–4 hours as opposed to 17 hours when the same amount of water is applied in the evening.

On heavier soils, it is desirable not to apply too much water at each irrigation event to avoid exceeding the capacity for drainage, which leads to anaerobic conditions in the underlying soil. Such conditions often result in both poor seedling growth and an explosion of worm casting, which potentially brings many weed seeds to the sowing mulch surface, hence breaching the weed seed cordon sanitaire, leading to much greater weeding requirements.

Managing slug damage to seedlings

In climates where these invertebrates are abundant, slug grazing can be a major cause of seedling mortality. As adults, herbaceous plants vary hugely in their palatability to slugs. Where slugs and snails are a ubiquitous part of the local ecology, such as in maritime parts of Western Europe and the Pacific Northwest, many plant species have evolved a range of chemical (including highly toxic alkaloids in the tissues) and physical defences (spine-like hairs on leaves, high levels of silicon crystals in grass leaves) to discourage slug grazing. Because these defences all require a substantial commitment of carbohydrates and other molecules that could otherwise be used to manufacture seeds, where slugs are not significant factors in a habitat, the species in these habitats have generally not invested in this evolutionary insurance policy and are often defenceless when grown in areas where slugs are abundant.

Many continental North American species lack defences against slug herbivory. There are often few obvious patterns in this. *Veronicastrum virginicum*, which is unpalatable to slugs, grows side by side in wet swales in prairies with the slug caviar better known as *Arnoglossum atriplicifolium* and *Echinacea purpurea*. The relative palatability to slugs of some of the species likely to be used in meadow-like vegetation is shown in the eight tables at the end of the previous chapter. Damage from slugs in at least the first few years can be minimized by selecting sand as a sowing mulch.

When plants are at the seedling stage, chemical and physical defences have yet to kick in, even in species that are able to do this, so they too are potentially very vulnerable. Slug grazing is mainly nocturnal and unseen, and it can lead to close to 100 per cent loss of the most palatable species.

The highest levels of slug damage are most likely to occur with:

- sowings close to edges with hedges or long grass (these support very high slug densities)
- sowings on north- or east-facing slopes (where slugs graze for longer during the day)
- climates with above-average spring and early-summer rainfall
- sowing mulches that stay wet for long periods of time (clay subsoil and composted green waste, as opposed to sharp sand)

Using a diversity of species in a sowing mix is one way to reduce catastrophic seedling loss, as it is unlikely that all species will be equally palatable to slugs or indeed sensitive to moisture stress. The tell-tale signs of slug grazing on small seedlings are the disappearance of one or more cotyledons, or parts thereof, and in extreme cases the seedling being reduced to just a leafless stump. You have to get your head close to the sowing mulch to see this. The best way (because it is simple, environmentally benign, and long term) to manage slug grazing during the seedling stage is to use sand sowing mulches. Where grazing is really extreme, perhaps on the edge of sowings near a hedge, the application of a molluscide (such as those based on metaldehyde) as a band might need to be considered as a temporary measure during the establishment period. In many public landscapes, however, this is generally not tenable due to perception of risk to hedgehogs, dogs, and children. This can be mitigated in many cases by temporary fencing around sown schemes, which is often required to prevent curious locals trafficking the sowings. Although less effective than metaldehyde when the soil surface is dry, molluscides based around iron phosphate and approved of by the organic movement provide some control and have lower mammalian and avian toxicity. The best strategy is to mark out a few 1 × 1 m squares near the edge of sowings and then scrutinize these for signs of damage before losing too much sleep over the perils of slugs.

If making meadows in your own garden, you can go out at night with a head lamp and kill the slugs you find on the surface. This process can be made more efficient by baiting at intervals with dollops of tinned cat food. Slugs love cat food and make a beeline for this, where they can easily be collected up. Don't worry about your control activities leading to local slug extinction events; even when molluscide pellets are deliberately used repeatedly, the slug populations return to prebaiting densities by about 6 weeks after the cessation of baiting. Slugs are very abundant organisms in wet places like the United Kingdom.

Weed management

The use of sowing mulches is a powerful way of greatly reducing weed seed establishment during the first growing season. There will always be some blow-in weed seeds, however, or some emergence from the soil below or from weed seeds present in the sowing mulches.

Weed emergence often occurs because, unless the soil is very level when sowing mulch is spread, the depth of the mulch is often too shallow on top of soil ridges to prevent emergence through the sowing mulch at these points. Another source of weed contamination is where worm casting is heavy, depositing weed seeds onto the surface. Whether you need to take action against these weeds depends heavily on the goals of the sowing, as well as the density and the particular species of weeds.

As ever, context and expectation are important. If you have, for example, a native wildflower meadow that is not closely inspected by people, then blow-in weeds (many annual or biennial forbs and grasses plus some perennial forbs and grasses) might be tolerable if densities are low, say, less than 10 plants/m². At higher weed densities, competition (particularly from grasses) with the slower growing forbs becomes problematic, as weeds are highly competitive. In one of our meadow research studies, the presence of annual and biennial weeds such as sow thistle (*Sonchus oleraceus*) did not have any measurable impact on how the meadow developed. In contrast, in the same experiment, native perennial grasses such as Yorkshire fog (*Holcus lanatus*), when not removed, led to the loss of many of the perennial native forb species by the second year. This was not just a reduction in total number of seedlings present, but also a dramatic loss in the species diversity. This mechanism explains why, on productive soil types, many native wildflower meadows often produce disappointing results.

If you are producing a more horticultural meadow in which many or at least some of the species are less well fitted climatically and hence potentially more sensitive to competition from weeds, then weeding will definitely be necessary. Except in garden-scale sowings, it is generally impossible to remove all of the weeds. The goal is to reduce the competitive pressure so that by the end of the first growing season (mid autumn) most of the standing biomass is composed of the sown species rather than weeds. If this can be achieved, the sown species (providing they are dense enough) will close canopy and are then well on the way to achieving dominance of the site. If dominance is not achieved by the end of the first growing season, weed problems tend to continue on into the future. Spending time weeding in the first year results in much better appearance and species performance in subsequent years and much less long-term management. The first year is the time when you need to be prepared to throw resources at the problem.

The obvious difficulty in weeding meadow-like sown communities from early summer on (by then the sown seedlings are generally large enough to potentially be identified) is how to distinguish between the sown species and the weeds. This is also a major issue in professional practice, where it is rare to work with maintenance staff (outside of some botanic gardens) that can reliably identify common weeds when small. There is almost no chance that these staff will know what the sown seedlings look like. Why should they? The way I address these issues in practice is to delay weeding until early summer. By this time, identification is getting easier and the sown species are generally large enough not to be accidentally uprooted when removing weed species.

You need to get down close to see what's emerging, both desired and not. The 1.2-m-wide channels created by the jute erosion matting are very obvious in this image.

When possible, we normally sow a 9-cm-diameter pot with approximately thirty to forty seeds of each species present in the sowing mix and label these, so it is possible to train maintenance staff what the sown species look like. To assist this process, close-up photographs of seedlings of the sown species, as a series of thumbprints on a laminated card, improve weeding decision-making. These cards hang around the neck of the weeders on a lanyard. We undertake the same process for the common weeds on the site. In most cases, the protocol is that you only remove seedlings that you are sure are weeds. This is generally easier for weeders to get their heads around than not removing seedlings that resemble the sown species.

Weed species nearly always germinate earlier and grow much faster than the sown species, so they are conspicuously larger, a useful rule of thumb. Removal by hand is generally the most effective approach, especially when sand mulches are used and plants pull out from these very easily. At the first weeding, I often wear soft kneeling pads (not hard shell, which are bad for the seedlings) and crawl on all fours through the sowings. Rather than just wander around hither and thither, the weeding process is much faster and effective where string lines are used to create a 1-m-wide channel across the sowings. You can then focus on what is in front of you, and motivation is boosted as you can really see what you have achieved. Where jute erosion matting is used, it has the advantage of automatically creating these corridors (1.2 m wide). Where weeding is undertaken on a sunny day in summer, small weed seedlings can just be left to dry out and die on the soil surface. Damage to the desired seedlings is reduced if thick walking socks are pulled over workboots or soft-soled shoes are worn.

In 2004 I hand-weeded an 800-m^2 sowing of prairie species at the Sheffield Botanical Gardens to maintain it essentially weed free for the first growing season. This took me a total of 15 hours, spread over about five weeding visits of about 3 hours each. This sowing was done on a sand mulch, and it represented the lower to middle end of the weediness spectrum. Tom Stuart-Smith's prairie garden (see case study) involved at least double this amount of weeding due to mass worm casting (perhaps encouraged by a heavy soil and possible overirrigation) containing creeping buttercup and other weeds. This prairie is now a paragon. Getting on top of the problem in the first year is good value, although it may not seem like this at the time. Try to avoid uprooting large amounts of sowing mulch when weeding; with larger weeds, pushing down onto the sowing mulch with one hand while pulling up with the other reduces the unintentional uprooting of adjacent desired species.

If there is insufficient time to remove all weeds, a more strategic approach can be used to remove weeds that will be most detrimental in future months and years. A ranking based on greatest future risk needs to factor in the nature of the vegetation and how it might be managed. In general, however, the species that are most problematic in the longer term are perennial clump-forming or rhizomatous grasses and their nongrassy equivalents, such as nettles, docks, bindweeds, and creeping thistles. All of these species ultimately form patches from which the sown species are gradually extirpated, leading to the collapse of the visual content in the vegetation. Clovers and creeping buttercup are also bad, but because they are shorter they do not eliminate all of the sown species.

Unless the sowing mulch is insufficiently deep or heavily contaminated by seed rain from these species prior to spreading, these weeds tend to be less common initially. Hence, their removal is extremely good value in terms of the long-term benefits obtained from the limited inputs. Most of the species that are likely to be most numerous initially are annuals (ruderals) that will disappear after a couple of years in vegetation that is closed for much of the year. Such species may, however, persist in low vegetation that is relatively open, as in steppe-type sowings, particularly from late autumn to spring.

Sown species management

As with weed management, removal of excess sown species is also worth considering in the first growing season. It is rarely possible to micro-manage overall composition in sown meadow-like vegetation, except when these are relatively small in scale. Removals are therefore most likely going to involve species which are sown at low densities, normally because they are large plants with the potential to be competitively dominant. The reason for including these plants in the first place is generally to provide very occasional large emergents. If the actual seedling emergence rates are higher in practice than allowed for in the seed mix calculations, the excess seedlings of these species will need to be removed. This is best done in the first year, especially with species with very deep roots that are difficult to remove or kill. Classic examples of this are *Silphium laciniatum* and *Silphium terebinthinaceum*, which in flower reach more than 3 m and have deeply questing tap roots. Removal of these by hand is entirely feasible in the first year, but requires herbicides and other complications from the second year on.

Sometimes it is not possible to visually conceptualize densities until later in the summer of the first year. Even then, sometimes it is desirable to only remove half the anticipated surplus, as an insurance policy against unforeseen circumstances in the second year.

Boosting growth in the first year

The quicker the canopy fuses together in the first year, the more weed invasion from outside is reduced. It just becomes much more difficult for invaders to establish because of the shade at soil level. Hence, there is often a desire to speed up canopy closure where it seems to be proceeding too slowly. This can be achieved via two routes.

The first route is to extend irrigation (during dry periods) beyond the normal early-summer cut-off, as by this time germination from winter sowings is normally pretty much completed. This extended irrigation is most effective when undertaken at weekly intervals rather than every few days, as the latter tends to exacerbate weed colonization by maintaining a constantly wet surface.

The second approach is to apply nutrients. Since most normal soils (that is, those that are not industrial spoil-demolished building substrates) are generally more productive than required for meadows, using fertilizers to boost growth is normally an ultimately self-defeating strategy to be avoided at all costs. The exception to this is when there is clear evidence that the soil underlying the sowing mulches has been heavily compacted by the process of trucking in and spreading these mulches. Compaction normally manifests itself as patches of very slowly growing, stunted seedlings surrounded by areas of seedlings (in non-compacted soils) seemingly growing at normal rates.

Conversely there are other situations where the soils used have been manufactured from sand and various crushed building materials, such as concrete and brick, and often mixed with organic debris. These materials usually have good physical properties—and with concrete and crushed brick quite high phosphorus and potassium contents—but they are chronically short of nitrogen. Even plants of very low nutrient habitats grow incredibly slowly in these, giving the often-false perception of failure, and hence it is often politically important to accelerate growth.

With both compaction and nutrient deficiency, the best way to accelerate growth is to apply a nitrogen-only fertilizer, such as nitro chalk, a granular fertilizer used for cereal crops with the same nitrogen content (33 per cent) as ammonium nitrate but without the capacity of the latter to be turned into an explosive. In many countries, one's ability to purchase ammonium nitrate is restricted for this reason. The greatest advantage of these nitrogen-only fertilizers is they boost growth immediately after application, but contribute relatively little to the long-term fertility of the soil. The nitrogen they contain is either absorbed by roots of the plants or leached out of the profile in drainage water. They do not compromise the future by permanently increasing soil productivity, leading to increasing pressure from weedy species.

An alternative is to use hoof and horn meal or dried blood, but while these fertilizers are more sustainable energy wise, they are also much more expensive per unit area, so are problematic on a really large scale. You can use legumes to supply nitrogen as part of the seed mix, but these are often extremely aggressive and unpredictable when used on soils with moderate phosphorus levels but little nitrogen. I gave in to this conventional wisdom when co-designing the native meadow mixes at the Queen Elizabeth Olympic Park in London. It was soon apparent, however, that we had created a monster through my foolish decision, as the legumes began to eliminate everything else, requiring extensive cutting and nitrogen application to maintain some competitive balance between legumes and other plants in the mix.

LONG-TERM MANAGEMENT

Most sown communities will have fused or almost fused together to produce a sward of foliage by the end of the first year. Competition for light increases week by week in this first year as each seedling gets larger. Although it is rarely visually evident, many late-emerging seedlings of slower growing species will already have been eliminated by the end of the first year.

Sowings have an entirely different dynamic in the second year. The sugars and starches accumulated from the first year's growth and stored over winter are available in spring, and the size of the individual plants increases exponentially. What looked at the end of the first year as very immature vegetation now looks as if it has been in situ for years. This dramatic increase in the size of the component plants has both positive and negative effects, and the role of management is to try to balance these as best as possible in the second and subsequent years.

General principles behind the management of sown communities

The critical issue in long-term management is whether you do or don't have a vision for what you want the vegetation to become. If you don't have a vision and broadly speaking are perfectly happy for it to become what it wants to become, management is simplified to standard, generic, repetitive activities. The manager becomes largely a functionary. This is what happens in many public landscape sites, where because of a lack of skills, time, ambition, understanding, or resources (or all five) naturalistic vegetation is just allowed to do its thing. In one sense, this is a very elegant management philosophy in

Sown naturalistic herbaceous vegetation has a very complex structure. Where are the weeds here? Are there any? Are there too many? Getting your head around these issues of conceptualization can be challenging.

that fewer resources are required. The problem with this philosophy is when the users of the landscape in question have a much more defined set of expectations that then leads to conflict. In little-visited rural landscapes and in habitat restoration schemes, minimal input management is generally more tenable.

The process of managing vegetation effectively involves looking at it carefully month by month and trying to conceptualize what is happening, what is declining, what is increasing, and what is invading. The process involves looking and then processing in your head what is going on, with frequent back-check comparisons with the year before to try to confirm the pattern of what appears to be happening is real. This is always quite a challenging process, as sometimes it is hard to perceive clear patterns, due to either insufficient familiarity or because you can't remember whether similar things happened the previous year and hence might be normal.

With naturalistic vegetation this process is more challenging because what you are looking at is, compared to, for example, block planting of herbaceous plants, much more complex in space and time. To the uninitiated, this vegetation—especially before it flowers and becomes defined at least by colour—just looks like a random sort of minestrone soup. You can, however, train your optical system and brain to be more critical of these chaotic scenes, to filter out the distractions. This happens both through experience and through using tools like taking photos from the same location every couple of weeks, so you have a record and can compare how the patterns change in space and time. To make sense of these patterns, however, you do need to have some framework for what is acceptable to you, and this involves setting notional densities for individual species and the community as a whole.

In most urban situations it is generally a good idea to construct at least a framework vision for action. If you are not able to construct such a vision it will be very difficult, if not impossible, for you to manage naturalistic vegetation effectively. Such a framework needs to specify essentially a series of red lines, thresholds for action including the level of invasion of unsown species that is tolerable, the density of sown species that is tolerable, and the acceptable density of a particular species.

The level of invasion of unsown species that is tolerable

In a garden situation, you might be able to tolerate no more than 10 per cent of the standing biomass being composed of weeds, whereas in a large-scale public site this might be as high as 50 per cent. One thing to be aware of in making these judgements is the notion of the tipping point. As sown or planted vegetation gradually accrues weeds, it often gets to a point beyond which decline of the surviving sown or planted vegetation becomes very rapid. Sometimes this is because once a threshold amount of weed biomass is exceeded the remaining sown species are placed under untenable levels of competition. In other cases it is because as the weedy vegetation (and in particular grasses) increases, there is a major increase in the number of slugs per square metre and damage to palatable species, most of which will be sown. This combination of increasing competition with weedy species and being grazed is very damaging. It's necessary to be vigilant to try to assess whether a sowing or planting is stable or at or approaching these tipping points. The problem with tipping points is that they are most obvious retrospectively and therefore require managers to try to project forward what is likely to happen next year in the absence of action this year.

The density of sown species that is tolerable

In most sowings and plantings, sooner or later a dominant or a few dominant species emerge, plants that are well fitted to the site conditions and do well. Because competition between plants in communities is a relative process, these species need not be highly vigorous or aggressive to establish dominance. They often just need to have a slightly greater growth rate or foliage height. Sometimes they are just slightly less palatable to herbivores. If you sow a range of candelabra *Primula* species in wet locales such as northern Britain, the dominant species is normally *Primula pulverulenta*. This is hardly an aggressive plant, but in the relative context of the other *Primula* species it just has the edge, and hence it dominates.

The prairie-steppe vegetation we created at RHS Garden Wisley in 2007 (see case study) reached its zenith of visual drama in summer 2011, with very high densities of flowering in *Echinacea pallida*. The summer of 2012 was very wet, and the asters growing with the echinacea grew taller than normal, shading the basal foliage of the echinacea. This foliage was more heavily defoliated by the larger slug population. I didn't visit this planting in 2012, but by spring 2013 it was evident that the *Echinacea* population had crashed. I don't think any of this was evident to the garden staff at Wisley at that time. In this case, the tipping point was precipitated by the over successful growth of the sown neighbours, not invading weeds.

The acceptable density of a particular species

To some degree you have to be a little philosophical about what is an acceptable density of any particular species. When you establish, say, thirty species as part of a community, it is almost inevitable that you will find that at least 25 per cent of these will subsequently prove to be unfit for the site and will either rapidly (often due to slug predation) or slowly (competition plus poor fit with soils and climate) disappear. If like King Canute you try to stop the tide of water or the change in species complements, you will either be disappointed or have to use lots of resources to try and halt the decline of a species, often unsuccessfully.

One of the reasons why traditional horticultural planting tends to be very labour intensive is because we try to protect and prop up species that are clearly not well suited to the site. In an ecological mode of thinking, decline of some species is just normal. Think of it in a positive sense, it is freeing up spaces for other species to develop in. It can, of course, be very irritating if the species that decline are the ones that you really need to deliver on your aesthetic purpose or some functional role such as feeding a particular invertebrate. Even when you are fully aware of the inevitability of the decline of some species, it is also useful, while operating within this ecological realization, to have notional and lower and upper limits which trip management actions, or at least consideration of action. If, for example, you have lots of rosette-forming forbs in a grassy meadow, their numbers will tend to decline over time just because they are subject to too much shade in summer as the vegetation becomes taller. This decline can often be halted or even reversed by changing the cutting time from, say, September to early July. This reduces the duration of shading of the rosette-forming species by taller species, leading to lower mortality. In some cases management action will not be appropriate, perhaps because the decline of a species is due to factors beyond your control, for example, because it is short lived or highly palatable to slugs and snails.

Targeting weeds at the critical developmental stages to maximize long-term control

In horticultural plantings, there is a tendency to play down the implications of the developmental stages weeds are at before removing them. For example, are the weeds about to liberate their seed or are they months away from this? In these types of plantings there is often a human rather than ecologically oriented timescale for management action. In naturalistic plantings ecologically oriented timescales are much more important, as using the same energy to remove weeds at a stage when they are most vulnerable to extinction from the site is much more effective in achieving positive change. Ideally you want to try to break the cycle that leads to the next generation of weed seedlings or the increase in biomass of vegetative weeds. A classic example might involve removing the seed heads of biennials such as Canadian fleabane (*Erigeron canadensis*), a common invader of forb-dominated herbaceous plantings in late summer, before it has started to release its seeds. If you leave it a few weeks, the seeds have been dispersed into your plantings, and you will have to then contend with thousands of new seedlings for next year. Going backwards is a very poor management trajectory.

With perennial weeds, the optimal time for control is often from winter to early spring when the plant community is likely to be at its most open and hence access to the perennial weeds is easiest. With weeds that are winter dormant, this activity has to wait until spring and the emergence of the new foliage. Whether control is achieved by spot painting the foliage of weeds such as docks with glyphosate-containing herbicides or attempting to physically remove as much of the roots as possible, doing this in spring means that any regrowth from the weeds will have to compete with the closing, shade-generating canopy of the sown or planted species, thus reducing the regrowth and reproductive capacity of the weeds.

The effect of community type on subsequent management

The specific management requirements of naturalistic herbaceous plant communities depend heavily on the nature of those communities. In temperate climates, most herbaceous vegetation types generally grow from spring to autumn with a period of dormancy or quiescence imposed by low temperature in winter. In Mediterranean climates in which the mean winter temperature normally exceeds 5°C, the window of growth is more typically autumn to late spring, with dormancy or quiescence from mid summer to autumn. These patterns are shown in the chart in relation to the months in which weed colonization from seed is most likely to occur in Western European maritime climates. The window for this to occur is often shorter in continental climates (such as the north-eastern United States or central Europe), restricted further due to the lower winter temperatures. This lack of need for management in winter is an advantage of these colder climates.

Typical main growth periods of designed herbaceous plant communities in Western European maritime climates in relation to the key windows for weed seed germination and establishment

CLIMATE REGION	COMMUNITY TYPE	MAIN MANAGEMENT TECHNIQUES	JAN	FEB	MAR	APR	MAY	JUN	JUL	AUG	SEP	OCT	NOV	DEC
Temperate	**Forb dominated**													
	Prairie-like	cut and remove or burn in spring												
	Steppe-like	cut and remove or burn in spring												
	Woodland understorey-like	cut and remove in autumn or winter												
	Grass dominated													
	Meadow-like	cut and remove in summer												
	Prairie-like	cut and remove or burn in spring												
	Steppe-like	cut and remove or burn in spring												
Mediterranean	**Forb dominated**													
	Steppe-like	cut and remove or burn in late summer or autumn												
	Geophyte dominated													
	Steppe-like	cut and remove or burn in late summer or autumn												

 main period of active growth

 main period of likely weed invasion

The chart provides a general picture of how weed invasion from seed is most likely to take place in response to the climatic patterns of the region, and in particular when the soil is moist enough and warm enough for germination to take place. It also hints at how some plant communities might be more invasible than others, because of the nature of the plants present and the resulting overall structure. The grass-dominated temperate communities have the shortest period of likely weed establishment, because in these the persistent green foliage or persistent overwintering dead foliage limits weed seedling establishment. In contrast, forb-only communities are more invasible simply because most species do not typically retain leaves over the period favourable for weed establishment; there is a large window of opportunity for weeds to germinate and establish during these periods.

Forb-dominated vegetation

Although forb-dominated vegetation can potentially be quite varied, when established from seed or seed and planting it is likely to be similar to a prairie or steppe community stereotype. Most of the species in these communities are winter deciduous. Hence, in mild winter climates there is physical space and light at soil level for winter- and spring-germinating weeds to establish. These problems can be reduced by adding more grasses or other forbs with evergreen winter foliage or persistent dead foliage to the community. The presence of grasses, and particularly tall grasses, however, has a negative effect on the capacity to maintain a high density and diversity of forb species which are often critical in delivering dramatic flowering displays and also pollen and nectar for pollinators. As a result of this fundamental ecological conflict, in many urban situations forb-rich communities, while inherently vulnerable to invasion, are still a highly attractive option.

Prairie-like vegetation

The key management activities in plantings composed of true prairie species in maritime Western Europe and equivalent climates in north-western North America are preventing weed invasion between winter and spring. Several plant selection strategies can influence this, some of which are available at the design stage, for example, by selecting long-persistent species with dense basal foliage to close down gaps, plus species with good self-seeding capacity.

Management of prairie vegetation relies on restricting the access of light to the soil surface for as long as possible during the growing and dormant seasons. Factors that contribute positively to this are fostering high plant density, leaving the canopy of the plants in situ for as long as possible, and allowing the dead stems to trap autumn leaf litter. The dead stems can then be cut off and removed in spring. This restricts light availability for existing or newly germinated weed seedlings prior to the re-emergence of the prairie plant canopy, after which many of these weed seedlings will be killed by shading. If the

Meadow vegetation is cut down with a brushcutter-mounted hedge trimming blade.

Flash burning was performed over the prairie at the Sheffield Botanical Gardens immediately after cutting the vegetation and removing it from the site in March. When done on a dry day there is very little smoke. Burning vegetation strikes a cord with many people, perhaps as some cultural throwback to the time when humans regularly relied on fire to manage the landscape around us.

canopy is removed in autumn or winter, especially in maritime climates, the weeds are much larger by the time of prairie growth recommencement and are not so effectively suppressed by the emerging canopy. In continental climates, winter weed establishment and growth in prairie-like vegetation is much reduced or nonexistent.

For cutting down dead prairie plant stems to 20–50 mm above ground level in spring, the best tool is generally a reciprocating hedge trimmer mounted at 45° on a brushcutter frame. Heavy-duty cord strimmers or steel brush cutter blades are also satisfactory. The cut material is then raked up and removed from the site.

This approach to management has to be amended if spring-flowering geophytes are planted in prairie-like vegetation. Geophytes such as dwarf *Narcissus* and *Crocus* add another season of interest, but there is a cost. This requires cutting the vegetation down in mid winter to allow bulb foliage to emerge into the light, but before it is so well developed that it will be either cut off or damaged by trampling during the cutting process. In large-scale sowings with limited management capacity the bulbs are best left out, especially in maritime climates where winter weed invasion is potentially a significant problem. Another option is to use non-geophyte, spring-flowering forbs that come into growth just slightly earlier than the main wave of prairie forbs. In Britain, *Pulsatilla vulgaris* has proved to be surprisingly successful in this role in relatively open prairie communities, as has *Dodecatheon meadia* (see RHS Garden Wisley prairie-steppe case study). *Ranunculus gramineus* and *Incarvillea zhongdianensis* also seem to have potential in this May-flowering role, but probably only on relatively unproductive soils.

Large, very obvious weeds can be tackled immediately before cutting down, although smaller weeds will often be hidden. Control of new weed seedlings is further maximized if after the stems are cut down in early spring the surface of the sowing mulch is flash burnt using a triple-head burner, fuelled by propane or a biofuel. At this time of the year there are many weeds in growth or coming into growth, but the prairie forbs and grasses are generally still dormant, giving an opportunity to apply differential management pressure to the weeds. Triple-head burners are intended for use by contractors who need to soften tarmac in the course of small-scale road repairs. The three burner heads are mounted across a T-bar lance and when held approximately 300 mm above the soil surface provide temperatures of approximately 500°C at the soil surface.

This cutting-and-burning approach is most likely to be used on a large scale in public landscapes, where physical removal of small weeds is simply not resourceable. Flash burning is relatively quick to do, and it boils the water in the leaves of weed seedlings. If done more slowly, it carbonizes the leaves and stems. Annual weeds are killed by this treatment, as are some biennials and very small perennials. The degree of damage to both desired and undesired vegetation and the consumption of fuel depend on how slowly or quickly the lance is moved across each square metre. When it is moved slowly, heat conductance through the aboveground tissues of plants into the stem-root interface is greater, as is the chance of killing short-lived perennials such as many weedy *Epilobium* hybrids. Established perennial weeds that are in leaf are merely defoliated, but this checking of growth of perennial weeds appears to favour the dominance of the prairie species which are not defoliated.

A research study into the effect of spring burning on persistence and weediness of designed prairie vegetation in Berlin found this practice made no difference compared to just cutting down and removal. This is not the case in more maritime climates, such as the United Kingdom, where in contrast to the situation in central or Eastern Europe weeds grow throughout the winter and hence are abundant and highly competitive when the prairie species emerge in April. Most of these weeds are cool-season species; if not checked, they have a major competitive advantage over the more warmth-demanding prairie species. Perennial weeds that cannot be controlled by burning (such as docks, creeping buttercup, and creeping thistle) resprout very quickly post burning—normally within 7 days—and are easily seen against the blackened sowing mulch surface. This helps in making them really stand out so their removal can be prioritized (where this is sensible to try) or they can be painted with a glyphosate gel where physical removal is ineffective or just plain impossible (for example, creeping thistle, docks, couch grass, and bindweed).

Flash burning sounds very radical and dramatic until you see it in practice. If done on a dry windless day in early spring, no one will be aware of it until they are a couple of metres away from the burning. There is little if any smoke, and on a sunny day the flames are almost invisible. Invertebrates overwintering on the dead stems are removed to composting with the cut vegetation beforehand and are not burnt.

An alternative to flash burning is to substitute overspraying with an organic herbicide in which the active ingredient is concentrated vinegar (acetic acid). This herbicide is registered for use in public landscapes in many European countries. It has very similar defoliant effects to burning, but with no effect on tissues that are not in direct contact with the spray. It cannot kill most perennial species and is probably less effective on short-lived ruderal perennials such as hybrid *Epilobium* than burning, but it is much cheaper and more energy efficient.

Engaging in these additional weed control techniques is only justified where there is good evidence that additional levels of control are necessary. Where the density of the sown and planted vegetation is high and weed control through the initial establishment period was good, this may not be required. This has largely been true in the Sheffield Botanical Gardens' prairie (see case study).

By late spring, in most cases the canopy of the prairie will have fused together. Little additional management is now possible due to the closed nature of the vegetation, other than to occasionally pull out any weeds that punch through the prairie foliage layer.

If you want to manipulate the composition of the prairie vegetation by adding species, a good time to do this is in the winter-dormant period, from immediately after leaf fall to cutting down, as you can now see where there are gaps. It is, however, often difficult to successfully establish new plants into these established plant communities, such is the intensity of competition. Where you wish to remove excess plants of some species, the easiest way to do this is often to paint the emerging leaves of the plants scheduled for termination with a glyphosate gel. There is always something of a risk of collateral damage with this technique, as where organic matter or clay is absent from the sowing mulch (as with sand) glyphosate can be absorbed directly by the roots of adjacent species.

A critical idea in prairie-like and all other naturalistic vegetation types is that removal of excess desired plants or weeds should proceed at the rate at which the surrounding prairie species can close the gaps that will be created. If you create large gaps, these soon become islands of the weedy species you were trying to get rid of. This is where horticulturally inspired ideas of going back to a cultivated weed-free surface just don't work in dynamic systems with limited management inputs.

Steppe-like vegetation

Although steppe-like vegetation is typically shorter than prairie-like vegetation and hence more invasible by weeds, the fact that more of the species have overwintering, evergreen, or near-evergreen foliage helps compensate for this to some degree. Many steppe species also come into growth earlier than is the norm with prairie-like vegetation, hence contributing to earlier gap closure. The archetypal image of steppe as a design metaphor is of a short, rather open vegetation of the type historically favoured in German planting design. In actual steppe habitats, however, the openness of the community is a function of rainfall and soil fertility. Steppe in central Eastern Europe growing on good soils can be quite dense and tall, in essence prairie-like, while on much drier, less-fertile soils it is much more open (the archetypal steppe of the German Hansen School).

The management of steppe also varies considerably. Agricultural steppe remnants in eastern Austria, for example, are often burnt in spring to improve the palatability to domestic grazing animals, whereas much less productive steppes are normally managed by low-intensity grazing.

Many steppe species have some degree of fire tolerance, but in a competitive situation it seems reasonable to assume that evergreen species may be disadvantaged by flash burning relative to winter-deciduous species. In the prairie-steppe sowing at RHS Garden Wisley (see case study), the evergreen *Dianthus carthusianorum* survives annual spring

Despite nearly the same species being present in this community, on sloping hillsides with deeper soils, a tall, almost closed, prairie-like vegetation develops.

Forbs that grow actively from late winter, as in the case of *Primula elatior*, are effective at reducing the development of winter weed seedlings.

burning and continues to be able to compete with its neighbours on the edges of the sowing. Where more heavily shaded by taller prairie species in the middle of the sowing, this species has largely disappeared. In mountain steppe in western North America, many species of *Penstemon* appear to be severely damaged in fires. Most herbaceous *Penstemon* species have near-woody short horizontal stems at or just below the surface that are likely to be killed by intense fire, and particularly so when this is projected downwards from a triple-head burner. *Penstemon barbatus* and *Penstemon cobaea* (a more properly herbaceous *Penstemon* species) have survived repeated spring burnings in my designed vegetation sites in the United Kingdom.

The most problematic plants in steppe sowings in relation to spring burning are geophytes, as these are nearly all in growth and even flowering at that time. In large-scale designed steppe, unless management resources are abundant, geophytes are probably best left out (as in the case of prairie), as their presence potentially restricts the management of the core species. In small-scale sowings where hand weeding can be used, geophytes are a very attractive addition.

In general, the management approaches listed under prairie—a combination of cutting and removal in spring with or without burning—are also appropriate for many summer-growing steppe-like communities.

Woodland understorey

Although grasses and sedges are significant components of some shaded subcanopy habitats, these plants will often be reduced in designed woodland understorey vegetation. These communities tend to be dominated by relatively low growing sheet- or

The same can be achieved by summer-growing highly shade tolerant species that are winter evergreen or retain their dead foliage over winter, such as this sedge on a woodland edge in Liaoning Province, north-eastern China.

rosette-forming forbs, many of which are evergreen or semi-evergreen. Those species that do go dormant or quiescent tend to do so in summer in response to very low light levels and high moisture stress due to the removal of soil water by the roots of the woody over-storey. These two factors also restrict weed establishment in these communities during the summer. At times of the year when soil moisture and light levels are more favourable to invasion, the canopies of these understorey species is more closed in semi-natural communities. As with steppe communities, this and the greater degree of evergreenness discourage weed invasion despite the relatively shallow canopy depth of the understorey species.

In terms of recurrent management, woodland understoreys generally need very little management beyond cutting down and raking off senescent and untidy foliage, normally in autumn. The overall aim is to keep the canopy closed for as long as possible. Some understorey species have one-off management needs, which sometimes may have to be sacrificed for the greater good. With evergreen *Epimedium*, for example, cutting the foliage off a few weeks before the flowers appear in mid spring increases the visual drama, most probably without materially increasing weed invasion, but as this is the time when most understorey species are flowering this task may simply be untenable in large-scale mixed sowings and plantings.

In addition to the use of shade-tolerant woodland species under trees and shrubs, these species can also be used to form an understorey under tall summer- to autumn-flowering herbaceous plants: a sort of herbaceous woodland. From a management perspective, these two communities complement one another. The woodland understorey, which largely grows in late winter to early summer, keeps the gaps beneath the summer-flowering species essentially closed until the latter come into growth in mid spring, leading to a

Where have the grasses gone in early spring in the Italian Alps? The green is the foliage of bulbs and emerging forbs, not grasses.

two-layer system that once established is highly resistant to weed invasion. The taller species are cut back to 100 mm in early winter and this material removed from the site to increase light and allow the woodland understorey species light and space to emerge into. This cutting and removal is also beneficial to seedling regeneration within the community (both desired and weedy species). If low-growing woodland understorey species such as *Primula elatior* and *Primula vulgaris* are chosen, there is little need for management beyond the early-winter cut down and removal from the site. Bulbous species are fine in these systems, as the cutting to the ground will have taken place before most geophytes have started to emerge from the soil.

Grass-dominated vegetation

In typical lowland meadow vegetation, at least 50 per cent of the biomass is generally composed of grasses.

Meadow-like vegetation

In the most forb-rich meadows, such as those found in alpine regions where low soil productivity plus almost 6 months of shading from deep snow pack disadvantages grasses, the biomass of grasses may be less than 10 per cent.. Conversely, in typical temperate productive lowland meadows in Western Europe, grass frequently comprises more than 90 per cent of the biomass. In the areas of the world ideal for the growth of cool-season (C3) grasses, grass biomass is always much greater than that of forbs, except where productivity is reduced through management. This includes the introduction of hemi-parasites such as *Rhinanthus* through oversowing. In these meadows, grasses are often present at very high densities, perhaps more than 500 plants/m². This imposes substantial competition on both would-be invading weeds and the sown forb species that have to coexist with the grasses. This often leads to loss of forb diversity or, at the very least, forb density.

Contrast this to the situation where the forbs and geophytes, like this *Colchicum bulbocodium*, have to emerge into a dense sward of meadow grasses.

Most of the management strategies for grass-dominated meadow-like vegetation involve some form of cutting and removal of the biomass, often during the growing season. This is designed to impose stress on the community, and in particular to check the growth of potential competitive dominants (such as grasses), as well as to create temporary canopy gaps to allow the regeneration of species from within the community from seed. The sudden removal through cutting of many of the carbohydrates present in each plant and the means of producing replacement carbohydrates at the peak of photosynthesis restricts the height of the meadow, and in doing so helps restrict the elimination of the forbs in the system through competition for light.

This same process inhibits the growth of weeds with tall leafy stems such as nettles, which often invade herbaceous vegetation. Soil productivity plays an important role in these processes. As productivity increases, the effectiveness of cutting as a weed control technique decreases, and it becomes increasingly difficult to retain slowly growing small species unless they are highly shade tolerant and unpalatable.

Grass-dominated summer-cut meadows are a neat system for low-input herbaceous vegetation. The management challenge is keeping sufficient forb diversity and density for them to be interesting to ordinary members of the public and to provide nectar and pollen to invertebrates.

The standard agricultural hay meadow management prescription in Europe is generally to cut in the first half of July. This cutting regime is ancient in origin and evolved in agricultural societies to maximize production of hay. It's purely chance that it also tends to increase total species diversity because this regime favours smaller species that are intolerant of being shaded by taller plants. The effect of various cutting regime options on meadow forbs are shown in the table.

Effect of cutting time on key aspects of grass-dominated meadows

EFFECT	CUT AND REMOVE IN LATE SPRING AND CUT AND REMOVE IN EARLY AUTUMN	CUT AND REMOVE IN MID SUMMER	CUT AND REMOVE IN EARLY AUTUMN
Impact on taller grasses and leafy-stem forbs (such as *Malva moschata*)	decrease or stay the same	decrease	increase
Impact on rosette-forming forbs and sheets (such as *Scabiosa columbaria*)	increase but not *Primula veris* due to seed removal	increase	decrease
Impact on tidiness (amount of standing biomass in summer)	increase	increase	decrease
Impact on management cost	increase	stays the same (standard baseline treatment)	stays the same

As the information in the table suggests, potentially the most attractive option is the dual cut in late spring and early autumn. This approach arose out of research we undertook at the Queen Elizabeth Olympic Park in London to work out how to delay flowering of native wildflower meadows that would normally peak in the middle of June to the opening day of the games on July 28. We found that cutting in early May achieved this for many of the species present. By pushing the flowering peak back into July, providing there was sufficient rain after May, we were able to delay the onset of the post-flowering senescence until late August. This dual cut reduces conflict in highly urban areas with human expectations that meadows should be attractive during the holiday season when urban greenspace is most used.

This process also extends the window of opportunity for native invertebrates into a time when most meadows are not flowering. Because May cutting prevents seed production in important native European meadow species such as cowslips (*Primula veris*) and potentially meadow buttercup (*Ranunculus acris*), it is necessary to alternate a July cut in the management regime every 3–4 years to ensure that populations of these forbs are sufficiently well retained.

WINTER SURFACE SCARIFICATION

There is anecdotal evidence that meadows subject to severe disturbance during the winter months have lower grass dominance and higher forb density and diversity. This disturbance comes about in semi-natural meadows by two main routes: animal grazing and mechanical damage to the surface by the hooves of these animals, as well as deep snow cover shading the underlying vegetation and greatly reducing vigour of the more vigorous grasses (most of which are winter evergreen and shade sensitive). In urban meadows,

Rhinanthus is the visual dominant in
mid-altitude meadows in the European
Alps.

practices which deliberately abrade the surface in winter are an interesting possibility, using, for example, tractor-mounted flailing of the surface during the winter months. I know of no deliberate attempts to try this in practice, but it is an intriguing possibility that it could help in the creation of some really special meadows.

INTRODUCTION OF NEW SPECIES

In general, it is very difficult to change the composition of heavily grass dominated urban wildflower meadows quickly. This process is ongoing naturally whenever there is seed rain into urban meadows from outside, but it is a very slow process. The two groups of plants that might be established as part of long-term management strategy are hemi-parasites and desirable forbs absent from the meadow.

Depending where you live in the world, hemi-parasites mainly involve species of *Castilleja*, *Pedicularis*, and *Rhinanthus*. The last genus is the least interesting visually but the most powerful biologically, in that when these plants attach onto the roots of their meadow neighbours, they appropriate their carbohydrates and use them to produce *Rhinanthus* biomass. This utilization process is not very efficient in energy terms, so the net effect is to produce less meadow biomass in total than were the hemi-parasites absent.

ESTABLISHMENT AND MANAGEMENT

The world centre of diversity for *Pedicularis* is western China. This is the 450-mm-tall *Pedicularis davidii*.

Pedicularis semitorta is another native of western China.

Castilleja integra has proved amenable in my work in the United Kingdom, here growing in research tubs of *Festuca ovina*.

Rhinanthus therefore potentially leads to dramatic reductions in the productivity of meadows. Although the widespread belief is that *Rhinanthus* selectively targets grasses, this is not the case. *Rhinanthus* tends to parasitize the most common plants because they are the species most likely to be, purely by chance, growing adjacent to each *Rhinanthus* seedling. These are often grasses but, if preference is involved, it is more likely to be for nitrogen-rich legumes, such as clovers. All in all, what this means is that if the dominant plant in a meadow is ox-eye daisy it will be debilitated by the introduction of *Rhinanthus*. If grasses are dominant, they will be reduced and so on. Hence, in the short term the introduction of *Rhinanthus* is a little bit like Russian roulette. In the longer term, these issues seem to sort themselves out in semi-natural situations where there is ongoing seed rain of desirable species from outside. In urban situations, however, this doesn't normally happen, so heavily preferred species may go extinct in the absence of seed rain from outside. Most high-quality European natural grasslands contain *Rhinanthus*, but that's not the same as being able to say they are species rich because of the *Rhinanthus*.

Rhinanthus is an annual with a very long chilling requirement and really needs to be sown in early autumn to get good germination in late winter (it's very early to do this). Cut the meadow very close to the ground and scarify heavily post sowing. The seed is relatively expensive but it is probably a good investment; once its bridgehead is secure, it moves through the meadows in a wave.

The other genera of hemi-parasites are perennials and much more exciting visually, but the bad news is that they don't seem to reduce productivity of the meadows they grow in at all. At the scale of the home garden meadow, *Pedicularis* and *Castilleja* are fun to play with to create some amazing surprises in less-productive meadows.

Oversowing with seed of desirable species of other forbs is very slow to effect change in a meadow, as the chance of a seed producing a seedling that actually survives

Castilleja integra in the edges of prairie-like vegetation at Oxford Botanic Garden, with *Phlox pilosa* and *Penstemon strictus*.

to flowering in these competitive environments is very low. Nursery-grown meadow forbs in pots are probably better value, but even then it is hit and miss what establishes. Establishment is most difficult on highly productive soils with large grass biomasses. The forbs that do this best are plants with large biomass themselves, such as *Geranium* species; those with tall leafy stems, such as *Knautia*, *Centaurea*, and *Malva*; or highly shade tolerant evergreen rosettes that are not palatable to slugs, including *Primula veris* and *Succisa pratensis*. Planting short-lived species like ox-eye daisies is a bit of a waste of time and money.

Planting as 9-cm-diameter pots in late summer or early autumn is probably the optimal approach as evaporation is decreasing and the sward has recently been mown very short, so competition for light is reduced. Plugs typically have very high mortality in closed swards and are not recommended. Research on the factors affecting establishment suggests that creating a 150-mm-radius gap around each pot plant increases plant size in the first year, but once the gap closes after about 4 months there is no lasting benefit that inevitably leads to successful establishment. Species and individuals that are well fitted to the microsite into which they are planted establish, and those that are not eventually fade away. It's very much a case of what will be will be, so planting many individuals of lots of different species is a good strategy for eventually finding some winners. But don't expect it to be a quick process.

Prairie- and steppe-like vegetation

As in forb-dominated vegetation, most of the species in these communities are winter deciduous. In regions with little snow cover, this means there is sufficient light and space for weeds to germinate in winter and spring. Adding more grasses or forbs with evergreen winter foliage or persistent dead foliage to the community can help to alleviate these problems.

Practices such as spring burning on a regular basis tend to increase the dominance of warm-season (C4) grasses in these designed communities (most prairie grasses are C4 plants). The soil blackening raises the soil temperature post fire, and the window of time that normally exists between the emergence of the cool-season forbs and the warm-season grasses is shortened. Hence, forbs experience more competition, and their biomass as a percentage of the prairie declines. The overall picture is that the presence of grasses will make these communities less invasible but also less attractive in terms of flower impact. Burning should therefore be used only at intervals, perhaps every 3 to 4 years, with cutting and removal as an annual treatment.

Mediterranean vegetation

Mediterranean is used in this book to refer to areas of the world which have dry hot summers and mild wet winters. This includes, for example, southern Europe, California, western South Africa, Western Australia, and Chile. Much of the nonwoody vegetation of the Mediterranean regions is probably best described as steppe-like in that it is composed of relatively low, open communities of forbs, sub-shrubs (plants with a woody base from which annually resprout herbaceous shoots), and geophytes, with occasional grasses and in some systems large numbers of winter-growing annuals. The actual detail of the communities varies hugely depending on the Mediterranean region in question or where the species being used in this vegetation are drawn from. It is often possible to pick and mix species from very different Mediterranean regions that share broadly similar habitat requirements.

From a management perspective, the essential characteristics of Mediterranean vegetation is that it is relatively open due to exposure to lengthy periods of summer moisture stress. It is most open in summer and most closed in spring. This structure is fundamentally prone to invasion by weeds and other species, and thus it is no surprise that the most invaded semi-natural plant communities on Earth are mainly Mediterranean or near-Mediterranean.

When Mediterranean species are transposed to create new designed vegetation in areas which are less subject to extreme summer moisture stress, the species that can tolerate these new conditions produce a more closed vegetation that is easier to manage. For example, many high-altitude geophytes of the western Cape region in South Africa including *Aristea*, *Bulbinella*, and *Kniphofia* species, and particularly those of seasonally moist habitats, potentially form dense closed canopies in urban heat island microclimates in Britain and maritime Western Europe. With sensible plant selection, it is possible in these new habitats to close the canopy and increase manageability, but it is still necessary to deal with the different growth cycles compared to those of temperate vegetation, as shown in the chart of key windows for weed seed germination and establishment.

In actual Mediterranean climates, many species show a burst of growth after the first heavy rains of autumn and then enter a period of reduced growth or quiescence in winter, depending on how cold these are. This is followed by a final burst of growth and flowering in spring and then foliage senescence or complete loss in summer-deciduous species, although there are often significant numbers of species which are summer evergreen or semi-evergreen. This is the typical low-altitude pattern of growth.

At high altitudes in the Mediterranean regions, growth takes place in autumn but then there is often little or no growth in winter. In some species, growth does not resume until late spring with flowering pushed into summer. That is, the growth cycles begin to resemble those associated with temperate climates. This is precisely what has been demonstrated in our research in Sheffield on high-altitude Mediterranean flora.

The standard management approaches for these rather broad groups of species are generally to cut down and remove the previous year's growth before the recommencement of growth in late summer and autumn. Weeds are targeted in the window immediately after the cutting, potentially by using flash burning on a biennial or triennial basis where this is warranted and tolerated. This can only be done, however, when all or most of the species are tolerant of and able to reshoot post burning. The classic species that are almost universally tolerant of this are geophytes, both evergreen and summer deciduous,

Sown and planted mixtures of *Bulbinella latifolia*, *Watsonia borbonica*, and autumn- to early-summer-growing *Kniphofia sarmentosa* form a dense weed-suppressing community in spring.

Weeds are also suppressed in September, as *Kniphofia* returns into full growth. (Ye Hang's Ph.D. research, Department of Landscape, University of Sheffield)

followed by perennial forbs, which often show high tolerance (for example, *Gazania* and *Corymbium* in the South African flora). Shrubs and sub-shrubs are much more varied in their response to fire. Most species are reseeders—they are killed by fire and then regenerate from liberated seed—but this is very unreliable in weedy urban contexts.

The remainder of Mediterranean species resprout from dormant or newly initiated buds on the roots, basal stem regions, or in species that form these, an underground swelling known as a lignotuber. Some species that behave as reseeders when burnt are able to resprout passably well when instead managed by coppicing or severe pruning; the sub-shrubby *Scabiosa africana* is one such species that behaves in this way. The least tolerant of burning as a management strategy are often succulents and especially woody species, although some of these can resprout. The advantages of burning as a management strategy (other than it kills annual weeds) is that it promotes abundant flowering in some Mediterranean geophytes, particularly some species from south-western South Africa, which otherwise may only flower sporadically in cultivation.

One of the key difficulties in managing designed Mediterranean vegetation in urban contexts is how to deal with species which have large amounts of foliage that is potentially extremely unattractive during the summer senescence phase. The most problematic of these species are those native to moist productive sites that allow for the production of tall leafy foliage prior to flowering, including the larger *Bulbinella* species (such as *B. latifolia* and *B. elata*), *Kniphofia sarmentosa*, *Kniphofia uvaria*, and summer-dormant *Watsonia* (*W. borbonica*, *W. stokoei*). Of course, this visual post-flowering decline can be managed by selective removal of senescent leaves when resources permit, but this is not possible in many situations.

One option is to mix these species with summer leafy species from other parts of the world that are effective at screening the declining foliage prior to cutting to the ground in late summer. The advantages of these screening species is that they are amenable to being cut down to the ground at this time and are then capable of reshooting in autumn. One grass that fits this bill and would be ideal with the previously mentioned species of wet sites is tufted hairgrass, *Deschampsia cespitosa*. The international turf grass company Barenbrug sells seed of a variety of this tussock grass as 'Barcampsia' that they developed as a turf grass for moist shaded environments. This variety establishes very easily from field sowing.

Another strategy is to build communities dominated by species with evergreen foliage that has an acceptable appearance in summer or is even attractive (such as *Aristea inaequalis*) to provide a structure which houses species that show some summer decline. Mediterranean species from drier habitats generally have less messy or at least less voluminous foliage and in some cases more permanently evergreen foliage. In the South African Mediterranean flora, this is the case with *Agapanthus africanus*, *Agapanthus praecox*, *Aristea*, *Dilatris*, *Lanaria*, and some dwarf restios.

CASE STUDIES
OF SOWN PRAIRIES,
MEADOWS, AND
STEPPE

Over the past 20 years I have created a large number of sown vegetation types, as part of the ongoing dialogue between my research and practice. Here, I present some of these projects as case studies to provide much greater understanding of how and why sown vegetation or sown and planted hybrids work or don't work. For me, this interplay between the rigour of measuring what happens in experiments and then seeing if the same works on much larger scales with much less control in practice has been very stimulating. It can also be a bit terrifying and depressing, when it becomes apparent that it isn't going to work as anticipated.

I have selected projects which represent the timeline from commencing this work in the 1990s up to the present day. Generally speaking, the work has become more sophisticated in terms of design and ecological ideas across this period and my willingness to take more risks to push the boat out has increased. I have also tried to highlight the diversity of the plant communities. With the assistance of Ph.D. and master's students, I have conceptualized potential communities for various sites, laboriously counted seedlings to understand the seasonal dynamics of the communities, and finally road tested in practice. I have tried to be as honest as possible about success and failure, as the most useful lessons learnt often come from failure as much as from success.

The Eden Project

St Austell, Cornwall, England

PLANT COMMUNITIES North American prairie sown onto manufactured soil of decomposed granite with composted organic waste

SEED SOURCE Seed mainly from Prairie Nursery

CLIENT AND CONDITIONS The Eden Project is an innovative museum of human interaction with the vegetation and ecosystems of the world. The site has an extreme maritime climate, with warm but rarely hot summers and average winters which are close to frost free. Average rainfall exceeds 1000 mm and occurs at frequent intervals year round, but with peaks in winter. RHS Hardiness Zone H3, USDA 9b/10a.

AREA OF PROJECT 1250 m²

TIMESCALE Site prepared in 1999, sown in late January 2000

HISTORY AND DESIGN APPROACH

I had contributed to the development of the Eden Project from the mid 1990s as part of their Brains Trust. I was asked to create an area of North American prairie vegetation to interpret the relationship between seemingly natural vegetation (such as prairie) and how it was shaped or even created through human agency, in this case spring burning by Native Americans.

The Eden Project is situated in an enormous 70-m-deep china clay pit. The soil consists of free-draining decomposed granite grit, with some organic debris added. The sowing site is a steep, wedge-shaped, south-west-facing slope with a gradient of between 20° and 45°. Quite how the site would work in ecological terms was something of a mystery at the time of designing the plant community. The soil was very low in nutrients (and in particular nitrogen). I guessed that the plants could be exposed to significant moisture stress but that this would be compensated for by the regular rainfall. The top of the slope is extremely steep, almost 45°, and particularly challenging for plants on this soil type. As a result of these imponderables, I designed a community that included plants of both moist and dry prairies to provide the opportunity for species to sort themselves out on the slope in the longer term. Some nitrogen-fixing legumes were added to provide the nutrient that seemed likely to be severely limiting.

Because the site had to be sown just 2–3 months before the project opened to the paying public in March 2000, I decided that we would plant a 3-m-wide edge band of prairie plants around the whole site at a mean density of 7 plants/m². In order to reduce the cost and time taken for establishment without reducing the initial impact for visitors, the planting density progressively declined from the 1-m-wide strip next to the paths where visitors would walk. Three of the largest species in the community (*Silphium laciniatum*, *Silphium terebinthinaceum*, and *Sorghastrum nutans*) were planted as random elements across the whole site at a density of approximately 0.2 plants/m². Planting was completed in January 2000, and then the seed mix was sown across the entire site to fill in the space between. No sowing mulch was used because the soil did not contain a weed seed bank, other than the few clovers and grasses accidentally added during hydroseeding work on the steep walls of the china clay pit. The prairie species sown are listed in the table.

To provide contrast to the sown species plus some height on this reasonably large site and to reinforce the educational message about aboriginal people, fire, and prairie, approximately ten large carbonized tree trunks were placed on the site as vertical elements. These were up to 4 m tall with a diameter of about 600 mm, with attractive tessellated patterns on the very black surfaces. These trunks were manufactured on a large bonfire, using a mechanical digger in lieu of giant barbecue tongs to turn and manage the degree of burning.

Edge planting mix of the smaller planted species

SPECIES	NUMBERS REQUIRED FOR 1 M WIDE × 5 M LONG PLANTING UNITS			TOTAL FOR THREE 5-M PLANTING STRIPS	TOTAL PLANTS REQUIRED FOR EDGES (170 M)
	FIRST STRIP (75% DENSITY)	SECOND STRIP (50% DENSITY)	THIRD STRIP (25% DENSITY)		
Asclepias tuberosa	3	2	1	6	204
Aster laevis	2	2	1	5	170
Baptisia alba	2	1	1	4	136
Baptisia australis var. *minor*	2	2	1	5	170
Coreopsis palmata	2	2	1	5	170
Dodecatheon meadia	2	1	1	4	136
Echinacea pallida	2	1	1	4	136
Echinacea purpurea	3	2	1	6	204
Geum triflorum	2	1	1	4	136
Liatris aspera	3	2	1	6	204
Ratibida pinnata	2	2	1	5	170
Rudbeckia subtomentosa	2	1	1	4	136
Schizachyrium scoparium	2	2	1	5	170
Solidago speciosa	2	1	1	4	136
Sporobolus heterolepis	3	1	1	5	170
Totals	34	23	15	72	2448

Emergent species planting mix used across the site

LARGE SPECIES USED AS RANDOM EMERGENTS PLACED THROUGHOUT THE AREA	NUMBER OF PLANTS REQUIRED FOR TOTAL SOWN AREA (1250 M²)
Silphium laciniatum	30
Silphium terebinthinaceum	50
Sorghastrum nutans	130
	210

Prairie seed mix sown across the site

SPECIES	TARGET SEEDLINGS/M²
Aster laevis	10
Aster oolentangiensis	15
Dalea purpurea	10
Echinacea pallida	10
Echinacea purpurea	15
Euphorbia corollata	10
Helianthus mollis	5
Helianthus occidentalis	10
Liatris aspera	10
Liatris pycnostachya	10
Ratibida pinnata	10
Rudbeckia subtomentosa	10
Silphium integrifolium	2
Solidago rigida	10
Solidago speciosa	10
	147

WHAT WORKED AND WHAT DIDN'T

This site is over 400 km from my home in Sheffield, so it was not possible to visit frequently during the establishment period. At the first visit in summer 2000, it was apparent that *Echinacea pallida*, *Echinacea purpurea*, *Liatris aspera*, and *Liatris pycnostachya* were way below the expected seedling densities. This was also true of the legume *Dalea purpurea*, which subsequently I have found to almost always fail in U.K. sowings, but which is robust when sown in the hot summers of north-eastern China.

The failure of the first four species was probably because both of the *Echinacea* species are highly palatable to slugs, which were likely to be rapidly building up on the site in this very wet climate. Alternatively, it may have been due to insufficient irrigation during the germination window on this south-facing slope. The *Liatris* species are also likely to have suffered from the tendency in this genus for seedlings to have malformed root tips, which leads to seedling failure. The failure of these particular species was unfortunate in that it meant the bulk of the species flowering in summer were now almost all yellow, with few colour contrasts. This was only my second public sowing project, and I was probably too focused on using species that had proved very reliable and successful in my initial underpinning research. Minimizing the risk of failure rather than thinking about

The prairie at the bottom of the slope in early summer with large shrub-like clumps of *Baptisia alba* and a sea of *Rudbeckia subtomentosa* not yet in flower.

the long-term aesthetic consequences was foremost in my mind. This balance between pushing the boat out aesthetically and not failing is always challenging in public sites. The site came to be dominated by two of the most unpalatable, tall, and vigorous yellow daisies, *Rudbeckia subtomentosa* and *Silphium integrifolium*.

The clovers from the hydroseeding also proved troublesome in the first few years. Where there is sufficient phosphorus for legumes, but little nitrogen, nitrogen-fixers have a serious competitive advantage.

As of 2015 the prairie is 15 years old, and it is clear that species have re-sorted themselves as they should according to ecological theory. The most diverse prairie is at the top of the slope and includes the species that favour dry conditions, such as *Liatris aspera*, *Schizachyrium scoparium*, and *Geum triflorum*. Unfortunately, due to a road train ferrying the public from a car park, the public cannot access this best bit. The damper bottom of the slope is dominated by *Rudbeckia subtomentosa*. The most interesting thing about this site is that it is still there years later; that is, there was sufficient fitness among the rather short list of species to select out at least some winners in a slug-rich, maritime environment.

Maintenance involves strimming off the vegetation in March and tackling any significant weeds in the window of time before the canopy regrows and fuses together in May.

Penstemon digitalis, **Schizachyrium scoparium**, and **Solidago speciosa** prevail at the top of the slope (in November), where the vegetation is much more diverse and open due to moisture and nutrient stress.

Suckering stems of planted *Rhus typhina* provide some vivid autumn tones among *Baptisia* and *Solidago*.

RHS Garden Harlow Carr Primula Meadows

Harrogate, North Yorkshire, England

PLANT COMMUNITIES Western Chinese bog candelabra *Primula* intermixed with European *Primula* and other forbs of wet grassland sown onto 75 mm of composted green waste and subsoil clay (1:1 mix)

SEED SOURCES Seed mainly produced from my research plots, with additions from Jelitto Perennial Seeds and *Dodecatheon* from Western Native Seed

CLIENT AND CONDITIONS This was a scientific experiment, which the Royal Horticultural Society kindly allowed me to undertake at Harlow Carr. RHS Garden Harlow Carr is the society's most northern garden in the United Kingdom, in Harrogate, Yorkshire, at an altitude of 150 m. The site has relatively cool summers, even in the context of the United Kingdom, and potentially quite cold winters (minima of −15°C), although these extreme events are increasingly rare. Average rainfall is around 800 mm. RHS Hardiness Zone H4, USDA 8b/9a. The site was at the base of a meadow-covered slope, and the combination of downslope drainage and a heavy clay loam soil (pH 5.5) meant it was waterlogged for most of the year outside of July, August, and September.

AREA OF PROJECT 140 m^2 of experimental plots surrounded by about 150 m^2 of the same species sown to form an organically shaped meadow to integrate the rectangular plots into the garden landscape

TIMESCALE Site prepared in summer 2004, sown in August 2004, and maintained as an experiment until October 2011

Primula alpicola is an extremely beautiful species of wet meadows, here growing in the wild in western Sichuan.

HISTORY AND DESIGN APPROACH

This was the last of a series of experiments that commenced in 1999 to investigate whether it was possible to use the candelabra and sikkimensis primulas of western China as glamorous meadow vegetation for wet sustainable drainage swales in urban housing and similar situations. This final study looked at how soil wetness and management (meadow cut in September or November) affected competition between fifteen sown *Primula* species and six other forbs as well as their long-term survival. I also wanted to see what such a community would look like. Could it be as glamorous as these *Primula* species used almost as perennial bedding out in the streamside garden within Harlow Carr (for which the site is famous) and other gardens in the wettest parts of north-western Europe?

Although no scientific studies have confirmed this, in the wild habitat it seems likely that these species shed their seed in late August and September, when it is warm and wet in western China. At 20°C seed of these *Primula* species germinate rapidly, and the small seedlings then overwinter under a blanket of protective snow. In previous experiments, we had sown these species in winter and early spring in an attempt to use chilling to overcome the dormancy present in dry seed in most species. These sowings just didn't work, probably because the temperatures were too low in a U.K. spring. We eventually set up our own seed production plots for the species we were working with to produce fresh seed of species that were not available from Jelitto Perennial Seeds as chemically treated nondormant seeds (Gold Nugget). When sown in August, this seed germinated within 10 days of sowing. The only problem with this approach is that the seedlings are still quite small by the time growth stops in late autumn, and if the site doesn't have reliable snow cover many of the seedlings will be uprooted by winter rain erosion and frost-thaw cycles. In this experiment, we prevented this by covering our sown experimental plots with horticultural fleece in their first winter.

The *Primula* species were sown in August onto weed-free soil that had been covered with a 75-mm layer of a 1:1 mixture of composted green waste and (mostly weed-seed-free) clay subsoil. Composted green waste by itself would probably have been fine. After sowing, the seed was lightly raked in, and the plots were covered with standard jute erosion matting. Because this was an experiment, we did not use target emergence values as in practice. Instead, all species were sown at 100 seeds/m², with the exception of *Primula rosea*, which has particularly tiny seeds and had shown reduced emergence in previous research.

The six non-*Primula* species were oversown in early winter to allow their chilling requirements to be met.

Primula and other forbs of wet grasslands sown in the experiment

SPECIES	NUMBER OF SEEDS SOWN/M²
Cardamine pratensis	100
Dodecatheon jeffreyi	100
Persicaria milletii	100
Primula alpicola	100
Primula beesiana	100
Primula bulleyana	100
Primula burmanica	100
Primula chionantha	100
Primula denticulata	100
Primula japonica	100
Primula poissonii	100
Primula prolifera	100
Primula pulverulenta	100
Primula rosea 'Gigas'	150
Primula secundiflora	100
Primula sikkimensis	100
Primula veris	100
Primula vulgaris	100
Primula waltonii	100
Ranunculus acris	100
Silene flos-cuculi	100
Succisa pratensis	100

Additional forbs of wet to moist grassland added to the *Primula* sowing mix and sown into the meadow surrounding the plots

SPECIES	NUMBER OF SEEDS SOWN/M²
Alchemilla epipsilla	100
Cardamine pratensis	100
Cruciata laevipes	100
Persicaria milletii	100
Potentilla nepalensis	100
Ranunculus acris	100
Sanguisorba officinalis	100
Silene chalcedonica	100
Silene flos-cuculi	100
Stachys officinalis	100
Succisa pratensis	100
Veronica longifolia	100

Seedlings in April 2005, 8 months after sowing.

WHAT WORKED AND WHAT DIDN'T

There was heavy rain a couple of days after sowing and germination occurred rapidly in all of the Chinese *Primula*, although distinguishing between these species when very small was challenging. In terms of percentage emergence, the most successful species was *Primula pulverulenta* (approximately 40 per cent). As a result, this species became the community dominant from the outset. In spring 2005 we weeded the plots, mainly to remove grasses whose seed had washed in from the meadows further up the slope. After this no further weeding was undertaken. The rosette-like foliage of the primulas had generally fused by July 2005 and proved to be highly resistant to weed invasion. Flowering commenced in spring 2006 with *Primula rosea*, *Primula denticulata*, and *Primula vulgaris*, creating a slightly odd-looking version of park polyanthus bedding out. As the flowering whorls of the candelabra species emerged from the spring-flowering layer, a quite extraordinary succession of flowering took place, with the last species to flower finishing in late July early August. Had emergence of the winter-oversown forb species not been so poor, with higher densities of *Succisa* and *Persicaria* the plots would have continued to be attractive into September.

The meadow started to flower in March and April 2006 during its second growing season.

Primula denticulata and *Primula rosea* are intermixed with *Primula veris* and *Primula vulgaris*.

By early May, the emerging flower spikes of *Primula pulverulenta* are obscuring the spring species.

Primula pulverulenta came into full flower in early June.

By late June and early July, the yellow *Primula prolifera*, orange *Primula bulleyana*, and cerise purple *Primula burmanica* and *Primula poissonii* are strongly evident.

By the seventh year of the experiment, the species that showed no decline in numbers were *Primula pulverulenta* and *Primula rosea*. It was too wet for *Primula denticulata* and *Primula veris* and these species declined markedly, as did *Primula japonica* (slug damage). Other species were intermediate in persistence. The main factor in the slow decline of the species that were well suited to the site seemed to be competition with *P. pulverulenta*. In future sowings, I would use a target density approach to control the dominance of this species. There was no difference in persistence of species whether we cut the meadow off while growing (September) or after the first frosts had killed the leaves of the deciduous species (November), although plant size and flowering impact were greater when cut in November. A more useful management comparison would have been cutting in March, before the first primula started flowering, and in October. By cutting in March the evergreen species would have been able to continue photosynthesizing over winter, and the deciduous species would not be disadvantaged by losing their leaves prematurely. Competition from invading grasses and rushes would also have been reduced.

Sheffield Botanical Gardens Prairie

Sheffield, South Yorkshire, England

PLANT COMMUNITIES North American prairie sown onto 75–100 mm of sharp sand

SEED SOURCES Seed mainly purchased from Prairie Nursery, with a few species from Jelitto Perennial Seeds and Prairie Moon Nursery

CLIENT AND CONDITIONS Sheffield Botanical Gardens is essentially a horticulturally souped-up city park run by the local authority. In the context of the United Kingdom, the site has summer growing conditions which are a little warmer than might be expected by the latitude (July mean 16°C), due to being right in the middle of England. Winters are surprisingly mild, due to the large urban heat island effect and hilly terrain creating good cold air drainage, with typical minima of –5°C and extreme minima of –10°C. Annual rainfall is 800–900 mm. Slug population densities are high to very high. RHS Hardiness Zone H4, USDA 8b/9a. Soils are high-quality clay loams and highly productive (pH 5–6).

AREA OF PROJECT 800 m²

TIMESCALE Site prepared in summer 2003, sown in early February 2004

HISTORY AND DESIGN APPROACH

The Sheffield Botanical Gardens had several years previously been awarded a £7 million restoration grant from the National Heritage Lottery. In addition to completely renovating the 1833 glasshouses and other core infrastructure, there was a desire to add some contemporary planting. The site borders the tall southern boundary wall of the garden, and parts of it are lightly shaded by adjacent trees and shrubs. The soil is generally highly productive, especially the lowest portion of the area, which was once a pond.

To deal with the range of shade conditions across the site, I designed two main seed mixes, one for sun and one for shade, with the sun mix being split into an edge and core mix. The edge mix contained lower densities of the larger, potentially more dominant species, and correspondingly more smaller species. Because of the relatively sparse seedling emergence at the Eden Project, I decided to substantially increase the sowing rates to achieve targets up to 192 seedlings/m². This would ensure, in the absence of any planting, that the site would be well clothed in vegetation. The botanical gardens did not have the resources to intensively manage the site, so this seemed an imperative during the design phase. I recognized during the design process that this was a very productive soil, and so I knew that in the longer term the site would be dominated by the tall leafy-stemmed species, but I thought it would be a useful learning experience to see how far one could stretch the less productive species.

This project represented an evolution in my practice to explicitly recognize the need to respond to shade gradients by changing the mix (rather than just hoping for sufficient adaptation from within a single mix). It also addressed the idea of the edge as requiring visual continuity but also more diversity and perhaps a more controlled appearance.

Sunny core mix, with the seedling targets for each species

SPECIES	TARGET SEEDLINGS/M²
Aster laevis	10
Aster novae-angliae 'Septemberrubin'	2
Aster oolentangiensis	7
Aster turbinellus	10
Baptisia australis	3
Castilleja coccinea	5
Echinacea pallida	20
Echinacea purpurea	20
Eupatorium fistulosum 'Atropurpureum'	1
Helianthus mollis	10
Helenium autumnale	5
Liatris aspera	10
Monarda fistulosa	5
Pedicularis canadensis	5
Penstemon digitalis	7
Ratibida pinnata	10
Rudbeckia fulgida var. *deamii*	10
Rudbeckia subtomentosa	5
Silphium integrifolium	0.5
Silphium laciniatum	0.25
Silphium terebinthinaceum	0.25
Solidago rigida	5
Solidago speciosa	20
Sorghastrum nutans	1
Tradescantia ohiensis	10
Veronicastrum virginicum	5
Zizia aptera	5
	192

Sunny edge sowing mix, with the seedling targets for each species

SPECIES	TARGET SEEDLINGS/M²
Asclepias tuberosa	10
Aster oolentangiensis	7
Aster turbinellus	10
Baptisia australis	2
Baptisia leucantha	3
Castilleja coccinea	5
Echinacea pallida	20
Echinacea purpurea	20
Helianthus mollis	5
Helianthus occidentalis	10
Liatris aspera	10
Penstemon digitalis	10
Phlox pilosa	10
Schizachyrium scoparium	20
Silphium terebinthinaceum	0.25
Silphium laciniatum	0.25
Solidago speciosa	15
Sporobolus heterolepis	15
Tradescantia ohiensis	10
Zizia aptera	5
	187.5

Shady areas sowing mix, with the seedling targets for each species

SPECIES	TARGET SEEDLINGS/M²
Aster divaricatus	30
Aster macrophyllus	30
Aster novae-angliae 'Septemberrubin'	2
Eupatorium fistulosum 'Atropurpureum'	2
Helianthus hirsutus	2
Penstemon digitalis	7
Phlox maculata	10
Rudbeckia fulgida var. deamii	40
Rudbeckia subtomentosa	10
Silphium perfoliatum	2
Solidago flexicaulis	10
Veronicastrum virginicum	5
Zizia aptera	5
	155

Additional species oversown in January 2005 which were not available or not available in sufficient quantity in 2004

SPECIES	TARGET SEEDLINGS/M²
Castilleja coccinea	5
Lobelia cardinalis	10
Liatris pycnostachya	5
Solidago ohioensis	5
	25

WHAT WORKED AND WHAT DIDN'T

Unlike most projects I have worked on, this one had no irrigation. Fortunately, spring 2004 had relatively frequent rainfall, and good emergence was evident from May on, in part because of the high sowing targets. Some species, however, were surprisingly poorly represented from the beginning, most noticeably the two *Echinacea* species which were sown to achieve around 40 seedlings/m² and hence be the dominant visual element in the sowings. It seemed that this must be due to poor-quality seed, rather than moisture stress or post-emergence competition. This shaped my future work in deciding to primarily use seed from Jelitto Perennial Seeds to ensure the emergence of key species. The most striking aspect of the vegetation is that—even allowing for greatly reduced numbers of *Echinacea*—high soil productivity meant the vegetation closed together very quickly. Most of the site had a fused canopy by August, which allowed for relatively little management input. I had decided to weed the site in the first year, and this took me approximately 15 hours total to achieve a nearly weed-free prairie by October.

This rapid canopy closure pleased the client, but it led to a more rapid loss of the more slowly emerging and growing species than would otherwise have occurred. Species that need high summer temperatures to be robust, such as *Asclepias tuberosa*, *Helianthus*

This project was sown at a high target density of **190 seedlings/m²**.

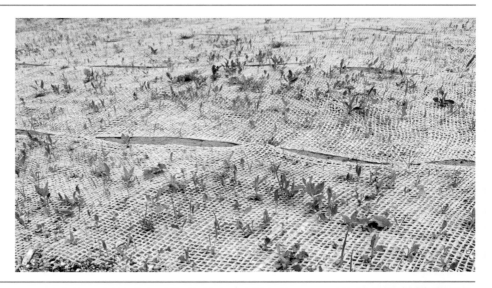

In **May 2004**, at 4 months after sowing, many seedlings are emerging.

The site is very productive, and plants had grown very rapidly by September 2004.

The prairie was in full flower in early September 2005.

The garden curator tries to walk the now disappeared bark path in September 2005.

Penstemon digitalis, an early species, flowers in June 2006. This species was subsequently eliminated through shading on this productive site.

occidentalis, and prairie grasses (*Schizachyrium scoparium*, *Sorghastrum nutans*, and *Sporobolus heterolepis*), were, I suspect, eliminated through shading by faster growing neighbours in this first year. Despite this, by the second year the prairie had a good diversity of species, with smaller species such as the biennial *Castilleja coccinea* and the perennials *Penstemon digitalis* and *Phlox pilosa* strongly evident. In the first 4 years after sowing, the site was managed by cutting down and flash burning in spring. Since then, this has been replaced by cutting down and removal only. As time has passed, there has been a loss of diversity but no loss of cover. Species that were present in the second year but have now disappeared (probably due to slug grazing) include *Echinacea purpurea*, *Monarda fistulosa*, and *Ratibida pinnata*. Sunny portions of the site are now dominated by *Aster* species, *Baptisia australis*, *Helenium autumnale*, *Helianthus mollis*, *Rudbeckia subtomentosa*, *Silphium integrifolium*, and *Solidago speciosa*.

The wild form of *Helenium autumnale* and *Silphium perfoliatum* were poor choices. These species are just too dominant for use in productive situations, where diversity is desired. As far as I could see, none of the species oversown in winter 2004–2005 established on the site; this practice is probably a waste of time except in very open plant communities.

In summary, the prairie plant community established on this site has proved to be extremely robust and long persistent. The site has not been weeded since 2004, and yet it is mostly weed free. This is really quite extraordinary and shows how important high seedling density, combined with ecologically nuanced management (not removing the dead biomass until just before shoot re-emergence in spring), is in restricting weed invasion and promoting low maintenance over the long term. The outcome of this project also shows that the combination of productive soils and high levels of slug grazing limits the range of species that can persist in northern regions with relatively cool summers. There are clear parallels with what happened at the Eden Project in relation to tall leafy-stemmed species employed at minimal maintenance levels.

Echinacea purpurea emerged from self-sown seed following spring burning in 2006.

The prairie in October 2014, looking much the same as it did 10 years earlier, but with no weeding performed for 9 years.

RHS Garden Wisley Steppe-Prairie

Wisley, Surrey, England

PLANT COMMUNITIES North American prairie with western North American and Eurasian steppe elements sown onto 100 mm of sand mulch, with open-weave jute erosion blanket; plug planting used at low levels, including 200 plugs of *Pulsatilla vulgaris* and *Dodecatheon meadia* 'Goliath' across the site

SEED SOURCES Seed mainly from Jelitto Perennial Seeds

CLIENT AND CONDITIONS This is the Royal Horticultural Society's oldest and most heavily visited garden, very much a prestige horticultural location. The site has relatively warm summers for the United Kingdom and potentially quite cold winters (minima of −15°C, although only very occasionally so). Average rainfall is 650 mm. RHS Hardiness Zone H4, USDA 8b/9a. Soils are very sandy, moderately productive, and prone to episodes of severe drought.

AREA OF PROJECT 600 m²

TIMESCALE Site prepared in summer 2007, sown in January 2008

HISTORY AND DESIGN APPROACH

I was invited by the Royal Horticultural Society (via Tom Stuart-Smith Design, who were designing the bicentennial borders around the garden's new glasshouse) to undertake this project. My 600 m² were the final and wildest portion of the planting sequence. It was an opportunity to respond to a different sort of site—one with relatively dry, drought-prone soils and a warm (for the United Kingdom) climate—with an expert horticultural work-force. I came up with a hybrid vegetation, based partly on North American prairie species often associated with mid-range to dry sites, combined with what were essentially steppe species from the central to southern Rocky Mountains and Eurasia.

This project was also an opportunity to further develop the spatial form of my designed communities. To date, I had mainly worked with prairie species that formed a 1-m-tall layer out of which arose occasional large emergents. When sown at high densities, such as at the Sheffield Botanical Gardens, this creates a meadow-like vegetation with a topographically rather uniform, almost flat surface. At RHS Garden Wisley, I wanted to investigate whether with seeding alone it was possible to produce a much more topographically varied surface. To try to achieve this, I worked with a community composed of three layers of foliage: a ground layer of flat rosettes to low mounds up to 300 mm tall, primarily of steppe species; an intermediate layer of mounds or upright stems to 600 mm tall, mainly composed of prairie species; and then relatively few species with foliage taller than 600 mm, such as *Aster turbinellus*, and the basal foliage of giant forbs such as *Silphium laciniatum*.

To reduce shading of the generally shade intolerant lowest layer, the aim was to progressively decrease the density of species proportionate to their foliage height. This can be seen in the table, with some *Penstemon* (foliage mainly in ground-level rosettes) at up to 6 seedlings/m² and *Silphium* at 0.25 seedlings/m². I used a spreadsheet to help conceptualize how many target seedlings would be allocated to each of the three canopy layers. Of a total target density of 77 seedlings/m², 56 of these were allocated to the lower foliage species, 16 to the intermediate layer, and 5 to the tallest foliage layer. The actual values are not hugely important; it is the relativities that are key.

Nearly all of the taller species chosen had leafless stems, that is, largely basal foliage with flowering stems with few leaves present. This both reduces shading and creates see-through visual effects. The other innovation was to reduce the target seedling rate, from 150-plus in my earlier prairie sowings to less than 80 in this scheme. This was a slightly scary decision to make in this high-profile site, with a preponderance of small and slowly growing steppe species, but a necessary one if a more complex topography more reminiscent of central European matrix planting was to be achieved.

In essence, the entire site was sown with an edge mix. Although it seemed certain that the prairie species would eventually dominate the planting, it was unclear just how quickly this would happen. I anticipated that most of the steppe-like species would ultimately be eliminated except on the edges, where there was more light. Given the high-profile nature of the site and the horticultural expertise of the staff, I believed there was a good chance that these processes could be successfully managed.

Target densities of the species sown

SPECIES	TARGET SEEDLINGS/M²
Amsonia hubrichtii	0.1
Asclepias tuberosa	3
Aster oblongifolius	1
Aster oolentangiensis	2
Baptisia australis var. minor	0.2
Baptisia bracteata var. glabrescens	0.3
Castilleja coccinea	2.3
Dianthus carthusianorum	3
Dodecatheon meadia 'Goliath'	4
Dracocephalum rupestre	3
Echinacea pallida	3
Echinacea paradoxa	1.5
Eryngium yuccifolium	1
Euphorbia corollata	2
Geum triflorum	4
Helichrysum aureum	2
Oenothera macrocarpa subsp. incana	2.7
Oenothera tetragona	2
Penstemon ×mexicanus 'Sunburst Ruby'	1.5
Penstemon barbatus 'Coccineus'	2
Penstemon cobaea subsp. purpureus	3
Penstemon cyananthus	3
Penstemon strictus	6
Phlox pilosa	10
Pulsatilla vulgaris	2
Ruellia humilis	2
Schizachyrium scoparium	1.5
Scutellaria baicalensis	5
Silphium laciniatum	0.25
Silphium terebinthinaceum	0.25
Solidago speciosa	1
Sporobolus heterolepis	1
Viola pedatifida	2
	77.6

Species for partly shaded areas (adjacent to a tree and hedges), with the seedling targets for each species

SPECIES	TARGET SEEDLINGS/M²
Aster oolentangiensis	4
Aster divaricatus	6
Aster oblongifolius	1
Castilleja coccinea	5
Dianthus carthusianorum	4
Dodecatheon meadia 'Goliath'	4
Dracocephalum rupestre	3
Eryngium yuccifolium	1
Euphorbia corollata	3
Geum triflorum	3
Heuchera villosa	5
Oenothera tetragona	2
Penstemon digitalis	1
Penstemon smallii	5
Phlox pilosa	10
Polemonium reptans	5
Rudbeckia maxima	1
Silphium laciniatum	0.25
Silphium terebinthinaceum	0.25
Solidago speciosa	3
Sporobolus heterolepis	1
Viola pedatifida	2
	69.5

By August 2008, the vegetation had achieved approximately 50 per cent surface cover.

WHAT WORKED AND WHAT DIDN'T

I first visited the site in May 2008 for a meeting with the Wisley staff, who I think were convinced the sowing was a complete failure. At the one-leaf stage, 70 to 80 seedlings/m² looks like no seedlings at all to the uninitiated. It was obvious to me that, despite their concerns, emergence was mostly on target. The site had been irrigated from March to my visit, and this continued to the end of June.

By September 2008, the site was approximately 50–75 per cent covered in the foliage of the sown species. There was much less shading by the sown species than in the more conventional prairie sowings, so weeding continued as required across the summer. The vegetation was cut down and the limited amount of dead material removed in spring 2009. Flowering started in earnest in May 2009 with *Penstemon* and *Dianthus*, and it was quite an extraordinary sight. Most of the Rocky Mountain species worked very well, including *Oenothera macrocarpa* subsp. *incana*, which often fails to perform in mixed communities in Sheffield, where summers are just too cool.

In 2010 the community was flash burnt in spring for the first time to check the build-up of annual winter-growing weeds, such as winter grass (*Poa annua*). This burning is tolerated by *Dianthus* and some *Penstemon*, but it probably accelerated the switch to prairie dominance. In late July 2011 *Echinacea pallida* was visually dominant, signalling the anticipated switch over from steppe to prairie dominance.

The site has also provided an interesting study of how maintenance staff interact with naturalistic vegetation. From 2009 on, the Royal Horticultural Society was in a state of flux, with the departure of many senior gardening staff. The average gardener is now much younger, and the rotation of garden team supervisors on a regular basis has led to issues of continuity in understanding this planting. The latter is a general issue in the management of this type of vegetation.

Because of my London Olympics commitments in 2012, I did not visit in that year. By 2013 it was apparent that there was a pressing need to remove excessive *Aster oblongifolius*

Many of the steppe species were coming into flower by late May 2009, here dominated by *Dianthus carthusianorum* and blue *Penstemon strictus*, along with pink *Phlox pilosa* and scarlet *Castilleja coccinea*.

The drama increased further by mid June 2009.

By early August 2011, the structural composition had changed from steppe to prairie.

The planting is now dominated by prairie species such as *Echinacea pallida* and *Eryngium yuccifolium*.

In autumn 2013, the prairie was a mass of lilac and purple from *Aster turbinellus* and *Aster oblongifolius*.

The rare European native *Pulsatilla vulgaris*, with attractive flowers in March and April, has proved to be robust and has established throughout the prairie from the original seedlings.

Pulsatilla vulgaris also produces exceptionally attractive seed heads in May.

and *Aster turbinellus*, which were beginning to dominate and shade out the other species, including *Echinacea*. In Tom Stuart-Smith's home garden the same species also began to dominate (see case study), but Tom as the guiding force saw the need to respond to this early on. At Wisley this did not happen until I hit the panic button in 2013, and when it did, the approach by the new supervisor was to clear large areas of asters, thus creating large openings, rather than remove plants selectively bit by bit. Predictably, these big gaps just became weedy patches, making matters worse not better.

Staff rotation has made it difficult to develop an understanding of how to work more ecologically. Since 2013 management has been more proactive, but there are still issues with prioritizing maintenance resources. Because these areas are viewed as "natural" or "wild", the management of weeds appears to be seen as discretionary, to the detriment of visual quality.

Despite these problems, the vegetation in the main continues to look reasonably good. The major events are in April, when the long-persistent and effective self-seeder *Pulsatilla vulgaris* comes into flower, then mid summer with *Echinacea pallida* and *Asclepias tuberosa*, and then the asters from September on. The major problem is the August gap, as not much flowers at this peak time. Although we have identified species to address this gap, these have rarely materialized.

If I was to design another version of this vegetation for a similarly dry site, I would increase the density of the steppe layer, decrease the density of the intermediate and tall foliage layers, and probably add *Parthenium integrifolium*, and *Liatris scariosa* or *Liatris pycnostachya* for August interest. I would also increase the grassy component, but prairie grasses are problematic in these not quite warm enough summer climates; the large ones potentially shade too much and the small ones tend to get eliminated by shading. *Sporobolus heterolepis* persists but is both very expensive and quite difficult to establish via sowing.

Fidelity International

Tonbridge, Kent, England

PLANT COMMUNITIES North American prairie, with some Eurasian and western North American steppe elements, sown onto 100 mm of sand mulch; mainly European woodland understorey and edge sown onto 75 mm of composted bark mulch; and native U.K. meadow sown onto Olympic Park low-nutrient topsoil (mainly sand with some organic debris added)

SEED SOURCES All non-native seed from Jelitto Perennial Seeds, native species from Emorsgate Seeds

CLIENT AND CONDITIONS The Kent campus of Fidelity International, an investment management company; this site is not open to the public. Project was undertaken in conjunction with Tom Stuart-Smith Design and the landscape contractor Willerby Landscapes. The site has relatively warm summers for the United Kingdom and potentially quite cold winters (minima of −15°C, although only very occasionally so). Average rainfall is 700 mm. RHS Hardiness Zone H4, USDA 8b/9a. Original soil type was very heavy, poorly drained clay. Many of the soils for this project were manufactured on site.

AREA OF PROJECT 2985 m² of prairie, 1700 m² of woodland understorey and edge, 1500 m² of native wildflower meadow

TIMESCALE Site prepared in 2009, prairie and woodland vegetation sown in February 2010, native wildflower meadow sown in February 2011

Most of the Fidelity International buildings are surrounded by Tom Stuart-Smith's herbaceous planting, rather than lawn.

HISTORY AND DESIGN APPROACH

Fidelity International is a company with a very strong commitment to providing high-quality attractive landscapes around their offices and have worked with Tom Stuart-Smith to achieve this for many years. They have a highly trained horticultural staff at each of their centres, and this long-term informed management approach allowed this project to be much more ambitious than the typical business park landscape.

Set on the rural-urban edge, the site's vegetation consists of alternating areas of more conventional horticultural and naturalistic planting, set within woodland and parkland tree planting. The spatial and planting master plan by Tom Stuart-Smith was designed, where possible, to bring exciting planting right up to the building and create constantly changing vegetation in the foreground that gives way to more distant views of the countryside. The brief was to maximize the range of seasonal events for staff, so that the external landscape is interesting throughout the year.

The largest areas of herbaceous vegetation in this project are those established by sowing. They include native wildflower meadows and a prairie-like plant community, including both North American and Eurasian elements to maximize the season of interest. One of the largest areas of this prairie-like vegetation overlies a subterranean car park, and here the soil was manufactured on site to utilize waste materials that would otherwise have to be removed. The waste materials were crushed concrete and rubble (fines to 35–40 mm) from the demolition of the original buildings on site, and deep subsoil clay from the car park excavation. These materials were mixed on site prior to laying, creating a highly infertile, high-pH soil. Surface drainage was improved through the incorporation of grit.

Although the soil type was challenging, it was also an interesting opportunity to work with a supportive client to be as sustainable as possible and to work from a very unproductive set of conditions to create a unique, relatively self-sustaining vegetation.

Prairie-like seed mix, with the seedling targets for each species

SPECIES	TARGET SEEDLINGS/M²
Agastache rupestris	3
Asclepias tuberosa	3
Aster oblongifolius	1
Baptisia australis var. *minor*	0.2
Dianthus carthusianorum	4
Dracocephalum rupestre	4
Echinacea pallida	3
Echinacea paradoxa	3
Echinacea tennesseensis 'Rocky Top' hybrids	1
Eryngium yuccifolium	0.75
Euphorbia corollata	2
Geum triflorum	5
Liatris aspera	3
Liatris ligulistylis	2
Liatris scariosa 'Alba'	2
Oenothera macrocarpa subsp. *incana*	5
Oenothera tetragona	2
Penstemon barbatus 'Coccineus'	4
Penstemon cobaea subsp. *purpureus*	4
Penstemon digitalis 'Huskers Red'	2
Penstemon strictus	3
Phlox pilosa	5
Rudbeckia fulgida var. *deamii*	3
Rudbeckia maxima	0.25
Rudbeckia missouriensis	2
Schizachyrium scoparium	7
Scutellaria baicalensis	10
Silphium laciniatum	0.25
Silphium terebinthinaceum	0.25
	84.7

Native meadow mix

SPECIES	TARGET SEEDLINGS/M²
Achillea millefolium	5
Calamintha nepeta subsp. *nepeta* 'Blue Cloud'	15
Campanula glomerata	10
Centaurea scabiosa	3
Daucus carota	5
Echium vulgare	2
Festuca ovina	10
Galium mollugo	1
Galium verum	15
Geranium pratense	2
Geranium sanguineum	3
Knautia arvensis	3
Leucanthemum vulgare	6
Linaria vulgaris	5
Malva moschata	2
Onobrychis viciifolia	2
Origanum vulgare	15
Primula veris	15
Prunella vulgaris	10
Ranunculus acris	10
Salvia pratensis	5
Sanguisorba officinalis	2
Scabiosa columbaria	10
Stachys officinalis	5
Trifolium pratense	5
Verbascum nigrum	2
	168

Woodland understorey and edge mix

SPECIES	TARGET SEEDLINGS/M²
Aster divaricatus	5
Euphorbia amygdaloides 'Purpurea'	0.5
Gillenia trifoliata	0.5
Heuchera villosa	10
Lathyrus vernus	2
Papaver pilosum subsp. *spicatum*	3
Polemonium reptans	15
Primula elatior	15
Primula sieboldii	5
Primula vulgaris	15
Rudbeckia fulgida var. *deamii*	10
Viola odorata 'Queen Charlotte'	1
	82

The soil is very low in nitrogen, but with adequate phosphorus and potassium levels. To provide an initially highly oxygenated and root-penetrable buffering surface for seedlings to establish in before having to punch their roots into the physically more hostile underlying soil, a 100-mm layer of sharp sand was spread across the surface in January 2010. The prairie-like plant community used was based on the design ideas previously discussed under RHS Garden Wisley, with a basal layer of small species, an intermediate emergent layer, and tall emergents. Sowing was at relatively low target densities to develop a more open, topographically interesting community.

The woodland understorey and edge sowing mix was mainly sown in conjunction with established trees, and a fine composted bark sowing mix was used to provide moister conditions on top of the root plates of these trees. The sowing mix was designed to provide a major spring-flowering display through native woodland species, such as *Primula elatior*, and then a display in late summer to autumn through woodland asters and *Rudbeckia fulgida*.

The wildflower meadow mix included a range of species native to southern England and was similar to some of the mixes I had previously designed for the Queen Elizabeth Olympic Park in London.

The sown prairie almost touches the building façade.

WHAT WORKED AND WHAT DIDN'T

Willerby Landscapes, the landscape contractor, did a fine job in terms of irrigating the sowings, and target emergence was obtained for the prairie-like vegetation, both for the large areas sown in early February and sowings delayed until May. Seed for the latter was chilled in bags of moist sand in a refrigerator for 3 months prior.

Emergence and establishment of the woodland species on the composted pine bark was far inferior, and seedlings that did germinate grew poorly and in many instances declined. Low emergence in the woodland species was in part due to the chilling requirements of the two woodland primulas not being fully met by the February sowing, even with a refrigerator chilling period in moist sand a month prior to sowing. My experience with these *Primula* species is that if you want really good emergence you need to sow in mid to late autumn. These species naturally emerge in late winter and early spring, and even when artificially chilled establishment is poor in the first year. Good emergence may also occur in the following spring, but this runs the risk of many losses from competition

Staff enjoy views from within the building through and across the prairie to the rural landscape.

with existing plants. Another factor in the poor performance of the woodland species seemed to be either chronic nitrogen lockup in the composted bark or the presence of toxins through inadequate composting. It's possible both were operating. When combined with the rapidly drying clay soil under the mulch as the trees came into leaf, the woodland edge and understories were not particularly successful.

By 2012, following onsite discussions, we decided to convert the single largest area of the sowings under a dense tree canopy to a spring meadow. We did this by oversowing in autumn with *Festuca longifolia* and leaving this uncut until summer to allow growth and seed production, and then cutting to ground level and removing in July. This has worked successfully for the spring species, especially the primulas and violets, which are now abundant. Elsewhere on site we have persevered with this vegetation, and there is a version of the originally envisaged understorey vegetation, including large patches of *Rudbeckia fulgida* var. *deamii*, which wilts in dry periods in summer but perks up remarkably after rain.

The grass *Schizachyrium scoparium* turns orange-buff in the prairie in winter.

Invasion of grass weeds from the lawn edge has been a problem. In winter 2014–2015 the garden staff sprayed a contact herbicide on an experimental 1-m-wide band on this edge. This treatment eliminated nearly all of the weeds in this band with no loss of desired species.

The overall learning from the project is that it is difficult to get shade-tolerant sowings, especially in warmer climates, to perform to the same timescale as vegetation in full sun. Even for shade-tolerant species, the shortage of light and moisture under trees means everything happens very slowly. In current projects involving these situations, I have increasingly used plantings of *Epimedium* and other woodland species to provide a scaffold of vegetation which is then oversown as early as possible, using sand as the sowing mulch. Composted green waste is another alternative, but it is sometimes very weed rich.

We had anticipated greatly reduced growth on the crushed building soil and applied a nitrogen-only fertilizer in the first growing season to the more slowly growing patches. The intention was to try to increase the size and vigour of the seedlings to allow them

In July 2015, the same edge has lush prairie vegetation.

to begin to break into the underlying soil. We have been reluctant to do this annually as this might swing the balance in the favour of the weeds. As a result, we have tolerated a situation of relatively small prairie plants but also lower weed density.

Regeneration from self-sown seed of competition-sensitive species such as *Liatris* has been excellent, as has prairie regeneration in general. At the March 2015 site management meeting, we agreed that this vegetation looked too bonsai-like in this prominent location, and an 8 × 8 m test square was treated with a nitrogen-only fertilizer. This transformed the prairie into an extraordinary floral extravaganza, but it also increased the predominant weed, the nitrogen-fixing legume *Medicago*. In 2016 the staff will use a slow-release nitrogen fertilizer to try to gain the same level of "wow" without boosting the weeds as much.

One prairie species that grows particularly well and is robust on this site is the heat-demanding *Asclepias tuberosa*. The sand mulch prevents the fleshy shoots being eaten out by slugs during the winter months, which is its normal fate in Britain.

The two *Silphium* species used to provide tall emergent stems and yellow daisies have proved to be excessively free seeding, requiring control methods to be developed by the horticultural staff. This has been achieved by injection of glyphosate into the stems using a proprietary system designed for Japanese knotweed control.

Oenothera macrocarpa subsp. *incana* shows the growth-reducing effect of the rubble and clay substrate on its growth. Plants to the left are growing in this material, whereas those to the right are in soil with much less crushed concrete.

The large native U.K. wildflower meadow is at the front of the complex and is seen by all who arrive at the reception area. The meadow established very well, and each year it has been dominated by different species from within the mix. Its floral display has been extended further by plantings of early-flowering *Crocus chrysanthus* and September- to October-flowering *Crocus speciosus* and *Colchicum*. In 2015 the garden staff tested a new cutting regime as an alternative to the standard cut in late July to early August. This involves a winter mow before the crocus emerge, followed by a hay cut at the end of May after the cowslip and buttercups flower. The meadow is then allowed to regrow, pushing back the flowering periods of species like *Geranium pratense* into July and August. This approach was taken to reduce the strawy look in August and to check the dominance of tall leafy-stemmed species as well as the growth of the annual leguminous arable weed tere (*Vicia tetrasperma*), which this cutting regime seems to have done.

The real innovation at the Fidelity International site is that the client financially supports three management review meetings per year for the planting design team (Tom Stuart-Smith, Andy Hamilton, and myself), in which a whole day is spent with the garden's management team (led by Joe Ransley, senior horticulturist), leading to an agreed list of issues and management actions to resolve these. There is complete buy-in by the garden's staff. If something is not working, we can specify what might be a better alternative. New species are added as plugs, burning times are experimented with to maximize efficiency, and so on.

What has also been very interesting to observe is how the staff within the building have come to really value the relatively disordered naturalistic vegetation on the other side of their windows. When the wildflower meadow is cut down, there are emails asking "Why has our meadow been cut off?"

Visitors to the site have to drive or walk through native meadows to get to the reception area.

By July 2012, the initial dominance of wild carrot (*Daucus carota*) and sainfoin (*Onobrychis viciifolia*) was gradually weakening.

Tom Stuart-Smith's Home Prairie Garden

Near St Albans, Hertfordshire, England

PLANT COMMUNITIES North American prairie with some South African and European elements sown onto 100 mm of sand mulch

SEED SOURCES Seed mainly from Jelitto Perennial Seeds, with *Castilleja* from Western Native Seed, *Gentiana andrewsii* and *Melanthium virginicum* from Prairie Moon, and the South African species from my research plots

CLIENT AND CONDITIONS The English landscape architect and garden designer Tom Stuart-Smith. The site has relatively warm summers for the United Kingdom and potentially quite cold winters (minima of −15°C, although only very occasionally so). Average rainfall is 700 mm. RHS Hardiness Zone H4, USDA 8b/9a.

AREA OF PROJECT 1500 m^2

TIMESCALE Site prepared in 2010, sown in January 2011

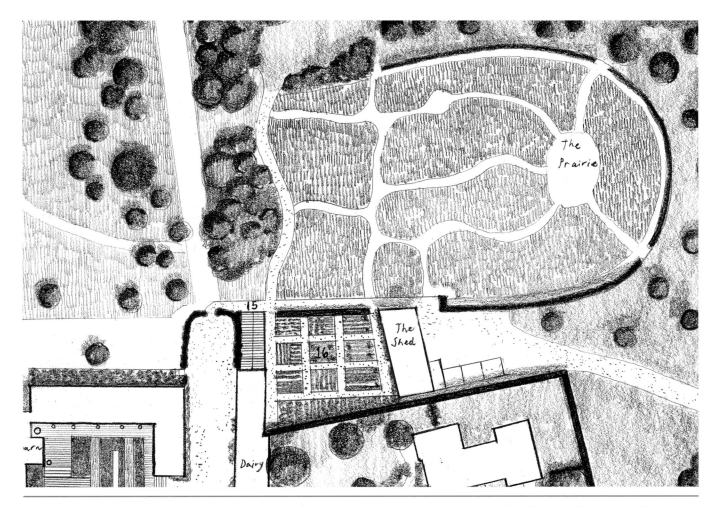

HISTORY AND DESIGN APPROACH

Tom Stuart-Smith is an internationally renowned landscape architect, and he and I have
collaborated on design projects since 2005. The garden site was previously species-poor
meadow grassland. Tom had designed the bed layout: sinuous organic shapes separated
by 2-m-wide mown grass paths with a gravel path on the side nearest the house.

The scheme straddles two contrasting soil types; a heavy clay predominates in the
eastern part of the site, and the western end is sandier. Tom asked me to design two seed
mixes for these contrasting soil types, based around North American prairie species.
Some species are common to both mixes, providing a sense of visual continuity at certain
times of the year. Because I was heavily involved in research on South African Drakensberg species at this time, I incorporated several geophytic genera such as *Kniphofia* into
the mixes, to create a quirky, prairie-based hybrid. The sowing densities in terms of target
seedlings per square metre were a bit higher than I normally use, at 96 and 131 seedlings/
m². In part this was because, particularly in the sandy soil mix, I was experimenting with
some riskier species which had a high likelihood of not establishing, such as *Carex testacea* (1.5 seedlings/m²), the hemi-parasite *Castilleja integra* (10 seedlings/m²), *Gentiana
andrewsii* (10 seedlings/m²), and *Melanthium virginicum* (3 seedlings/m²).

Seed mix and origins of the species for clay soil areas, with the seedling targets for each species

SPECIES	NATURAL DISTRIBUTION OF SPECIES	TARGET SEEDLINGS/M^2
Amorpha canescens	central USA	3
Andropogon gerardii	central USA	0.5
Aster novae-angliae 'Septemberrubin'	central USA	1
Aster oblongifolius	central USA	15
Aster oolentangiensis	central USA	3
Aster turbinellus	central USA	0.5
Baptisia alba	central USA	0.25
Carex testacea	New Zealand	15
Coreopsis tripteris	central USA	0.5
Echinacea pallida	central USA	3
Echinacea purpurea 'Prairie Splendor'	central USA	10
Eryngium yuccifolium	central USA	2
Galtonia candicans	eastern South Africa	3
Hesperantha coccinea pink forms	eastern South Africa	5
Kniphofia uvaria eastern Cape form	eastern South Africa	1
Lobelia tupa	coastal Chile	0.25
Melanthium virginicum	central USA	3
Moraea spathulata	eastern South Africa	2
Rudbeckia fulgida var. *deamii*	central USA	15
Rudbeckia maxima	central USA	0.5
Silene regia	central USA	5
Silphium laciniatum	central USA	0.5
Silphium terebinthinaceum	central USA	1
Solidago speciosa	central USA	5
Sorghastrum nutans	central USA	1
		96

Seed mix and origins of the species for sandy soil areas, with the seedling targets for each species

SPECIES	NATURAL DISTRIBUTION OF SPECIES	TARGET SEEDLINGS/M²
Amorpha canescens	central USA	2
Andropogon gerardii	central USA	0.5
Asclepias tuberosa	central USA	3
Aster oblongifolius	central USA	5
Aster oolentangiensis	central USA	2
Callirhoe bushii	central USA	2
Carex testacea	New Zealand	10
Castilleja integra	south-western USA	10
Dianthus carthusianorum	Western Europe	5
Dracocephalum rupestre	western China	5
Echinacea pallida	central USA	3
Echinacea paradoxa	central USA	5
Echinacea purpurea 'Prairie Splendor'	central USA	1
Echinacea tennesseensis 'Rocky Top' hybrids	central USA	3
Eryngium yuccifolium	central USA	1
Euphorbia corollata	central USA	3
Galtonia candicans	eastern South Africa	3
Gentiana andrewsii	central USA	10
Gladiolus papilio ex 'Ruby'	eastern South Africa	3
Kniphofia triangularis	eastern South Africa	3
Kniphofia uvaria eastern Cape form	eastern South Africa	0.5
Liatris aspera	central USA	10
Liatris scariosa 'Alba'	central USA	5
Lobelia tupa	coastal Chile	0.25
Moraea spathulata	eastern South Africa	2
Oenothera macrocarpa subsp. *incana*	central USA	5
Penstemon barbatus 'Coccineus'	Mexico to south-western USA	3
Penstemon cobaea	central USA	3
Scutellaria baicalensis	Siberia to northern China	15
Silene regia	central USA	3
Silphium laciniatum	central USA	0.5
Silphium terebinthinaceum	central USA	1
Solidago speciosa	central USA	3
		131

WHAT WORKED AND WHAT DIDN'T

Through our past collaborations, Tom had quite a lot of experience of observing the establishment of sown vegetation, and he worked closely with his gardeners Brian Maslin and Fabian Lee to ensure irrigation was sufficient during the germination period. In fact, the site was probably irrigated a bit too much, resulting in much worm casting, which deposited many weed seeds on top of the sterile sand layer. This then required more weeding than is typical. In the process of doing this, quite a few of the South African geophytes appear to have been accidentally weeded out as grass weeds and are much sparser than intended. Grasses and grass look-alikes in sowings are always problematic in that, when young, distinguishing them from grass weeds is challenging. *Carex* survived weeding out because they are brownish and hence distinct. They do not tolerate the annual spring cutting off to ground level, however, so have mostly disappeared. *Carex testacea* is problematic to manage, and I no longer use it.

Castilleja established well, as did *Gentiana*, but not the elusive *Melanthium*. I sowed a few pots of *M. virginicum*, but no germination occurred even after two winter chilling cycles; the seed was almost certainly nonviable. *Lobelia tupa* did what it normally does, that is, not establish from seed. The seed of this species is just too small and sensitive, so I now plant it.

Most species were close to their target densities, but there was much more *Aster oblongifolius* than we wanted. In a previous sowing, this late-autumn-flowering species showed very poor emergence, so I increased target numbers up to 15 seedlings/m^2 just in case, only to then find extremely high emergence and an embarrassment of numbers. These have been progressively weeded out, but still require a substantial weeding programme (up to 100 hours per year) to prevent them dominating the prairie as they did at RHS Garden Wisley.

The first species to flower in this prairie is *Dianthus carthusianorum* (in May), followed by *Penstemon barbatus* and *Echinacea pallida*. Flowering continues into November. Since its initial establishment, Tom has experimented by adding autumn colouring shrubs such as *Cotinus* and other species to personalize the experience. He estimates the total annual input of maintenance for the 1500-m^2 planting is a maximum of 180 hours (excluding aster pulling), or about 12 hours per 100 m^2 per annum, and still under 20 hours with aster pulling included. This is more than typical values for native wildflower meadows (4 hours) but less than conventional herbaceous borders (20–40+ hours). The project has been really successful because from the outset Tom was prepared to make decisions about what to change, and his maintenance staff signed up to this. This is unlike some other prairie projects where a more laissez-faire approach prevailed, with predictably problematic outcomes.

The sandy soil portion of the prairie in June 2013 is dominated visually by *Dianthus carthusianorum*.

The same area and same species in early July 2015. With time, the community has become much more attractive in terms of naturally emerging patterns and textures.

By early September 2013, there was an enormous change within the same vegetation compared to June of that year.

The brown seed heads of the dianthus that was the visual dominant in June can be seen in the foreground.

Liatris pycnostachya is very dramatic in late summer.

The Merton Borders at University of Oxford Botanic Garden

University of Oxford, Oxford, England

PLANT COMMUNITIES North American prairie with some western North American steppe elements, South African Drakensberg grassland, and a Eurasian steppe community, all sown onto 100 mm of sand mulch

SEED SOURCES Seed mainly from Jelitto Perennial Seeds, with *Castilleja* from Western Native Seed and South African species from my research plots

CLIENT AND CONDITIONS The University of Oxford Botanic Garden is located in a bend in the river (replete with punts) in the historic core of the city and is managed by the university; it was originally there to supply plants and parts of plants for teaching, particularly in botany. The site is about as continental as the United Kingdom gets, with relatively warm summers (July average 16.5°C) and potentially very cold winters (minima of −20°C, although only very occasionally). Average rainfall is 660 mm. RHS Hardiness Zone H5, USDA 7b/8a. Soils (pH 8) are well-drained alluvial silts, but prone to winter flooding, as the planting is immediately adjacent to the River Cherwell.

AREA OF PROJECT 850 m²

TIMESCALE Site prepared in summer 2011, sown in December 2011

HISTORY AND DESIGN APPROACH

Established in 1621, Oxford is the oldest botanic garden in the United Kingdom, and much of the site is given over to historical order beds in vogue from the 17th century. As a contrast to these, the director and curators wanted to add a deliberately contemporary sustainable planting. An area shaped rather like an aircraft carrier deck in the lower garden had been master planned by landscape architect Kim Wilkie, and I was given free rein to develop interesting ideas for its planting. I decided on a ground pattern involving alternating wedges of three naturalistic plant communities that all came from parts of the world with warmer summers than currently experienced in Oxford and that had good tolerance of summer drought. The design narrative was all about showcasing plants and planting that might become more important in a future Oxford, which is shifting increasingly to a near-Mediterranean climate due to climate change. Where possible, I tried to use plants that were not very familiar in British gardens, although even the familiar ones were likely to appear novel when used in the naturalistic design context. The wedges would initially provide somewhat sharp divisions between one community and its different neighbour. These divisions would blur over time with self-seeding, ultimately leading to a fusion of the three, mediated by the site and the inclinations of the gardeners. To fast-track this process, I included *Aster oblongifolius*, *Kniphofia triangularis*, and *K. triangularis* 'Cameron' in all three mixes.

The three wedges of each community type provide a strong sense of repetition to counterbalance the chaos within each wedge. Laid over the top of the wedges are three rhomboidal phalanxes of *Eremurus stenophyllus* with plants at 2-m centres, to again provide some visual glue in July.

A small amount of planting was done to establish species that were too slow or difficult via seeding. These were mostly the tall emergents in the Eurasian steppe.

Sowing mix for the Eurasian steppe, with the seedling targets for each species

SPECIES	TARGET SEEDLINGS/M²	SPECIES	
Allium senescens	8	*Malva alcea* var. *fastigiata*	0.33
Aster oblongifolius	0.2	*Marrubium supinum*	1
Astragalus alopecurus	0.5	*Papaver orientale* 'Brilliant'	1
Campanula persicifolia 'Grandiflora'	2	*Paradisea lusitanica*	1
Dianthus carthusianorum	2	*Perovskia atriplicifolia*	1
Dianthus carthusianorum 'Rupert's Pink'	5	*Pulsatilla vulgaris*	2
Dracocephalum argunense 'Fuji Blue'	2	*Salvia* ×*sylvestris* 'Blaukönigin'	1
Echinops ritro	1	*Scabiosa comosa*	2
Eryngium maritimum	1	*Scabiosa ochroleuca* 'Moon Dance'	3
Eryngium planum 'Blaukappe'	1	*Scutellaria baicalensis*	3
Euphorbia epithymoides	0.5	*Sedum telephium* 'Emperor's Waves'	5
Euphorbia nicaeensis	3	*Silene schafta* 'Persian Carpet'	5
Galium verum	3	*Teucrium chamaedrys*	2
Hyssopus officinalis subsp. *aristatus*	3	*Veronica spicata* subsp. *incana*	5
Incarvillea delavayi 'Bees Pink'	1		76
Incarvillea zhongdianensis	1		

SPECIES	TARGET SEEDLINGS/M²	SPECIES	PLANTS/M² (1-L POTS)
Inula ensifolia	3	*Achnatherum calamagrostis*	0.25
Kniphofia triangularis	0.2	*Aster sedifolius* 'Nanus'	0.3
Kniphofia triangularis 'Cameron'	0.2	*Ferula communis*	0.1
Laserpitium siler	0.2	*Origanum* 'Rosenkuppel'	0.3
Limonium platyphyllum	3	*Stipa gigantea*	0.1
Linum narbonense	3		1

Sowing and planting mix for the prairie core, with the seedling targets for each species

SPECIES	TARGET SEEDLINGS/M²
Agastache rupestris	1
Amorpha canescens	1
Asclepias tuberosa subsp. interior	5
Aster oblongifolius	1
Echinacea pallida	2
Echinacea paradoxa	5
Echinacea purpurea 'Prairie Splendor'	4
Erigeron glaucus 'Albus'	2
Eryngium yuccifolium	2
Geum triflorum	5
Helianthella quinquenervis	1
Kniphofia triangularis	0.2
Kniphofia triangularis 'Cameron'	0.2
Liatris aspera	5
Liatris scariosa 'Alba'	5
Mirabilis multiflora	1
Oenothera macrocarpa subsp. incana	5
Penstemon barbatus 'Coccineus'	4
Penstemon cobaea	3
Phlox pilosa	5
Rudbeckia maxima	0.25
Rudbeckia missouriensis	3
Ruellia humilis	1.5
Silphium laciniatum	0.33
Silphium terebinthinaceum	0.33
Solidago speciosa	2
Stokesia laevis 'Omega Skyrocket'	1.5
	66

SPECIES	PLANTS/M² (1-L POTS)
Coreopsis verticillata 'Zagreb'	0.33
Schizachyrium scoparium 'Blaze'	0.33
	0.66

Sowing and planting mix for the prairie edge, with the seedling targets for each species

SPECIES	TARGET SEEDLINGS/M²
Agastache aurantiaca	2
Agastache rupestris	1
Amorpha canescens	0.2
Asclepias tuberosa subsp. interior	2
Aster oblongifolius	0.5
Castilleja integra	10
Echinacea pallida	0.5
Echinacea paradoxa	2
Echinacea purpurea 'Prairie Splendor'	1
Erigeron glaucus 'Albus'	2
Eryngium yuccifolium	0.5
Eryngium proteiflorum	3
Geum triflorum	5
Helianthella quinquenervis	0.5
Kniphofia triangularis	0.2
Kniphofia triangularis 'Cameron'	0.2
Liatris aspera	5
Liatris scariosa 'Alba'	5
Mirabilis multiflora	1
Oenothera macrocarpa subsp. incana	5
Penstemon barbatus 'Coccineus'	2
Penstemon cobaea	1
Penstemon ovatus	3
Penstemon pinifolius	5
Penstemon strictus	3
Phlox pilosa	5
Rudbeckia missouriensis	1
Ruellia humilis	1.8
Salvia pachyphylla	1
Silphium laciniatum	0.2
Silphium terebinthinaceum	0.33
Solidago speciosa	0.5
Stokesia laevis 'Omega Skyrocket'	1.5
Rudbeckia maxima	0.25
	72

SPECIES	PLANTS/M² (1-L POTS)
Coreopsis verticillata 'Zagreb'	0.5
Schizachyrium scoparium 'Blaze'	0.5
Zauschneria californica 'Olbrich Silver'	0.5
	1.5

**Sowing and planting mix for the Drakensberg grassland,
with the seedling targets for each species**

SPECIES	TARGET SEEDLINGS/M²
Berkheya macrospermus	0.5
Berkheya purpurea	2
Diascia integerrima	5
Diascia rigescens	2
Dierama pulcherrimum 'Dark Cerise'	0.5
Galtonia candicans	1
Gazania linearis	5
Geum capense	3
Gladiolus papilio 'Ruby'	1
Gladiolus saundersii	4
Haplocarpha scaposa	2
Helichrysum aureum	5
Kniphofia hirsuta 'Traffic Lights'	3
Kniphofia triangularis	2.5
Kniphofia triangularis 'Cameron'	2.5
Kniphofia uvaria	0.5
Moraea spathulata	1
Themeda triandra	4
Tritonia disticha	5
	49.5

SPECIES	PLANTS/M² (1-L POTS)
Agapanthus campanulatus	0.2
Crocosmia masoniorum	0.2
Eucomis comosa	0.1
	0.5

WHAT WORKED AND WHAT DIDN'T

This has been a really good project to work on because the client—and in particular the garden curator, Tom Price, and his team—have been incredibly positive and supportive throughout, despite, I am sure, behind the scenes pressures from mystified visitors during the first year. From May 2012 until late summer it just rained and rained, so emergence was on target or over target, but the resulting seedlings didn't really grow very much in such cool conditions. Given that I had specified a lower than normal sowing target density, to the uninitiated the sowings must have looked a flop in that first year. One always has to deal with this in the first year of sown vegetation, as expectation is nearly always much higher than can be delivered biologically. You have to hold your nerve, as does the client, when the politics are getting tricky.

A portion of the North American prairie part of the scheme in late August 2012, with Jim Penny (foreground) removing weeds. The larger plants with yellow flowers are planted *Coreopsis verticillata* 'Zagreb'.

By May 2013, however, the magical second year transition had taken place and people began to be wowed. As Tom Price said to me in an email, "They [the public] are mesmerized".

After having not flooded for a decade, the site flooded in January 2013 and then again in January 2014, with the site being underwater (except for the prairie wedge furthest from the river) for more than 5 days. This was least appreciated by *Eremurus*, most of which bid *adieu*, except at the least flooded end. It was also bad for *Penstemon* and some of the South African species, particularly *Berkheya*, *Diascia integerrima*, and *Galtonia candicans*. In autumn 2012 I had asked the staff to pull out *Berkheya* thought excess to requirements only for the flood to kill many of the remaining.

Oxford is potentially very cold for South African plants, even those from the 2500- to 3000-m Drakensberg Plateau, but the combination of winter flooding and potentially −20°C whittles down the possible species to use, so the visually least successful community has been the South African. To the average visitor it looks ok, but it doesn't sing in the way I know it can, so there is more to be done here. The target for the South African community was only 50 seedlings/m², simply because I did not have any more seed in my refrigerator of the grass, *Themeda triandra*. I wanted the very attractive South African forms of this widespread tussocky grass to be dominant in these plantings, rather than the more common, taller, ranker East Asian forms.

The other two communities are splendid, with the Eurasian something of a revelation, looking good starting with *Pulsatilla* and *Primula veris* from spring to late September. *Eryngium planum* has turned out to like Oxford very much through its self-seeding, but this will probably pass as the system sorts itself out. Because this community contains more winter evergreen species, its weed management needs are less than those of the prairie.

The Eurasian steppe-like vegetation in April 2013, with *Euphorbia epithymoides* in flower and the planted tussocks of the structural elements, *Stipa gigantea* and *Ferula communis*, evident.

In June the *Stipa* flowers create a pulsating bronze haze, with *Galium* and *Salvia* in the ground level.

The purple blue theme is carried on into August by *Eryngium planum* 'Blauknappe'.

In August *Eryngium planum* and pink *Malva alcea* are in bloom.

This community has proved to be long flowering. Here in mid September it is still highly attractive.

I was very ambitious with some of the species in the North American prairie edge, choosing small quirky things that I thought were worth giving a run. I like the shrubby Californian *Salvia pachyphylla* very much, and some of these are still in the edge in the least flooded bit, as are May-flowering orange red *Castilleja integra* and Pacific Northwestern *Penstemon ovatus*. As at the Fidelity International site (see case study), *Penstemon cobaea* (found on limestone prairies) seems to like the alkaline soil and looks as if it can persist here. Some things didn't work, however. Mexican *Eryngium proteiflorum* would not play ball (as it does in Sheffield). I gave the Rocky Mountain sunflower *Helianthella quinquenervis* its final outing in my sowings, and as normal it simply refuses to establish in the United Kingdom or at least where I have tried it. In contrast to the failures, *Phlox pilosa* seems well suited here; I love its cerise-ness, but my experience with it in many projects has been for it to thrive for a couple of years and then disappear, for reasons that are not always clear. We shall see.

The North American prairie vegetation commences with *Geum triflorum*, which I like despite its floral modesty, and deep blue Pacific Northwest *Penstemon ovatus*, followed by electric pink *Phlox pilosa*.

Penstemon barbatus (red) follows in June and July and is persistent where the canopy does not become too shady.

Penstemon cobaea is highlighted against the wonderful leaves of *Silphium terebinthinaceum* in July.

By early August, *Echinacea pallida* is in its prime.

Diascia species are normally very pink, but here sub-shrubby coral pink *Diascia rigescens* grows with pale pink *Diascia vigilis*.

The cumulus acid-yellow flowers of *Solidago speciosa* with orange red *Kniphofia uvaria* grow in the edge between the South African Drakensberg grassland and the North American prairie.

Overall the project is a great success. As always, this is largely due to the management being switched on to make the necessary proactive decisions about what is happening in front of them. All of these vegetation communities were designed to be burnable in spring if annual winter weeds were getting out of control, but this does not look as if it is going to happen here. The key management is to keep an eye out for the larger species becoming too dominant and thus eliminating the smaller species.

Queen Elizabeth Olympic Park U.K. Native Wildflower Meadows

Stratford, London, England

PLANT COMMUNITIES Dry and moister hay meadows sown onto 300 mm of low-nutrient topsoil overlying subsoil and a meadow-like community sown into the stormwater drainage swales

SEED SOURCES Seed from a variety of native seed suppliers in the United Kingdom, but mainly Emorsgate Seeds and British Seed Houses

CLIENT AND CONDITIONS The Olympic Delivery Authority, one of the two main agencies that organized the London Olympic Games in 2012. The site has a climate typical for the United Kingdom, with warm summers and generally mild winters (rarely lower than −5°C due to being on the edge of the London heat island). Average rainfall is 550 mm, but the frequency is rather erratic; long droughts in spring and early summer are almost the norm. RHS Hardiness Zone H3–H4, USDA 8b/9a. Soils (pH 6) are entirely manufactured (from sand and composted wood fibre) to be free draining with very low nutrient levels.

AREA OF PROJECT More than 100,000 m²

TIMESCALE Site prepared in autumn 2010, sown from January to April 2011

HISTORY AND DESIGN APPROACH

My colleague Professor Nigel Dunnett and I were appointed as primary planting design and horticultural consultants to the Queen Elizabeth Olympic Park in 2008, with a brief to design the naturalistic herbaceous vegetation that was to be the key vegetation cover of the site. Our work started with rethinking the planting strategy for the entire site, then performing detailed design through to implementation and management on the ground, and finally ensuring that the meadows were in full flower on July 28, 2012, the opening day of the games. When combined with the annual meadows sown elsewhere in the park, this project was almost certainly the largest area (more than 20 ha) of complex naturalistic designed vegetation ever created by sowing in a single site. This case study deals with the native wildflower meadows that were used throughout the park, but most specifically to clothe the slopes of North Park and Eton Manor.

Rather than adopt a literal restoration ecology approach based on plant community specifications drawn from the U.K. National Vegetation Classification (Rodwell et al., *British Plant Communities*), we decided to adopt an ecologically informed but design-led, politically savvy approach. The challenge was to produce vegetation types that would be visually dramatic during the Olympic festival, both to excite the public's imagination and to build positive support for greater use of native meadows as an alternative to mown grass in public spaces in Britain. At the time of having to design the seed mixes in 2008 and 2009, we had no real idea of what the soils we would actually sow onto would be. Hence, a simplified more generic approach seemed the most sensible. For the summer-cut hay meadows, we decided on two basic plant communities that shared some common core species as well as species with more specialized habitat preferences to try and deal with the site variation we knew would exist.

At this time the landscape architectural master planners LDA Design and Hargreaves Associates were redesigning the final site topography. It was becoming evident that there were going to be west- and south-facing slopes, east- and occasionally north-facing slopes, and drainage swales at the base of every slope into which drainage water would be directed. These topographic characteristics created a range of conditions from hot and dry through to wet and semi-shady and led to us designing several seed mixes shown here.

Meadow mix for dry sunny slopes, with the seedling targets for each species

SPECIES	TARGET SEEDLINGS/M²
Calamintha nepeta subsp. *nepeta*	10
Campanula glomerata	10
Centaurea scabiosa	10
Daucus carota	10
Echium vulgare	5
Festuca ovina	10
Galium verum	20
Leontodon hispidus	10
Leucanthemum vulgare	10
Linaria vulgaris	5
Lotus corniculatus	5
Malva moschata	5
Origanum vulgare	20
Primula veris	20
Prunella vulgaris	10
Salvia pratensis	5
Scabiosa columbaria	20
Thymus praecox subsp. *polytrichus*	20
	205

Meadow mix for moister, slightly shaded slopes, with the seedling targets for each species

SPECIES	TARGET SEEDLINGS/M²
Achillea millefolium	5
Agrimonia eupatoria	1
Centaurea scabiosa	3
Deschampsia cespitosa	5
Festuca ovina	20
Galium mollugo	5
Galium verum	15
Geranium pratense	5
Geranium sanguineum	3
Knautia arvensis	5
Leucanthemum vulgare	10
Linaria vulgaris	10
Malva moschata	5
Origanum vulgare	15
Primula veris	15
Prunella vulgaris	10
Ranunculus acris	10
Sanguisorba officinalis	5
Stachys officinalis	10
Succisa pratensis	5
Trifolium pratense	1
	163

Meadow mixes for drainage swales which fluctuate from wet to relatively dry, with the seedling targets for each species

SPECIES FOR SWALE SLOPING SIDES	TARGET SEEDLINGS/M²
Cardamine pratensis	50
Centaurea nigra	10
Geranium sylvaticum	10
Leucanthemum vulgare	40
Silene flos-cuculi	40
Stachys officinalis	10
	160

SPECIES FOR SWALE BASE	TARGET SEEDLINGS/M²
Cardamine pratensis	40
Eupatorium cannabinum	5
Geranium sylvaticum	5
Juncus effusus	30
Lythrum salicaria	5
Mentha aquatica	30
Silene flos-cuculi	40
Valeriana officinalis	5
	160

As shown in the tables of seed mixes, we diverged substantially from seed mix practice in the United Kingdom by greatly reducing the grass component of the sown meadows. The reason for doing this is that we wanted to maximize forb density and flowering drama during the Olympic Games, and grasses are just competitors in this regard. We also knew that the biodiversity planning consents required the meadows to be oversown during the transformation phase (post games) with grasses and some additional forbs, so the meadows would get their grasses come what may.

Eventually the choice of soil for the meadows came down to a manufactured material based on a deep sand deposit that was weed seed free mixed with composted wood fibre to hold moisture. Working with the soil scientists for the project, Tim O'Hare Associates, we agreed to a maximum of 14 ppm phosphorus for the meadow soils. This was based on analyses of phosphorus content in chalk grassland. With the benefit of hindsight, this value was really too low (30–40 ppm probably would have been better), but this 200- to 300-mm layer of weed-seed-free soil meant there was virtually no competition with weeds during the establishment period, a huge plus. Beneath the low-nutrient weed-free soil lay a subsoil that contained some clay fines. The drainage swale seed mixes were sown onto a 50-mm-deep sowing mulch (1:1 mix of grit and composted green waste) laid on top of the standard manufactured topsoil for the site, which had more clay fines in it and higher nutrient levels. The meadows were sown by hand. I trained teams from the two main landscape contractors on North Park, Frosts Landscapes and Gavin Jones, using the approaches previously discussed.

We enjoyed substantial latitude of decision-making with the project, with a very high level of client confidence from both the Olympic Delivery Authority and the LDA Design and Hargreaves team. The major limitation was that, in the pre-2008 planning consents, the choice of species for areas scheduled to be planted with native species only was restricted to species that were believed to have occurred on the site prior to development for the games. The interpretation of this was managed by staff from the U.K. Environment Agency. The agency officers undertaking this role took a very literal view on local nativeness. Even species that were native to, say, Essex, but were not previously known to occur in Stratford (the site of the park) could not be used. The consequences of this are discussed later in this case study.

The meadows had to be in full flower on July 28, 2012, when the games commenced. As most of the native species that we were likely to use in the mixes have a flowering peak in the London area well before this, we set up trials in 2010 to look at how we could cut off the meadows at ground level at different intervals prior to the games and then use irrigation to support regrowth so that the plants would flower at their peak in late July. These trials were studied at fortnightly intervals in 2011 by my Ph.D. student Helen Hoyle.

The first meadow was sowed at the Queen Elizabeth Olympic Park in London in January 2011. The soil surface is covered with the sawdust carrier.

Seedlings are emerging on the same slope in May 2011.

Ideal levels of emergence were achieved in meadows near the Olympic Stadium.

In 2011, trials were performed to hone the timing of using cutting to delay the meadow flowering until July 28, 2012.

The dry meadow mix was used on south-facing slopes, which terminate in a drainage swale sown with wet-tolerant species.

Meadows shaped much of the experience of the North Park landscape.

The drama of the meadows during the Olympic Games was much enhanced by the omission of most of the grasses from the meadow mixes.

WHAT WORKED AND WHAT DIDN'T

The period from March to May 2011 was dry, with very little rainfall. Because of problems with the supply of water to the site, the temporary irrigation designed to achieve emergence targets initially had to use water abstracted from the river. This was problematic, as it limited how much and how often areas could be irrigated, quite an issue on the steep slopes onto which most of the meadows were sown. Eventually the water problems were resolved and normal rainfall occurred. The meadows sown later (March and April) were far superior in terms of species representation and density, as compared to the earlier ones in which moisture stress clearly led to death of emerged seedlings or lack of emergence.

After emergence, the main problem was getting the seedlings to grow. The low-nutrient topsoil had been supplemented with a slow-release nitrogen source (hoof and horn) to compensate for the expected nitrogen use by bacteria as they decomposed the wood fibre. This nitrogen source, however, was clearly inadequate, and seedlings just sat there during the summer 2011 while the clock was ticking. We needed to get them growing so the roots could access the higher phosphorus levels in the underlying subsoil. To do this without increasing soil fertility to the levels where dominance by weedy species would be a problem in the future, we applied ammonium nitrate. This was also used to try to get the other forbs to compete with the legumes at the site, which began to dominate the meadows because they are able to fix nitrogen in their roots. To check the legumes, we also cut off the meadows to 50 mm above soil level two or three times in 2011, and gradually the other forbs got bigger and bigger. Running in parallel with the real meadows, my experiments in 2011 showed that cutting off all of the meadow to ground level 12 weeks before July 28, along with irrigation, gave the optimal flowering in the last week of July. But this would only work if the species were big enough beforehand to flower.

In May 2012, we duly cut down all of the meadows—to much general consternation— but all went to plan and the meadows were extraordinary for the Olympic Games. What we have typically found since then is that when the site has an exceptionally dry spring, as in 2015, the meadows on the south-west-facing slopes really struggle to perform on the sandy low-nutrient soil, particularly where the slopes are heavily trafficked by visitors.

Irrespective of the U.K. nativeness specifications in the pre-2008 planning consents, we have in essence created a little bit of central Europe on these slopes in Stratford. Although this was always a fear, it is also an opportunity to add by oversowing highly drought tolerant, near-steppe native species such as *Pulsatilla vulgaris*, plus similar near-native European species such as *Dianthus carthusianorum*, *Salvia nemorosa*, and *Teucrium chamaedrys*. Time will tell just what the outcome will be on these troublesome slopes and whether species such as *Dianthus* which we used in non-native plantings elsewhere in the park eventually find these ideal habitats through natural colonization.

The picture is much more positive on the cooler slopes and in the drainage swales, with biologically diverse and very attractive meadow communities now well established.

Queen Elizabeth Olympic Park Stitches

Stratford, London, England

PLANT COMMUNITIES Geophytes and short-lived perennials oversown with annuals, biennials, and perennials sown onto either 300 mm of Olympic Park low-nutrient topsoil or 50 mm of sowing mulch composed of a 1:1 mix of grit and composted green waste overlaying ordinary Olympic Park general topsoil

SEED SOURCES Seed mainly from Jelitto Perennial Seeds, Pictorial Meadows, and Emorsgate Seeds

CLIENT AND CONDITIONS The Olympic Delivery Authority, one of the two main agencies that organized the London Olympic Games in 2012. The site has a climate typical for the United Kingdom, with warm to hot summers and generally mild winters (rarely lower than −5°C due to being on the edge of the London heat island). Average rainfall is 550 mm, but the frequency is rather erratic; long droughts in spring and early summer are almost the norm. RHS Hardiness Zone H3–H4, USDA 8b/9a. Soils (pH 6) are entirely manufactured (from sand and composted wood fibre) to be free draining with very low nutrient levels. The meadows were all planted and sown by Frosts Landscapes.

AREA OF PROJECT 5000 m^2

TIMESCALE Site prepared commencing in winter 2012–2013, sown from February to June 2013

HISTORY AND DESIGN APPROACH

These sowings and plantings were designed in 2012 to provide vegetation that would run alongside the paths that, once the perimeter security fence was taken down, would allow people to move from one side of the park to the other. The term *stitch* was coined by LDA Design because these routes stitched across the park. The stiches involved generally 4- to 6-m-wide bands of vegetation between paths and development hoardings that screen sites that had been cleared of whatever function they had during the Olympic Games and were now development platforms awaiting building. Given the reverberations of the credit crunch, no one was sure how long it would take to develop these platforms. The brief was to provide a complex, colourful, and long-flowering vegetation that would persist for up to 5 years, but it might only be 2 years. Some of the stiches were open, whereas others had a succession of 1-m-tall 3 × 3 m planter boxes containing trees that had during the games been planted in places that subsequently were cleared as development platforms. The stitch mixes flowed around the boxes.

The stitch sowings were always going to be difficult because they were one of the last tasks of the outgoing contractors, and their establishment had not initially been factored into the specification of the incoming long-term maintenance contractor. In addition, they were mainly in locations where there was no or limited capacity to irrigate during germination. The seed and planting mixes were designed jointly by Nigel Dunnett and myself, and we tried to use species that had proved highly reliable in past sowings (such as *Dianthus carthusianorum*) and which could self-sow in open habitats. It was an opportunity to engage in a lot of theatre, rather than having to worry about a long distant future that these plantings would never have. The design form was to have a long-flowering ground layer of annuals, biennials, and perennials, many of which were strongly self-seeding, out of which would arise seasonally dramatic emergents, such as *Alcea* (hollyhocks), *Allium*, *Eremurus*, *Verbena bonariensis*, and *Verbascum olympicum*, while maintaining a strong see-through look. The site was planted with the geophytes, sub-shrubs, and other herbaceous plants, and then the seed was sown over the top and raked in.

Biennial and perennial sowing mix for the stiches, with the seedling targets for each species

SPECIES	TARGET SEEDLINGS/M²
Allium schoenoprasum	10
Asclepias tuberosa subsp. *interior*	5
Aster oblongifolius	3
Aubrieta deltoidea 'Purple'	5
Berkheya purpurea	3
Buphthalmum salicifolium	1
Centaurea scabiosa	1
Centranthus ruber 'Coccineus'	0.2
Chrysanthemum maximum 'Starburst'	3
Daucus carota	5
Dianthus carthusianorum	5
Echinacea pallida	2
Foeniculum vulgare 'Purpureum'	0.2
Galium verum	10
Gaura lindheimeri	0.5
Knautia arvensis	2
Linaria purpurea 'Canon Went'	3
Lychnis coronaria Atrosanguinea Group	3
Malva alcea var. *fastigiata*	0.2
Malva moschata 'Alba'	1
Oenothera biennis	0.1
Oenothera macrocarpa subsp. *incana*	10
Origanum vulgare	5
Penstemon barbatus 'Coccineus'	5
Primula veris	5
Rudbeckia hirta 'Marmalade'	2
Scabiosa lachnophylla 'Blue Horizon'	5
Sedum telephium 'Emperor's Waves'	10
Silene schafta 'Splendens'	10
Solidago speciosa	2
Verbascum chaixii 'Sixteen Candles'	0.1
Veronica spicata subsp. *incana*	10
	127

Annual seed mix for the stitches, with the seedling targets for each species

SPECIES	TARGET SEEDLINGS/M²
Centaurea cyanus 'Polka Dot Mixture'	10
Coreopsis tinctoria 'Standard Dwarf Mixture'	30
Gypsophila elegans 'Covent Garden'	10
Linaria maroccana 'Northern Lights'	10
Linum grandiflorum 'Rubrum'	15
Linum grandiflorum 'Bright Eyes'	10
Linum usitatissimum 'Sutton's Blue'	5
Viscaria oculata	10
	100

Planting mixes for the stitches

SPECIES	PLANTS/100 M²
Alcea rosea subsp. *ficifolia* hybrids	3
Alcea rugosa	3
Allium 'Globemaster'	3
Allium 'Purple Sensation'	5
Eremurus stenophyllus	5
Ferula communis	1
Kniphofia rooperi	3
Lobelia tupa	2
Onopordum acanthium	0.5
Perovskia atriplicifolia	5
Verbena bonariensis	5
	35.5

The stitch vegetation starts to look dramatic in late May (here in 2015). *Papaver orientale* and *Allium* grow in an area where the annual and biennial mix largely failed to germinate due to late sowing.

WHAT WORKED AND WHAT DIDN'T

Across the entire site, the stitches turned out to be a bit of a mixed bag. They ended up being sown much later than intended, and many species did not emerge until autumn 2013. Species that germinate best after winter chilling (such as cowslips, *Primula veris*) largely failed to emerge. There are very few *Echinacea* or *Solidago speciosa*. As a result, the sowings were much more open than we had anticipated, but what held it all together was the use of the Olympic mix low-nutrient topsoil or a sowing mulch of grit and composted green waste. These restricted weed invasion, so this openness wasn't the same disaster as it would have been on good soil. By using a long list of species, at least some of these found themselves able to establish under the conditions that materialized. Short lists of species are fine when you can control conditions during emergence and establishment, but less so when there is much unpredictability.

The areas in which the seed mix established well are very dramatic, here in early June 2014.

The annual and biennial seed mix in June 2014, with *Erem-urus stenophyllus* visually dominant.

One the positive side, the annuals that either overwintered or germinated in spring 2014 did a great job in this year in terms holding it all together visually and buying time for some of the biennials and perennials to grow large enough to flower, as did the planted material. Many of the stitches looked fantastic in summer 2014 and again in 2015, exceeding our expectations. Many of the species are good at self-sowing, and on the relatively low nutrient soils this is proving to be an effective form of regeneration. The stitches are even popular with the Olympic Park maintenance contractor, who recognizes that for the same level of maintenance input as the native wildflower meadows receive, a much longer season of interest both for people and for pollinating insects is produced. And, of course, they provide much, much more visual drama. The maintenance contractors cut the stitches down to ground level in early spring and remove the cut material. Weeds are then rogued out twice a year, and that's all. This community is an interesting model for temporary public spaces, or indeed as an installation type planting in city centres, where its extraordinary cycle of change will inspire many people to engage with notions of nature in the city.

RHS Garden Wisley
South African Meadow

Wisley, Surrey, England

PLANT COMMUNITIES South African Drakensberg alti-montane grassland sown onto 200–300 mm of sharp sand

SEED SOURCES Seed from a variety of suppliers, originally from Silverhill Seeds, but mainly from my South African research plots

CLIENT AND CONDITIONS This is the Royal Horticultural Society's oldest and most heavily visited garden, very much a prestige horticultural location. The site has relatively warm summers for the United Kingdom and potentially quite cold winters (minima of −15°C, although only very occasionally so). Average rainfall is 650 mm. RHS Hardiness Zone H4, USDA 8b/9a. Soils are very sandy, moderately productive, and prone to episodes of severe drought. The site is situated on the east side of a large mature oak tree, and about a third of the site is shaded by this.

AREA OF PROJECT 1200 m²

TIMESCALE Site prepared in autumn 2012, sown in March 2013

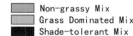

RHS Garden Wisley
New South African Border

design by James Hitchmough

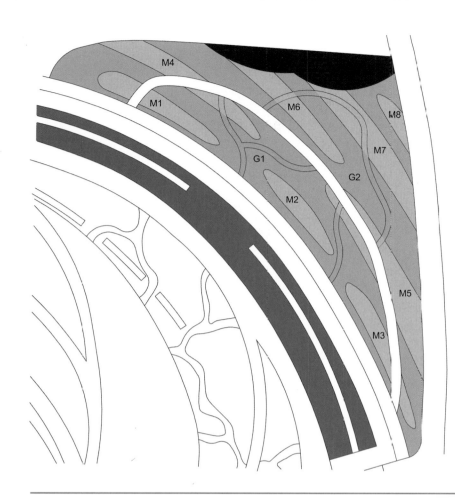

	Non-grassy Mix
	Grass Dominated Mix
	Shade-tolerant Mix

G1	263.3 m²
G2	405.6 m²
M1	45.2 m²
M2	34.9 m²
M3	40.2 m²
M4	56.1 m²
M5	80.8 m²
M6	50.0 m²
M7	80.3 m²
M8	15.2 m²
M9	105.4 m²

Distribution of the various plant community types across the area

HISTORY AND DESIGN APPROACH

This scheme grew out of the research into creating this type of vegetation that I had been undertaking with master's and Ph.D. students since 2005. We had large experimental sown communities in Sheffield which worked quite well, but we wanted to road test it in a public landscape, in a warmer summer climate than Sheffield, and without the very cold winters and flooding of the University of Oxford Botanic Garden. Jim Gardiner, the previous head of horticulture at Wisley, had a strong interest in *Dierama* and other South African species and was very supportive of a collaborative project that showcased the diversity of this flora. The design intention was to create initially a sown ground layer of forbs, grasses, and cold-tolerant succulents such as *Delosperma cooperi* and *Delosperma basuticum* that would gradually develop into a geophyte-dominated grassland. The aim was to produce a meadow-like vegetation with an unmatched diversity of South African montane grassland species. The geophytes would mainly be species with tall, leafless, see-through stems and would create a novel visual experience.

The site had a horsetail (*Equisetum arvense*) infestation near the main path and had previously supported an annual meadow. It was blanketed with a sand layer in January 2013 and sown in March 2013, as the South African species used do not have a chilling requirement for germination.

Main species sown to form the core of the plant community, with the seedling targets for each species

SPECIES	TARGET SEEDLINGS/M²	SPECIES	TARGET SEEDLINGS/M²
Agapanthus campanulatus 'Headbourne Blue'	1	Helichrysum aureum	5
Berkheya macrospermus	0.25	Hesperantha coccinea 'Major'	0.1
Berkheya multijuga	2	Hesperantha coccinea 'Sunrise'	0.1
Berkheya purpurea	2	Kniphofia caulescens	0.2
Crassula vaginata	5	Kniphofia hirsuta 'Fire Dance'	1
Delosperma cooperi	5	Kniphofia multiflora	0.1
Delosperma basuticum	5	Kniphofia northiae	0.1
Diascia integerrima	5	Kniphofia stricta	0.05
Dierama dracomontanum	0.02	Kniphofia triangularis	2
Dierama latifolium	0.02	Kniphofia triangularis 'Cameron'	1
Dierama latifolium JJA form	0.1	Kniphofia uvaria	0.5
Dierama mossii	0.1	Moraea alticola	0.1
Dierama pulcherrimum 'Dark Cerise'	0.2	Senecio macrospermus	0.2
Dierama trichorhizum	0.4	Themeda triandra	2
Dimorphotheca jucunda	0.5	Tritonia disticha	0.2
Galtonia candicans	1	Tritonia drakensbergensis	0.2
Gazania linearis	3.5	Watsonia confusa	0.2
Gladiolus dalenii ex 'Dunlop'	0.3	Watsonia densiflora	0.25
Gladiolus dalenii 'Red Form'	0.2	Watsonia galpinii 'Pale Pink'	0.5
Gladiolus flanaganii	0.3	Watsonia latifolia	0.1
Gladiolus longicollis	0.05	Watsonia lepida	0.2
Gladiolus oppositiflorus subsp. salmoneus	0.2	Watsonia pillansii	0.5
Gladiolus papilio yellow green	0.1	Watsonia pulchra	0.2
Haplocarpha scaposa	1	Watsonia strubeniae	1
			49

The tussock-forming grass *Themeda triandra* was sown to be present throughout, at low densities, but primarily concentrated into a series of bands that arched across the site, parallel with the main paths. In addition to the initial sowing, many rarer species would be established through planting from material either in my garden or present in research trials.

The species planted into the meadow from 2013 onward were *Agapanthus inapertus*, *Aloe cooperi*, *Crinum bulbispermum*, *Crinum macowanii*, *Crinum variabile*, *Crocosmia masoniorum*, *Crocosmia pearsei*, *Cymbopogon excavatus*, *Diascia rigescens*, *Diascia tugelensis*, *Erythrina zeyheri*, *Eucomis bicolor*, *Eucomis comosa*, *Geranium brycei*, *Geranium magniflorum*, *Geranium multisectum*, *Gladiolus saundersii*, *Greyia sutherlandii*, *Helichrysum splendidum*, *Hesperantha baurii*, *Hesperantha grandiflora*, *Kniphofia albomontana*, *Kniphofia caulescens* linear-leaved form, *Kniphofia ritualis*, *Kniphofia rooperi*, *Merxmuellera drakensbergensis*, *Moraea spathulata*, *Nerine angustifolia*, *Nerine bowdenii* JJA form, *Phygelius aequalis* 'Sani Pass', *Phygelius capensis* dwarf form, and *Watsonia latifolia*.

WHAT WORKED AND WHAT DIDN'T

Many South African geophytes are relatively immortal, but slow to germinate and relatively slow to establish. Emergence of the grass *Themeda triandra* was perplexingly low. As the summer went on, the growth of species that grew reasonably quickly in our trials in Sheffield was very slow. When we began to plant container-grown plants into the meadow in August 2013, it became apparent that the sand layer was up to 300 mm deep rather than the specified 100-mm layer, and that the soil beneath was much more heavily

A sea of *Gazania linearis* grows in the community in June 2015.

In response to irrigation and nitrogen fertilizer, by September 2015 the vegetation was beginning to develop a much more typical texture shaped by many emergent monocots, plus forbs such as *Berkheya purpurea* (in seed) in the foreground.

compacted than I had originally anticipated. There are large oak trees on the edge of the site whose roots dry out the soil beneath the sand, making for an extreme situation. In a standard 100-mm layer of sand, the roots of the sown species quickly reach the moister more nutrient rich soil beneath and their growth rapidly increases. In the Wisley meadow, however, seedlings are perched in a very dry layer of sand, overlying a dry and impenetrable compacted soil. This has proved to be rather hostile to many species, most of which come from relatively productive soils in their habitats; as a result, they have grown extremely slowly. On the plus side, the hostility also restricted weed vigour.

In such relatively open vegetation, we did not want to risk increasing weed invasion by boosting nutrient levels with fertilizer, so for the first 2 years we watched and waited. By June 2015 it was apparent that the vegetation was becoming dwarfed by the intensity of moisture and nutrient stress and an alternative course of action was required. A nitrogen-only fertilizer plus irrigation was applied to try to kick-start more rapid growth. The species that have been most successful to date in terms of growth rate are *Gazania*

Essentially the same vegetation in mid September in Sheffield on my research plots. On this much more productive soil, the community is dominated by a very good eastern Cape form of *Kniphofia uvaria*.

linearis and *Berkheya purpurea*, whose roots seem to have broken into the compacted soil beneath. On sand mulches, both of these species (especially *Gazania*) self-seed abundantly and fill all of the open spaces, and yet there are no signs of establishment in the garden beyond the sand mulch surface.

The site has a very high diversity of geophyte species from genera such as *Dierama*, *Kniphofia*, and *Watsonia*, but many of these individual plants are still too small to create the desired complex topography of emergents rising out of the base layer. At present the vegetation is just a little too low and flat, as the normally 1-m-plus emergents have not been able to attain these heights under the conditions. This meadow has been an interesting learning experience about when moisture and nutrient stress becomes a problem rather than an ally. We have added many more *Themeda* by planting plugs over the past year, with irrigation and nitrogen fertilization to encourage growth. We hope that a significant number of the geophytes will flower in 2016 and begin to create the drama this flora is capable of delivering.

Kaixian Eclectic Prairie–Meadow

Kaixian, Chongqing region of Sichuan, western China

PLANT COMMUNITIES North American prairie, with Chinese and Eurasian grassland species from regions with hot-summer climates, sown onto 100 mm of sharp sand overlying good-quality topsoil

SEED SOURCE Seed from Jelitto Perennial Seeds

CLIENT AND CONDITIONS Kaixian Urban and Rural Construction, China, the governmental body responsible for the development of Kaixian, a city with a population of approximately 300,000 people. The site is at an altitude of 300 m. The climate is summer monsoonal, with over 1000 mm of rain, primarily between March and October. Summer temperatures are very high, with maxima in excess of 35°C for much of the summer. Winters are relatively dry, with minima of −1 to −3°C. USDA Hardiness Zone 10b. Soils (pH 6) are typically fine-textured silts. The prairie-meadow is located primarily on a steeply sloping embankment wrapping around a public reception building within a lakeside public park.

AREA OF PROJECT 1000 m², L-shaped on a north-north-east–facing slope (up to 30°)

TIMESCALE Site prepared in winter 2014, sown in January 2015

HISTORY AND DESIGN APPROACH

I have been working as a consultant to Kaixian Urban and Rural Construction for almost 2 years, helping them to develop naturalistic flowering perennial plant communities for use in the developing city. This work has involved the construction of a field station in Kaixian, where more than 200 species have been tested for their capacity to germinate, emerge, grow, and flower satisfactorily, both as individual species and as mixed meadow-like communities. This work is the first of its type in China involving perennial species. The main challenge in Kaixian is that summers are relentlessly hot and often incredibly wet. As there is no real history of using herbaceous perennials in urban landscapes in this region, it's necessary to generate this from scratch by trial and error. The meadow is the first real project we have undertaken based on our initial research at the field station.

The design brief was very much left to me, but the key issues from a Chinese perspective are high levels of flowering drama for a long time and as tidy an appearance as possible. Untidy vegetation is very challenging to the average Chinese citizen's urban sensitivities. In the meadow, I tried to address this by using species with a mound-like form, with the multi-species ground layer typically no taller than 600 mm. It is punctuated by some taller species, such as *Echinacea purpurea* 'Magnus Superior' (very much liked by the locals), and two see-through species (with largely leafless stems), *Rudbeckia maxima* and the Chinese species *Patrinia scabiosifolia*.

The pressure to do things prematurely in China is just part of the cultural mix. Because we hadn't had long enough to evaluate the species on the field station, I had to design the seed mix through a mix of intuition and guesswork. The project was sown in January 2015 very much as a training event for staff from the construction team who would, all things being well, sow meadows in the future. The slope was steep and covered by a relatively unstable 100-mm-deep sand sowing mulch. Jute erosion matting was required to reduce the incidence of wash down the slope, but this had not arrived from India, so we had to sow anyway. The jute turned up 4 weeks later. The top of the slope was heavily trafficked by locals curious about and wanting to have a closer look at the slightly bizarre goings on.

Both single species and mixed communities are tested at the field station of the Department of Landscape, University of Sheffield at Kaixian.

Schizachyrium scoparium seems very well suited, as does the extraordinary pink-flowering grass *Muhlenbergia capillaris.* Grasses are prime invasion candidates, so we shall continue to observe whether these species self-sow at the field station before using them in practice.

Mixed communities are sown as 3×3 m microcosms.

Seed mix for the sunny areas, with the seedling targets for each species

SPECIES	TARGET SEEDLINGS/M²
Asclepias tuberosa	2
Aster oblongifolius	1
Calamagrostis brachytricha	0.5
Chrysanthemum maximum 'Silver Princess'	3
Commelina dianthifolia	5
Coreopsis major	5
Delphinium grandiflorum	5
Echinacea paradoxa	3
Echinacea purpurea 'Magnus Superior'	1
Galium verum	3
Geum chiloense 'Feuerball'	10
Kniphofia 'Border Ballet'	5
Liatris scariosa 'Alba'	3
Nipponanthemum nipponicum	5
Oenothera tetragona	10
Parthenium integrifolium	5
Pennisetum alopecuroides	1
Penstemon barbatus 'Coccineus'	5
Platycodon grandiflorus 'Mariesii'	3
Potentilla nepalensis 'Ron McBeath'	5
Rehmannia elata	3
Rudbeckia fulgida var. sullivantii 'Goldsturm'	3
Rudbeckia maxima	0.5
Ruellia humilis	5
Salvia ×sylvestris 'Blaukönigin'	3
Sanguisorba officinalis	5
Sporobolus heterolepis	5
Stokesia laevis 'Omega Skyrocket'	5
Scabiosa comosa	5
	115

Seed mix for the slightly shaded to shaded areas, with the seedling targets for each species

SPECIES	TARGET SEEDLINGS/M²
Aster divaricatus	5
Aster oblongifolius	1
Buphthalmum salicifolium 'Alpengold'	2
Commelina dianthifolia	5
Coreopsis major	5
Darmera peltata	1
Delphinium grandiflorum	5
Echinacea purpurea 'Prairie Splendor'	2
Euphorbia epithymoides	1
Geum chiloense 'Feuerball'	10
Heuchera villosa	5
Leucanthemum 'Silver Princess'	3
Monarda bradburiana	3
Nipponanthemum nipponicum	10
Patrinia scabiosifolia	1
Platycodon grandiflorus 'Mariesii'	3
Polemonium reptans	5
Potentilla nepalensis 'Ron McBeath'	5
Primula polyneura	15
Rehmannia elata	8
Rudbeckia fulgida var. sullivantii 'Goldsturm'	5
Sedum ussuriense	10
	110

The Kaixian staff was trained in sowing the prairie-meadow in January 2015.

By July 2015 *Delphinium grandiflorum* was flowering well.

WHAT WORKED AND WHAT DIDN'T

I was anxious that emergence would be poor, given the steep slope and sand mulch, but in fact emergence was excellent. Even with the collateral losses of seedlings when weeding out weedy grasses from the underlying soil (site preparation was rather rushed), density was good, with about 80 per cent of the sown species clearly present. *Aster divaricatus* didn't establish (as far as I can see), whereas *Aster oblongifolius* did. The only exception to this was the top of the slope, where there had been foot traffic prior to a temporary fence being installed.

The really extraordinary thing was just how fast the seedlings grew, with heavy rain and heat from March on. *Geum chiloense* 'Feuerball' started flowering after about 3 months, followed in July by *Delphinium grandiflorum*, a species native to the mountains of Sichuan (found right across northern China). This species then went into dormancy by August, but came back into growth in October. By August many of the species were flowering size, a process that takes approximately twice as long in Western Europe.

By the end of September, the vegetation was remarkably well developed. Here *Rudbeckia maxima* is beginning to flower.

Looking to the future, the main issue will be how the adult plants look post flowering in this very hot climate. Will they yellow and look ugly? Will it be possible to extend the display season into autumn, or will the high temperatures make species that in their cooler habitats flower in October be finished and in decline long before this? Curiously, some species such as *Aster oblongifolius* seem to flower at pretty much exactly the same time of year (late September on) as they do in the much cooler climate of the United Kingdom, and they show no signs of summer leaf scorch. As I write this in early October 2015, what seems to be happening (at least in the first year) is with the cooler weather many of the species have recommenced growth and many are now initiating flowers. The hot and wet summers of the south-eastern United States present very similar problems, so what happens on this project will be very important beyond China. In 2016, we hope to evaluate the response of the local users of the park to the planting.

METRIC CONVERSIONS

degrees Fahrenheit = (9/5 × degrees Celsius) + 32

TO CONVERT	MULTIPLY BY
km to miles	0.6
m to feet	3.3
cm to inches	0.4
mm to inches	0.04
m² to square feet	10.8
kg to pounds	2.2
g to ounces	0.04
L to gallons	0.26

RESOURCES

INFORMATION ON WILD HABITATS

Floras of Nepal, Chile, China, and North America
efloras.org

iSpot
ispotnature.org

U.S. Department of Agriculture's PLANTS database
plants.usda.gov

SOIL SAVER JUTE MATTING

Hy-tex (in the United Kingdom)
hy-tex.co.uk/index.php/products/biodegradables/
soil-saver

NYP Corp. (in the United States and Canada)
nyp-corp.com/jute-soil-saver-matting

R. L. Pritchard & Co.
(in the United States and Canada)
www.rlpritchard.com/jute_soil_saver.html

INDIVIDUAL SPECIES FOR MAKING SEED MIXES

WORLDWIDE
Jelitto Perennial Seeds
Jelitto Staudensamen GmbH, Postfach 1264, D-29685,
Schwarmstedt, Germany
jelitto.com

When the precise origin of the plants from within the total geographic distribution of a species is not so critical, as it might be in a restoration ecology situation, I purchase seed from Jelitto. They have outstanding seed storage and inventory management, and test their seed continuously to ensure it is above their 70 per cent minimum germinability criteria. They are entirely dependable and generally have higher and more uniform quality standards than the other suppliers that I have purchased from. Jelitto stock around 4000 different species and can sometimes procure other species that are not in their catalogue. Their range of nondormant (Jelitto Gold Nugget) seed of species that otherwise require extensive chilling is really useful when you must sow at the wrong time of year. Jelitto have agents in the United States, Britain, and Japan.

WESTERN EUROPEAN SPECIES
OF KNOWN GEOGRAPHIC ORIGIN
Emorsgate Seeds
Lynn Road, Tilney All Saints, King's Lynn, Norfolk PE34
4RT, UK
wildseed.co.uk

WESTERN EUROPEAN SPECIES
OF UNKNOWN GEOGRAPHIC ORIGIN
Rieger-Hofmann GmbH
In den Wildblumen 7, 74572 Blaufelden, Germany
rieger-hofmann.de

CENTRAL TO EASTERN
NORTH AMERICAN SPECIES
Prairie Moon Nursery
32115 Prairie Lane, Winona, MN 55987, USA
prairiemoon.com

Prairie Nursery
W7262 Dover Court, Westfield, WI 53964, USA
prairienursery.com

CENTRAL TO WESTERN
NORTH AMERICAN SPECIES
Alplains
PO Box 489, Kiowa, CO 80117-0489, USA
alplains.com

Rather like Silverhill, Alplains offers an extensive range
of fascinating largely western species available in small
volumes.

Western Native Seed
PO Box 188, Coaldale, CO 81222, USA
westernnativeseed.com

SOUTH AFRICAN SPECIES OF
UNKNOWN GEOGRAPHIC ORIGIN
Silverhill Seeds
PO Box 53108, Kenilworth, 7745 Cape Town,
South Africa
silverhillseeds.co.za

For each species seed is only available in limited
amounts, but they offer an extraordinary diversity of
species.

SEED MIXES

WORLDWIDE
Jelitto Perennial Seeds
Jelitto Staudensamen GmbH, Postfach 1264, D-29685,
Schwarmstedt, Germany
jelitto.com

Jelitto currently sell a prairie seed mix of my design.

Pictorial Meadows
Manor Oaks Farmhouse, 389 Manor Lane, Sheffield,
South Yorkshire S2 1UL, UK
pictorialmeadows.co.uk

I have collaborated with Pictorial Meadows for a number
of years, helping them to develop a range of perennial
seed mixes for urban landscapes that are as reliable as
possible, very attractive, and long flowering. We will
continue to collaborate to develop an increasing range of
mixes to eventually cover most of the types of communities discussed in this book. Their products are based
on extensive testing and an admirable expertise not
only in making up seed mixes but also in installing and
managing both sown meadow mixes and their specialist
wildflower turf across the United Kingdom.

U.K. NATIVE PLANT COMMUNITIES
Emorsgate Seeds
Lynn Road, Tilney All Saints, King's Lynn, Norfolk PE34
4RT, UK
wildseed.co.uk

EUROPEAN REGIONAL NATIVE PLANT COMMUNITIES
Rieger-Hofmann GmbH
In den Wildblumen 7, 74572 Blaufelden, Germany
rieger-hofmann.de

NORTH AMERICAN REGIONAL
NATIVE PLANT COMMUNITIES
Prairie Moon Nursery
32115 Prairie Lane, Winona, MN 55987, USA
prairiemoon.com

Prairie Nursery
W7262 Dover Court, Westfield, WI 53964, USA
prairienursery.com

Western Native Seed
PO Box 188, Coaldale, CO 81222, USA
westernnativeseed.com

REFERENCES

INTRODUCTION

Bekkers, G. 2003. *Jac. P. Thijsse Park: Designed Dutch Landscape*. Architectura and Natura, Amsterdam.

Dunnett, N., and J. D. Hitchmough. 2004. *The Dynamic Landscape: Design, Ecology and Management of Naturalistic Urban Planting*. Taylor and Francis, London.

Gerritsen, H., and A. Schlepers. 1993. *Spelen met de Natuur*. [*Playing with Nature*.] Terra, Warnsveld, the Netherlands. (In Dutch, but heavily illustrated)

Hansen, R., and F. Stahl. 1993. *Perennials and Their Garden Habitats*. Cambridge University Press, Cambridge.

Robinson, W. 1870. *The Wild Garden*. John Murray, London.

Thomas, C. D., and G. Palmer. 2015. Non-native plants add to the British flora without negative consequences for native diversity. *Proceedings of the National Academy of Sciences USA*, 112(14), 4389–4392.

Thompson, K. 2007. *No Nettles Required: The Truth About Wildlife Gardening*. Transworld Publishers, London.

Thompson, K. 2013. *Where Do Camels Belong? The Story and Science of Invasive Species*. Profile Books, London.

LOOKING TO NATURE FOR INSPIRATION AND DESIGN WISDOM

Brueldheide, H., and U. Scheidel. 1999. Slug herbivory as a limiting factor for the geographical range of *Arnica montana*. *Journal of Ecology*, 87(5), 839–848.

Ellenberg, H. 1988. *The Vegetation Ecology of Central Europe*. 4th ed. Cambridge University Press, Cambridge.

Grime, J. P. 2001. *Plant Strategies, Vegetation Processes, and Ecosystem Properties*. Wiley, Chichester, U.K.

Hitchmough, J. D., and H. Cummins. 2011. Cold hardiness of winter growing South African plants. *The Plantsman*, 10(2), 104–111.

Rice, G. 2006. *Royal Horticultural Society Encyclopaedia of Perennials*. Dorling Kindersley, London.

Taylor, J. 1996. *Weather in the Garden*. John Murray, London.

EUROPEAN LOW- TO MEDIUM-ALTITUDE HAY MEADOWS

Ellenberg, H. 1988. *The Vegetation Ecology of Central Europe*. 4th ed. Cambridge University Press, Cambridge.

Polunin, O., and M. Walters. 1985. *A Guide to the Vegetation of Britain and Europe*. Oxford University Press, Oxford.

Rodwell, J. S., C. D. Piggott, D. A. Ratcliffe, A. J. C. Malloch, H. J. B. Birks, M. C. F. Proctor, D. W. Shimwell, J. P. Huntley, E. Radford, M. J. Wigginton, and P. Wilkins. 1992. *British Plant Communities*. Vol. 3. *Grasslands and Montane Communities*. Cambridge University Press, Cambridge.

EUROPEAN AND EURASIAN ALPINE MEADOWS

Aeschimann, D., K. Lauber, D. M. Moser, and J.-P. Theurillat. 2004. *Flora Alpina*. Vols. 1–3. Belin, Paris.

Ellenberg, H. 1988. *The Vegetation Ecology of Central Europe*. 4th ed. Cambridge University Press, Cambridge.

Holubec, V., and P. Kriva. 2006. *The Caucasus and Its Flowers*. Loxia, Prague.

Pils, G. 2006. *Flowers of Turkey: A Photo Guide*. Friedrich VDV, Linz, Austria.

Polunin, O., and M. Walters. 1985. *A Guide to the Vegetation of Britain and Europe*. Oxford University Press, Oxford.

WESTERN NORTH AMERICAN ALPINE MEADOWS

Niehaus, T. F., and C. L. Ripper. 1976. *Pacific States Wildflowers*. Houghton Mifflin, Boston.

Pojar, J., and A. MacKinnon. 2013. *Alpine Plants of British Columbia, Alberta, and Northwest North America*. Lone Pine, Edmonton.

ASIAN ALPINE MEADOWS

Grey-Wilson, C., and P. Cribb. 2011. *Guide to the Flowers of Western China*. Kew Publishing, Royal Botanic Gardens, London.

EURASIAN STEPPE

Bone, M., D. Johnson, P. Kelaidis, M. Kintgen, and L. G. Vickerman. 2015. *Steppes: The Plants and Ecology of the World's Semi-Arid Regions*. Timber Press, Portland, Oregon.

Dallmann, P. R. 1998. *Plant Life in the World's Mediterranean Climates*. University of California Press, Berkeley.

Ellenberg, H. 1988. *The Vegetation Ecology of Central Europe*. 4th ed. Cambridge University Press, Cambridge.

Lafranchis, T., and G. Sfikas. 2009. *Flowers of Greece.* Vols. 1 and 2. Diatheo, Paris.

Pils, G. 2006. *Flowers of Turkey: A Photo Guide.* Friedrich VDV, Linz, Austria.

Polunin, O., and B. E. Smythies. 1988. *Flowers of South-West Europe: A Field Guide.* Oxford University Press, Oxford.

Polunin, O., and M. Walters. 1985. *A Guide to the Vegetation of Britain and Europe.* Oxford University Press, Oxford.

ASIAN STEPPE

Bone, M., D. Johnson, P. Kelaidis, M. Kintgen, and L. G. Vickerman. 2015. *Steppes: The Plants and Ecology of the World's Semi-Arid Regions.* Timber Press, Portland, Oregon.

Gardiner, C., and B. Gardiner. 2014. *Flora of the Silk Road.* I. B. Taurus, London.

Hauck, M. H. 2010. *Flowers of Mongolia.* Verlag Rudiger Biermann, Telgte, Germany.

WESTERN NORTH AMERICAN STEPPE

Bone, M., D. Johnson, P. Kelaidis, M. Kintgen, and L. G. Vickerman. 2015. *Steppes: The Plants and Ecology of the World's Semi-Arid Regions.* Timber Press, Portland, Oregon.

Pojar, J., and A. MacKinnon. 2013. *Alpine Plants of British Columbia, Alberta, and Northwest North America.* Lone Pine, Edmonton.

Robertson, L. 1999. *Southern Rocky Mountain Wildflowers.* Globe Pequot Press, Guilford, Connecticut.

SOUTH AMERICAN STEPPE

Sheader, M. 2015. *Flowers of the Patagonian Mountains.* Alpine Garden Society, Pershore, England.

SOUTH AFRICAN WINTER-RAINFALL STEPPE

Manning, J. 2007. *Field Guide to Fynbos.* Struik, Cape Town.

SOUTH AFRICAN SUMMER-RAINFALL GRASSLANDS

Pooley, E. 2003. *Mountain Flowers: A Field Guide to the Flora of the Drakensberg and Lesotho.* The Flora Publications Trust, Durban.

AUSTRALIAN STEPPE GRASSLAND

Williams, N. S. G., A. Marshall, and J. W. Morgan. 2015. *Land of Sweeping Plains: Managing and Restoring the Native Grasslands of South-eastern Australia.* CSIRO Publishing, Clayton South, Victoria.

NORTH AMERICAN PRAIRIE

Curtis, J. T. 1959. *The Vegetation of Wisconsin.* University of Wisconsin Press, Madison.

Ladd, D. 1995. *Tall Grass Prairie Wildflowers.* Falcon Press, Helena, Montana.

SUMMER-UNCUT TALL-FORB COMMUNITIES

Grey-Wilson, C., and P. Cribb. 2011. *Guide to the Flowers of Western China.* Kew Publishing, RBG, London.

Holubec, V., and P. Kriva. 2006. *The Caucasus and Its Flowers.* Loxia, Prague.

EURASIAN WOODLAND UNDERSTOREY AND EDGE COMMUNITIES

Ellenberg, H. 1988. *The Vegetation Ecology of Central Europe.* 4th ed. Cambridge University Press, Cambridge.

Holubec, V., and P. Kriva. 2006. *The Caucasus and Its Flowers.* Loxia, Prague.

Polunin, O., and M. Walters. 1985. *A Guide to the Vegetation of Britain and Europe.* Oxford University Press, Oxford.

TEMPERATE ASIAN WOODLAND UNDERSTOREY AND EDGE COMMUNITIES

Grey-Wilson, C., and P. Cribb. 2011. *Guide to the Flowers of Western China.* Kew Publishing, RBG, London.

EASTERN NORTH AMERICAN WOODLAND UNDERSTOREY AND EDGE COMMUNITIES

Hemmerly, T. E. 2000. *Appalachian Wildflowers.* University of Georgia Press, Athens.

Peterson, R. T., and M. McKenny. 1968. *A Field Guide to Wildflowers: Northeastern/North-Central North America.* Houghton Mifflin, Boston.

WESTERN NORTH AMERICAN WOODLAND UNDERSTOREY AND EDGE COMMUNITIES

Dallmann, P. R. 1998. *Plant Life in the World's Mediterranean Climates.* University of California Press, Berkeley.

Lyons, C. P., and B. Merilees. 1995. *Trees, Shrubs and Flowers to Know in Washington and British Columbia.* Lone Pine, Edmonton.

DESIGNING NATURALISTIC HERBACEOUS PLANT COMMUNITIES

Hansen, R., and F. Stahl. 1993. *Perennials and Their Garden Habitats*. Cambridge University Press, Cambridge.

Korn, P. 2013. *Peter Korn's Garden: Giving Plants What They Want*. Korn's Garden, Göteberg, Sweden.

Phillips, R., and M. Rix. 1991. *Early Perennials*. Vol. 1. Pan Books, London.

Phillips, R., and M. Rix. 1991. *Late Perennials*. Vol. 2. Pan Books, London.

Shapiro, A. M. 2002. The Californian urban butterfly population is dependent on alien plants. *Diversity and Distributions*, 8, 31–40.

CASE STUDIES

Rodwell, J. S., C. D. Piggott, D. A. Ratcliffe, A. J. C. Malloch, H. J. B. Birks, M. C. F. Proctor, D. W. Shimwell, J. P. Huntley, E. Radford, M. J. Wigginton, and P. Wilkins. 1992. *British Plant Communities*. Vol. 3. *Grasslands and Montane Communities*. Cambridge University Press, Cambridge.

ACKNOWLEDGEMENTS

Many people, too many to mention individually (mostly University of Melbourne horticultural colleagues and students and master's and Ph.D. students in the Department of Landscape, University of Sheffield), have helped me directly and indirectly to develop and road test these ideas over the past 30 years. Special thanks however are given to Hanim Ahmad, Marcus de la Fleur, Zoe Dunsiger, Ye Hang, Nadine Mitschunas, Zulhazmi Sayuti, and Markus Wagner. Mostly this has been a lot of fun but also, of course, a lot of tedium—that's the nature of research. Particular thanks go to Amanda for both tolerating and participating in my plant obsessions and expanding my horizons.

PHOTOGRAPHY AND ILLUSTRATION CREDITS

Cassian Schmidt, pages 6–7, 20 bottom, 21, 63, 73, 76, 89, 90, 91
Jingyu Cao, page 335
Mahsa Mohajer, page 72
Martin Schittle, page 74
Martin Sheader, pages 78, 79
Mt. Cuba Center / Sara Levin Stevenson, pages 106 bottom, 107
Noel Kingsbury, pages 86, 87
© RHS / Verity Bradbury, page 338
Shuke Gao, page 104
Tom Stuart-Smith, page 301
Travis Beck, page 105
Xiaoyu Wei, page 344 top
Ye Hang, pages 196, 197
Zhifu Yu, page 344 bottom

All other photos are by the author.

INDEX